Developing Metadata Application Profiles

Mariana Curado Malta
Polytechnic of Oporto, Portugal & Algoritmi Center, University of Minho, Portugal

Ana Alice Baptista
Algoritmi Center, University of Minho, Portugal

Paul Walk
University of Edinburgh, UK

A volume in the Advances in Web Technologies and Engineering (AWTE) Book Series

www.igi-global.com

Published in the United States of America by
    IGI Global
    Information Science Reference (an imprint of IGI Global)
    701 E. Chocolate Avenue
    Hershey PA 17033
    Tel: 717-533-8845
    Fax: 717-533-8661
    E-mail: cust@igi-global.com
    Web site: http://www.igi-global.com

Library of Congress Cataloging-in-Publication Data

Names: Malta, Mariana Curado, 1969- editor. | Baptista, Ana Alice, editor. |
  Walk, Paul, 1968- editor.
Title: Developing metadata application profiles / Mariana Curado Malta, Ana
  Alice Baptista, and Paul Walk, editors.
Description: Hershey, PA : Information Science Reference, [2017] | Includes
  bibliographical references and index.
Identifiers: LCCN 2016056939| ISBN 9781522522218 (hardcover) | ISBN
  9781522522225 (ebook)
Subjects: LCSH: Metadata--Standards.
Classification: LCC Z666.7 .D48 2017 | DDC 025.3--dc23 LC record available at https://lccn.loc.
gov/2016056939

This book is published in the IGI Global book series Advances in Web Technologies and Engineering (AWTE) (ISSN: 2328-2762; eISSN: 2328-2754)

British Cataloguing in Publication Data
A Cataloguing in Publication record for this book is available from the British Library.

Advances in Web Technologies and Engineering (AWTE) Book Series

ISSN:2328-2762
EISSN:2328-2754

MISSION

The **Advances in Web Technologies and Engineering (AWTE) Book Series** aims to provide a platform for research in the area of Information Technology (IT) concepts, tools, methodologies, and ethnography, in the contexts of global communication systems and Web engineered applications. Organizations are continuously overwhelmed by a variety of new information technologies, many are Web based. These new technologies are capitalizing on the widespread use of network and communication technologies for seamless integration of various issues in information and knowledge sharing within and among organizations. This emphasis on integrated approaches is unique to this book series and dictates cross platform and multidisciplinary strategy to research and practice.

The **Advances in Web Technologies and Engineering (AWTE) Book Series** seeks to create a stage where comprehensive publications are distributed for the objective of bettering and expanding the field of web systems, knowledge capture, and communication technologies. The series will provide researchers and practitioners with solutions for improving how technology is utilized for the purpose of a growing awareness of the importance of web applications and engineering.

COVERAGE

- Web Systems Architectures, Including Distributed, Grid Computer, and Communication Systems Processing
- Data analytics for business and government organizations
- Human factors and cultural impact of IT-based systems
- Security, integrity, privacy, and policy issues
- Web systems performance engineering studies
- Integrated Heterogeneous and Homogeneous Workflows and Databases within and Across Organizations and with Suppliers and Customers
- Web systems engineering design
- Mobile, location-aware, and ubiquitous computing
- IT readiness and technology transfer studies
- Ontology and semantic Web studies

IGI Global is currently accepting manuscripts for publication within this series. To submit a proposal for a volume in this series, please contact our Acquisition Editors at Acquisitions@igi-global.com or visit: http://www.igi-global.com/publish/.

Titles in this Series

For a list of additional titles in this series, please visit: www.igi-global.com

www.igi-global.com

701 East Chocolate Avenue, Hershey, PA 17033, USA
Tel: 717-533-8845 x100 • Fax: 717-533-8661
E-Mail: cust@igi-global.com • www.igi-global.com

Table of Contents

Detailed Table of Contents

Chapter 1
    Karen Coyle, Dublin Core Metadata Initiative, USA

Application profiles fulfill similar functions to other forms of metadata documentation, such as data dictionaries. The preference is for application profiles to be machine-readable and machine-actionable, so that they can provide validation and processing instructions, not unlike XML schema does for XML documents. These goals are behind the work of the Dublin Core Metadata Initiative in the work that has been done over the last decade to develop application profiles for data that uses the Resource Description Framework model of the World Wide Web Consortium.

Chapter 2
    Paul Walk, EDINA, University of Edinburgh, UK

This chapter describes an approach to the development of a metadata application profile. It is particularly concerned with the class of application profile which is optimised for a specific use-case, rather than those which are more concerned with supporting general interoperability in a broader domain. The example of the development of a particular application profile, RIOXX, is used to illustrate some of the methodology discussed. Much of the approach described in the chapter was designed during the course of the development of RIOXX. Issues which are given particular consideration include a focus on the close involvement of 'implementors' (normally software developers), the adoption of ideas from agile software development, continuous testing and open development, and ongoing maintenance and sustainability "on a shoestring".

Chapter 3

Alexander Ball, University of Bath, UK
Mansur Darlington, University of Bath, UK
Christopher McMahon, University of Bristol, UK

A Minimum Mandatory Metadata Set (M3S) was devised for the KIM (Knowledge and Information Management Through Life) Project to address two challenges. The first was to ensure the project's documents were sufficiently self-documented to allow them to be preserved in the long term. The second was to trial the M3S and supporting templates and tools as a possible approach that might be used by the aerospace, defence and construction industries. A different M3S was devised along similar principles by a later project called REDm-MED (Research Data Management for Mechanical Engineering Departments). The aim this time was to help specify a tool for documenting research data records and the associations between them, in support of both preservation and discovery. In both cases the emphasis was on collecting a minimal set of metadata at the time of object creation, on the understanding that later processes would be able to expand the set into a full metadata record.

Chapter 4

Jean-Christophe Desconnets, IRD, UMR ESPACE-DEV, France
Isabelle Mougenot, UM, UMR ESPACE-DEV, France
Hatim Chahdi, Université de Montpellier, IRD, UMR ESPACE-DEV,
    France

The satellite images have become an essential source of information to address and analyze environmental issues quickly, repeatedly and in a reliable way. The increasing number of remotely sensed images are the first impediments for data discovery, access and processing. In this context, it is critical to simplify efficient multi-sensors image-based data access and query processing to provide accessibility to a variety of users in remote sensing. Describing satellite images through a metadata application profile may leverage capabilities to promote easy use of satellite image for environmental analysis. Accordingly, an application profile conforming to the Dublin Core Application Profile guidelines and designed for Earth observations data have been developed. The aim is to provide insights of key methodological considerations in relation to the design of this profile called EOAP (Earth Observation Application Profile).

Chapter 5

Mariana Curado Malta, Polythechnic of Oporto, Portugal & Algoritmi Center, University of Minho, Portugal
Ana Alice Baptista, Algoritmi Center, Universidade do Minho, Portugal

This chapter presents the process of developing a Metadata Application Profile for the Social and Solidarity Economy (DCAP-SSE) using Me4MAP, a method for developing Application Profiles that was being put forth by the authors. The DCAP-SSE and Me4MAP were developed iteratively, feeding new developments into each other. This paper presents how the DCAP-SSE was developed showing the steps followed through the development of the activities and the techniques used, and the final deliverables obtained at the end of each activity. It also presents the work-team and how each profile of the team contributed for the DCAP-SSE development process. The DCAP-SSE has been endorsed by the SSE community and new perspectives of SSE activities have been defined for future enlargement of the DCAP-SSE. At the time of writing this chapter, Linked Open SSE Data is being published, they are the first examples of use of the DCAP-SSE.

Chapter 6

Panagiotis Zervas, Centre for Research and Technology Hellas, Greece
Demetrios G Sampson, Curtin University, Australia

With many Learning Object Repositories (LORs) implemented and maintained independently from different organizations or communities, valuable Learning Objects (LOs) are scattered over different LORs and making it difficult for end-users (namely, instructional designers, teachers and students) to easily find and access them. A suggested solution towards addressing this issue is to create federated LORs, which aim to harvest and aggregate LOs' metadata from different LORs towards facilitating LOs' discovery across these LORs through a single infrastructure.

However, a challenging issue during the development of federated LORs is the design of appropriate metadata application profile (AP) which supports harvesting heterogeneous metadata records from the aggregated LORs. Thus, the aim of this book chapter is twofold, namely (a) to present a methodology for developing metadata APs that can be used in building federated LORs and (b) to present a case study from the implementation of the proposed methodology for the development of the metadata AP used by the OpenDiscoverySpace federated LOR.

    Mariana Curado Malta, Polytechnic of Oporto, Portugal & LINHD-
       UNED, Spain
    Paloma Centenera, LINHD-UNED, Spain
    Elena Gonzalez-Blanco, LINHD-UNED, Spain

This chapter presents the early stages of a metadata application profile (MAP) development that uses a process of reverse engineering. The context of this development is the European poetry, more specifically the poetry metrics and all dimensions that exist around this context. This community of practice has a certain number of digital repertoires that store this information and that are not interoperable. This chapter presents some steps of the definition of the MAP Domain Model. It shows how the developers having as starting point these repertoires, and by means of a reverse engineering process are modeling the functional requirements of each repertoire using the use-case modeling technique and are analyzing every database logical models to extract the conceptual model of each repertoire. The final goal is to develop a common conceptual model in order to use it as basis, together with other sources of information, for the definition of the Domain Model.

    João Aguiar Castro, University of Porto, Portugal
    Ricardo Carvalho Amorim, University of Porto, Portugal
    Rúbia Gattelli, University of Porto, Portugal
    Yulia Karimova, University of Porto, Portugal
    João Rocha da Silva, University of Porto, Portugal
    Cristina Ribeiro, INESC TEC/ DEI - University of Porto, Portugal

Research data are the cornerstone of science and their current fast rate of production is disquieting researchers. Adequate research data management strongly depends on accurate metadata records that capture the production context of the datasets, thus enabling data interpretation and reuse. This chapter reports on the authors' experience in the development of the metadata models, formalized as ontologies, for several research domains, involving members from small research teams in the overall process. This process is instantiated with four case studies: vehicle simulation; hydrogen production; biological oceanography and social sciences. The authors also present a data description workflow that includes a research data management platform, named Dendro, where researchers can prepare their datasets for further deposit in external data repositories.

Foreword

The story of the Dublin Core is inextricably woven into the history of the Web, a metadata system conceived as a means of improving discovery at a time when the entire web consisted of perhaps 500,000 addressable resources. The naivete that characterizes our early efforts approaches the quaint: Can we identify a simple set of descriptors that authors might use to make their intellectual assets more discoverable, and therefore more accessible?

What we could not have envisioned in those earliest workshops was that the element set that took shape was but a small part (and perhaps the easiest part) of our achievement. The larger challenges were meeting the diverse needs of the many stakeholder communities that coalesced around the Dublin Core. These stakeholders were (are) as diverse as the Web itself, and to build an infrastructure that would serve their resource description needs has been an ongoing task of daunting proportion.

Diversity demands an approach to metadata that honors extensibility. From the first beginnings the community struggled to create a metadata architecture that made it possible to support multidisciplinary interoperability while providing the means to extend and enrich metadata to meet the specialized needs of any given community.

Doing so turns out to be a challenging objective that requires unambiguous specification of semantics that are both human-readable and machine-processable. Practitioners need to register, discover, declare, and reuse metadata terms and specifications in a world of decentralized metadata and web systems that continually undergo change. Dublin Core Application Profiles are the technical and social engineering response to this challenge.

The chapters in this book emerge from projects in the UK, Germany, Greece, Portugal, Spain, Brazil, and the United States. They cover projects that include scientific data repositories, metadata design, archive description and management, learning object repositories for education, engineering data management, and metadata systems to support non-governmental organizations. We see in these efforts examples of the diversity of domains, of functional requirements, of approaches to metadata, even of political philosophies. They represent a microcosm of the larger metadata world and the challenges of finding common descriptive properties on the one hand, while supporting the semantic detail that is essential to the richer descriptions necessary within a discipline or domain. The authors hope that their efforts and explanations will serve as guideposts for the next generation of metadata designers and practitioners in this ongoing challenge.

Stuart Weibel
OCLC Online Computer Library Center, Inc.
August 2016

Preface

This book is concerned with the processes for development of metadata application profiles, in an increasingly complex world of data, information standards and requirements for data exchange and interoperability.

The appearance of this book is timely. The rapid rise in the importance of data science is driving an urgent need for better metadata in order to manage and exploit the 'data deluge'. As interdisciplinary research becoming more prevalent, the issue of interoperability (or lack thereof) between contexts comes into sharp focus. Furthermore, the concept of 'metadata' has, in recent years, entered into mainstream consciousness. No longer an obscure concern for a small group of information professionals and researchers, metadata is fashionable and the average citizen now has at least heard the term and has some awareness that metadata is important.

Metadata application profiles equip systems - almost always based in software - to manage and exchange data. Application profiles allow us to gain some purchase on the complexity and variety of data, so that we might manage, use and re-use those data. However, as we will see in the chapters of this book, metadata application profiles are not easily constructed. Moreover, they cannot be developed in isolation. As Karen Coyle in the opening chapter says, issuing what might be heard as a 'call to arms':

The days in which one could invent their own metadata schema without concern for existing standards or data exchange are long over.

The chapters in this book cover a range of approaches to the development of metadata application profiles. Drawing on research and development work in disparate domains, taken together they illustrate how development methods must be tailored to fit the context. From the variety presented in these pages, it becomes clear that no single method can possibly solve every metadata application profile development use case.

The concept of the metadata application profile is defined by Heery and Patel (2000) as "data elements drawn from one or more namespace schemas combined together by implementers and optimised for a particular local application". This admirably neat and succinct definition accommodates a large range of possible types of implementation, the heterogeneity of which is apparent in the descriptions in the chapters to follow.

This book, then, is by and for those people who work with metadata schemas and application profiles. Once this audience might have been limited to a group consisting of librarians and related information professions, and a handful of researchers working in some branch of information science. However, the new importance of data and its management has meant that a much wider range of people have a stake in metadata, from software engineers to scientists working with research datasets in just about any discipline, to bureaucrats needing to account for public spending, to the growing army of 'data journalists'. Whether it is realised or not, metadata is everywhere, and a growing number of people need to have some understanding of how to work with it in a way that maximizes interoperability for use and re-use. And even if they are not actively employed in its development, if they truly want to understand metadata and how to maximise its interoperability, then they need to appreciate how it is constructed.

The authors of the different chapters in this book represent a mixture of research and practical interests and, as such, the book should have something to offer researchers and practitioners alike.

In Application Profiles - An Overview, the author offers an overview of current practice in metadata application profile development. Ranging from the relatively simple approach of the 'data dictionary', through to the more sophisticated Singapore Framework, this chapter reveals in general terms not only what has been achieved so far, but also how much is left to do if we are to realise the promise of fully interoperable metadata. As in several other chapters in this book, great emphasis is placed on developing approaches to creating 'machine-readable' profiles. Application profiles which are machine readable and even, in the author's words, "to the extent possible, machine-actionable" create opportunities for automated or, at least, semi-automated processing of various kinds. Standard modelling languages such as UML become useful in this context, while automated testing and validation become viable too. The Singapore Framework's 'Description Set Profile' is recommended as a "strong theoretical and practical" foundation for this kind of development, and the community is encouraged to continue development in this space.

The Development of an Optimised Metadata Application Profile describes a development methodology which departs from convention by largely ignoring concerns of wider interoperability in favour of a narrow focus on implementation (although, of course, the pragmatic decision to re-use existing namespaces - notably DCMI Metadata Terms - does introduce a degree of interoperability into the described metadata application profile, whether or not this is a priority for the developer).

Tied to a specific use-case, the methods used here are borrowed, in part, from the 'agile' school of software development practice. From this point of view, a metadata application profile becomes just one more component in an application which is optimised early in the development process. While opportunities for wider interoperability may present themselves, these are rejected "ruthlessly" in a single-minded effort to satisfy only the specific requirements being addressed by the project. Other chapters in this book have focused on developing documentation for application profiles which is machine-readable, promoting 'semantic interoperability' between documents. By contrast, the approach to documentation described in this chapter is to focus almost entirely on the needs of the developers of software. This is in keeping with the general thrust of this chapter which is to promote implementation above all other considerations.

The Minimum Mandatory Metadata Sets for the KIM Project and RAIDmap focuses on the development of M3S - Minimum Mandatory Metadata Set, for the KIM and RAIDMap project records. The authors notably present the historical context of the domain of digital preservation metadata focusing all evolution from the development of the OAIS Reference Model to that of schemas such as PREMIS, which became the basis for the KIM Minimum Mandatory Metadata Sets - M3S. All the stages of the process of deriving the KIM M3S from PREMIS are then explained and the decisions taken are conveniently justified. The same process was used to derive the RAIDmap M3S, albeit it had different requirements from those of the KIM M3S. Once again, all the stages and decisions are explained and justified. The results of the application of this process in these two distinct settings become apparent as the authors explain it step by step. The tables with the final results thus appear to the reader as a welcome evidence of the application of the process previously explained. At the end of the chapter, the authors provide valuable recommendations on the development of M3S.

In A Methodology For Effective Metadata Design In Earth Observation, the focus is squarely on interoperability. Having established the degree of "technical diversity" in instruments and sensors found on satellites, and the corresponding variety of data formats produced by them, the author goes on to describe the challenge of designing systems to discover images in this heterogenous mass of data and "domain specific" metadata. This chapter is notable for its application of a "model-driven" approach borrowed from software engineering, using this to complement DCMI's Singapore Framework (which makes an appearance in other chapters), with the result that functional requirements are able to be formally defined. In common with some other chapters, the work here is underpinned by the use of linked open data on the Web.

In The Development process of a Metadata Application Profile for the Social and Solidarity Economy, the authors show how a community specific application profile was built using the Me4MAP method. The development of this application profile has the singular characteristic of having been performed iteratively with the development of the Me4MAP method, which provided several feedback cycles between one development and the other. The chapter explains how the team was built and how each planned activity was carried on, and points to external sources for further information about the results.

In Developing Metadata Application Profiles for Open Educational Resources Federated Repositories - The Case of the Open Discovery Space Metadata Application Profile, the focus is on a method for developing application profiles federated Learning Object Repositories and an application scenario. The method consists of four steps targeted to define the metadata elements, their 'obligation status' and their 'value space'. The choice of metadata elements and value spaces is done using formulas that take into account several factors, including frequency. The chapter explains each of the steps and shows their application on a real world scenario, the Open Discovery Space, a federated repository of sixteen (16) learning object repositories. At the end of the chapter the reader may find a reflection over some aspects of the method.

In Using reverse engineering to define a Domain Model - The case of the development of a metadata application profile for European poetry, the focus is on the development of an application profile for a European poetry platform using the Me4MAP method. This platform aims to aggregate poetry metadata from various European platforms and provide services on this set of aggregated data, as well as make the data available as Linked Open Data. Of special interest is the way in which the authors used the Me4MAP method in a case where some of the activities provided by the method were already performed or partially performed. Thus, the focus is essentially on the design of the application profile from the analysis of the models of the various platforms / databases that provide metadata and that will inform the construction of the application profile at a later stage. At the end of the chapter the authors reflect on what went well and on which aspects to improve from the point of view of those who develop application profiles.

In Involving Data Creators in an Ontology-based Design Process for Metadata Models, the focus is in the process of determining and modeling the metadata elements and values for describing research data in specific domains. The resulting models are represented as lightweight ontologies which are used in the scope of the Dendro platform. The authors present the processes they used for different kinds of data through the presentation of four scenarios from four research domains: vehicle simulation, biological oceanography, hydrogen production and social sciences. The chapter emphasizes the user studies that the team conducted to determine how different types of data are produced and how they should be described to optimize retrieval. As in other chapters, at the end of this chapter the reader finds a section about the lessons learned.

By showing various approaches to the development of metadata application profiles, this book provides a starting point for those who want to develop this artefact and do not know where to begin. Each chapter focuses on the development process used and many of them reflect on the lessons learned, identifying aspects of methods which have yielded good results, together with those which need improvement, providing valuable reflection as a basis for future development. Together, the chapters provide, to the newcomer, a range of perspectives which will widen their understanding and better equip them to undertake development in this field.

This book also paves the way to an open, serious and in-depth discussion of methods for designing metadata application profiles. Until very recently the methods used in the development of metadata application profiles were based on those from other disciplines (especially computer and library sciences). In recent years, some tailored approaches to this subject have emerged, sometimes in distinct, but at other times in similar scenarios. The reader of this book is thus presented with some of these approaches, inviting them to reflection and action. It is then up to the metadata community to test, reflect and discuss the different approaches, the types of scenarios in which they may be applied and their validity and feasibility in a Linked Open Data environment.

REFERENCES

Heery, R., & Patel, M. (2000). Application profiles: Mixing and matching metadata schemas. *Ariadne*, *25*, 27–31.

Acknowledgment

The editors would like to thank the Advisory Board, the reviewers, and the authors of the chapters without whom the book could not exist. We would also like to acknowledge the communities of information professionals and researchers working to advance the state of the art of metadata management and, in particular, the Dublin Core Metadata Initiative for more than twenty years of work and leadership in this area.

Chapter 1
Application Profiles:
An Overview

Karen Coyle
Dublin Core Metadata Initiative, USA

ABSTRACT

Application profiles fulfill similar functions to other forms of metadata documentation, such as data dictionaries. The preference is for application profiles to be machine-readable and machine-actionable, so that they can provide validation and processing instructions, not unlike XML schema does for XML documents. These goals are behind the work of the Dublin Core Metadata Initiative in the work that has been done over the last decade to develop application profiles for data that uses the Resource Description Framework model of the World Wide Web Consortium.

INTRODUCTION

The days in which one could invent their own metadata schema without concern for existing standards or data exchange are long over. Today's data is social if not entirely promiscuous in its relationships with other data stores. The transition from closely held and private data to data that is intended to intermingle with the data of others calls for new tools to facilitate that sharing. Anyone who has undertaken to mix data from more than one source in a single application knows that there is much more that needs to be known beyond the names of data elements. Not only must one know what kind of data to expect, and how much of that data, but one also needs to know the choices that were made in the creation of the data.

DOI: 10.4018/978-1-5225-2221-8.ch001

Much effort takes place in data processing in the cultural heritage and scientific communities on the development of what are called "cross-walks." These are analyses that create equivalencies or near-equivalencies between different metadata schemas and that allow sharing data with others or aggregating data from multiple sources. The time and intellectual energy needed for creation of cross-walks and the subsequent programming to convert one set of metadata into a different metadata format is onerous. At least some of this is due to the lack of a standard to create a machine-readable schema definition that could be used by others. This is not just a data definition, such as "date = yyyymmdd" but information about the semantics of the schema itself. Is the date field required? Can there be more than one author? Does this community's ISBN field contain both ISBN-10's and ISBN-13's? What does "title" mean in this data - will it include subtitles or not?

Many programmers and analysts have experience in this kind of data transition, and many person-hours have been spent on it. Clearly this is an area where standardization could save a great deal of time.

Those exchanging data have commonly used documents to convey this information among their community of metadata sharing, but few of those documents are machine-actionable; a metadata schemas described in written documents are still very common. Although it has been acknowledged for a time that better and more standard documentation for data exchange is needed, we still do not have a satisfactory solution.

Some Examples of Data Documentation

The need to document and describe the elements and rules of computing practice are almost as old as computing itself. Early data definitions were not only not machine actionable, they were often paper documents with no actual connection to the machine-readable data. Many data standards still are issued as non-actionable documents, even in the major standards organizations like the International Standards Organization. The disadvantages of these paper schemas are obvious, from the problem of keeping them up to date to the fact that they cannot be tested against actual data. Over time, members of the computing community worked to rectify this disjunction between the machine-readable data and the human-readable documents that explain the data. Of these methods are data dictionaries, used with database management systems, formal modeling languages, like the Unified Modeling Language, and the schema standard for eXtensible Markup Language (XML) documents. These are familiar examples, but this is not a complete review of data profile methods.

Data Dictionaries

A data dictionary is a description of the data in a database. Data dictionaries almost always include a list of data elements and the conformance rules for the values that they can accept. More expansive data dictionaries can include descriptions of the data elements and their sources, dates on which the data elements were added to the database schema, and other explanatory fields.

Data dictionaries may be automatically generated from the database schema, but they are human-readable documents and are not intended for input to the data processing programs. Also, a data dictionary describes the data that resides in a database, which may differ significantly from the exchange formats of that same data.

An expansive data dictionary could include all of the information that is needed to populate the user interface and provide helpful information for the staff doing input of the data.

Given the potential for different audiences for information about the elements of the database, there may actually be more than one data dictionary; for example, a database administrator would need to see details that would not be meaningful to the input staff. Data dictionaries tend to be internal documents that are intended primarily for staff that is trained in the practices of the company. This method works where data input is controlled through enterprise systems and no sharing is done with un-initiated others.

Table 1. A simple data dictionary document

Field	Type	Notes
Customer ID	number	Automatically generated
Customer name	text	Max length 50
Customer ZIP code	number	Max length 5 Min length 5

Table 2. A data dictionary including input rules

Field	Type	Constraint	Input rules
Customer name	text	Max length 50	Input customer names in natural order, first name first, such as "John Smith". Use initials where first names are not known: "J. S. Smith". Do not include titles like "Mr." Or "Dr."

Data Models and Modeling

Parallel to the use of data dictionaries is the creation of visual models of enterprise data. These models can be realized at different levels depending on the need and the audience. A common high-level model shows the primary entities of an information domain and their relationship to each other, as illustrated in Figure 1.

Lower level diagrams can include increasing details such as entity attributes, data element names, and commentary. Diagrams, however, rarely include the quality control information found in data dictionaries, are not machine-actionable, and have a technically sophisticated intended audience.

XML and XML Schema

XML is a text-based format for structured documents. The documents may be prose, they may be sets of data elements, or they may be data of any type. An XML document can consist of any combination of data types and sources. XML documents are structured hierarchically in a tree format, with no limitations on how many branches can be encoded.

Any XML document can be test for well-formedness following the rules of the XML standard. However, mere well-formedness is not sufficient for most applications; it is necessary for the data itself to be clearly described and in such a way that

Figure 1. Simple data model

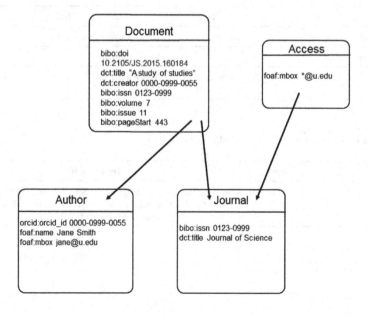

conformance of any individual XML document to its rules can be calculated. The World Wide Web Consortium (W3C) is the owner of the XML document standard and also of the standard XML schema language which can be used to document and define a set of rules for any given set of XML documents. XML schema is a formal language that expresses the syntax, structure, and value constraints of an XML document type. The XML schema defines conformance for instances of that XML document type, and can be used by applications to test conformance of the relevant XML documents. The XML schema language is itself expressed in XML.

The significance of XML and its schema language is that, unlike the previous generation of data usage, all XML documents and schemas can be understood and machine-processed by any applications that apply the XML standards. Where before each metadata standard and each database definition was unique to its context and application, XML is a generalized solution that greatly eases the cost of data sharing.

Unlike database management systems and their data dictionaries, XML can be used in the networked environment of the Internet, and makes use of the system of domain names that identify documents and entities on the Internet. XML allows the mixing of data elements from different namespaces by using URI names for the data elements.

In its basic form, XML schema provides data definitions: element names, data types, and cardinality constraints. This serves to document the data itself, but by extension XML schema can also provide human-readable documentation that serves the people who must understand the data so that it can be correctly created and applied.

Note that the goals of XML schema can also be achieved through other languages such as RELAX NG. (Clark, 2001) The variety of tools confirms the value of having conformance-defining languages for data sets.

Resource Description Framework

Throughout the 2000's, the W3C produced the core standards for the Resource Description Framework (RDF), a data standard designed to allow data to exist on the World Wide Web and to use the protocols of the Web as the foundation of its technology stack. RDF enables to so-called "web of data." Like the Web itself, RDF is structured as relationships between entities in a limitless network.

The openness of the web of RDF entities and relationships is its great strength, but also provides challenges for the creators and consumers of RDF data. There is at this moment no "schema" that would provide conformance rules for RDF such as there is for XML. This is not a simple oversight, as most users of RDF recognize this need. There are existing efforts in this direction, starting with the work of the Dublin Core Metadata Initiative, which began to address this question in the early development days of RDF.

Dublin Core Application Profiles

Many people think of Dublin Core as a fifteen data element scheme for simple metadata creation. (Dublin Core Metadata Initiative, 2012) That is a true characterization, but the real innovation of Dublin Core was the development of a set of metadata elements that were not tied to any record format, and that could be used in conjunction with other data elements without losing their semantics. Where most data definitions were directly tied to a single record-keeping environment and served a limited set of calculations, Dublin Core suggested that one could use its data elements in an unlimited number of situations. The history of the Dublin Core Metadata Initiative (DCMI) runs parallel to the rise of the Internet and the World Wide Web.

The Dublin Core initiative grew out of a meeting in 1994 at the second International World Wide Web Conference. (Dublin Core Metadata Initiative, undated) The format for Web documents, HTML, had been developed in its initial form by Tim Berners-Lee, the creator of the World Wide Web, in 1991. By the mid-1990's it was a standard both of the Internet Engineering Task Force and later of the World Wide Web Consortium, and was being used as the primary way to present human-readable information over the Internet. HTML is a document formatting and display language, but it did not include a method to consistently provide citation metadata in a standard, machine-readable format. At a meeting hosted by the Online Computer Library Center (OCLC) and the National Center for Supercomputing Applications (NCSA) in Dublin, Ohio in March of 1995, attendees agreed that this new information highway needed a core set of elements that would facilitate identification and retrieval of documents. The group of fifteen elements, known as "simple Dublin Core," were issued in 1998. Anyone could use these elements in any documents or applications. Dublin Core became one of the first general vocabularies that can be rendered in any number of serializations including key/value pairs, XML, HTML, and RDF.

Dublin Core on the Web

The W3C standard HyperText Markup Language, HTML (originally XHTML to indicate its encoding in XML) allows anyone to put documents onto the World Wide Web with a simple document structure of headers and paragraphs. Included in the HTML standard from its early days was the concept of "meta" information carried in the header of the document. One use of the HTML "<meta>" tag is to add Dublin Core document description information to the HTML document. The use of Dublin Core terms in HTML documents meant that the millions of creators of web pages could add some metadata to their pages without having to invent their own metadata formatting, and in a way that is generally understood by receiving systems.

```
<meta name="dc.language" CONTENT="US">
<meta name="dc.title" CONTENT="My Web Page">
<meta name="dc.creator" CONTENT="Mary Jones">
```

Dublin Core elements are used in many HTML-based content, such as in the Creative Commons rights metadata that accompanies many documents on the Web. It seems obvious that a rights license would include basic document description elements as well as naming the creators who were asserting rights. Rather than develop a set of data elements that are specific to the Creative Commons licenses, they were able to make use of the Dublin Core elements that were already commonly known by web content creators. This metadata, seen below, is expressed in HTML so that it can be included in web documents that are in HTML.

```
<a rel="license" href="http://creativecommons.org/licenses/
by/4.0/"></a>
Based on a work at <a xmlns:dct="http://purl.org/dc/terms/"
href="http://example.com/jane" rel="dct:source">http://example.
com/jane</a>
```

Examples like HTML's "<meta>" tag and the Creative Commons metadata show that the Dublin Core elements are useful in a wide range of applications. At the same time, it is evident that Dublin Core elements are often not sufficient in themselves for applications, but will be used together with other vocabularies. As data creators compile their metadata schemas from elements from different namespaces, there is a need to define such a schema in a standard, machine-readable way. This recognition was the beginning of the Dublin Core communities work on application profiles.

Dublin Core Application Profiles

The Dublin Core community began developing its concept of application profiles in 2000 after a workshop presented by Rachel Heery at its meeting in October of that year. The problem posed to the community was how to define, control and communicate the elements and rules of a metadata schema that was composed of data elements taken from existing vocabularies. It is easy to see that the Dublin Core community, with one of the vocabularies that is most often incorporated into schemas with a mix of namespaces, would be aware of and wish to find a resolution to this issue.

A key aspect of the concept presented by Heery was that application profiles would gather elements from existing namespaces, but would not define new elements. This defines an application profile solely as a *usage* of metadata elements, unlike most other metadata schemas. An application profile would provide further definition and constraints on the elements that it includes, yet these extensions to the semantics of the elements must not contradict the semantics of the elements as they are defined in their native namespaces. A Dublin Core application profile is therefore a meta level above the original element definitions. It also could contain significant enrichment of the context of the metadata and the meaning of the elements themselves.

This definition of an application profile informed the work of the Dublin Core community for the remainder of the 2000's.

At the Dublin Core meeting in Singapore in 2007, Mikael Nilsson presented a concept that he had developed called the "Description Set Profile" (DSP) (Nilsson, 2008). The DSP could provide the structure the metadata managers need to identify their data model and convey that information to others who might wish to use or interact with your data. The DSP, though, needed to be located in a technical and social context; it was only part of a much larger environment. Nilsson envisioned this context as a layered model, shown in Figure 2, which is named the Singapore Framework for the location of the meeting. (Nilsson, et al, 2008)

This is the current edition of the model, which became more advanced as members of the DCMI working groups elaborated this concept. The part of this model that is directly associated with the DSP came to be the Dublin Core Application Profile model. That model consists of:

Figure 2. Singapore Framework

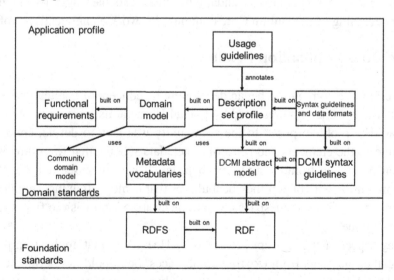

- Functional requirements
- A domain model
- A description set profile
- Usage guidelines
- Encoding syntax guidelines

Only the DSP is actually new in this model; the remaining elements are common in metadata design and maintenance. The functional requirements step is one that no designer should overlook: What are the goals for your data, and what functions do you wish to support? The domain model may be less well known, but it is often satisfied with an analysis that results in a list of entities, relationships, and values that sum up the data universe of that community, often in the form of an entity-relation or object-oriented diagram. Usage guidelines are known to library catalogers as cataloging rules, but other communities have a smaller set of guidelines for their users, such as those working with business data. Usage guidelines also include the information that one normally sees in a data dictionary: what type of input is allowed (integer, string, date); whether elements are mandatory or optional, and whether they can repeat; whether content must be taken from a specific list of allowed values, etc. The encoding syntax guidelines are the detailed specifications of data that you produce, explaining your data within format that you are using for your metadata, such XML or RDF.

In this model, the application profile is not a single document because it includes a domain analysis and usage guidelines (including cataloging rules), but the DSP is a machine-readable representation that will explain the metadata structure and content in a way that is sufficient for many internal functions and for most interactions with the larger community.

The DSP is a Dublin Core working draft from 2008. It is based on the Dublin Core Abstract Model, which defines a data structure similar to that of RDF, but with an emphasis on entity descriptions.

The DSP, as its name implies, is a set of descriptions. The general structure of the DSP is:

- Description set
  - Description
    - Statement
    - Statement
  - Description
    - Statement
    - Statement
  - Etc.

An example of a description could be the metadata used to describe persons. Another could be a set of metadata describing a manufactured product. There are no restrictions in what can be described. Statements are the specific metadata elements that describe the entity of that description. A statement can be "has name" or "manufactured on". The DSP also includes the rules that describe the data elements, such as the data type and the cardinality. A very simple description set for the description of a book is defined in pseudo-code in the Guidelines for Dublin Core Application Profiles (Coyle, 2009), and is reproduced here.

```
DescriptionSet: MyBookCase
  Description template: Book
    minimum = 1; maximum = 1
      Statement template: title
        minimum = 1; maximum = 1
        Property: http://purl.org/dc/terms/title
        Type of Value = "literal"
      Statement template: dateCreated
        minimum = 0; maximum = 1
        Property: http://purl.org/dc/terms/created
        Type of Value = "literal"
        Syntax Encoding Scheme IRI = http://purl.org/dc/
terms/W3CDTF
      Statement template: language
        minimum = 0; maximum = 3
        Property: http://purl.org/dc/terms/language
        Type of Value = "non-literal"
        takes list = yes
        Syntax Encoding Scheme IRI = http://purl.org/dc/
terms/ISO639-2
      Statement template: subject
        minimum = 0; maximum = unlimited
        Property: http://purl.org/dc/terms/LCSH
        Type of Value = "non-literal"
        takes list = yes
        Value Encoding Scheme IRI = http://lcsh.info/
      Statement template: author
        minimum = 0; maximum = 5
        Property: http://purl.org/dc/terms/creator
        Type of Value = "non-literal"
        defined as = person
```

At its upper level the DSP has a close resemblance to an entity-relation analysis. Each statement template represents an entity in the metadata schema. The DSP, however, is more than entities and relationships; its unique value is the detail that it can express about the descriptions, statements and values of the metadata schema. It also allows the developer to define the boundaries of a set of metadata that exist in the unbounded graph structure of RDF on the Web. In a way, this replicates the concept of "records" that is familiar to most developers, but that is not defined in the RDF standard of a potentially infinite graph. The record concept that is supported by the DSP permits the application of common quality control functions, such as allowing only a defined set of metadata elements to be allowed in ones application.

The DSP was defined in an XML schema. This was an alpha version of the DSP concept, and was tested briefly in a few metadata efforts, most notable the Scholarly Works Application Profile (SWAP). This was given a formal analysis, and some issues relating to the definition of validation were surfaced. Work on the DSP did not go further, although the basic structure and concepts of the DSP informed the creation of BIBFRAME profiles.

PROFILES IN PROGRESS

Dublin Core has arguably the strongest model for application profiles, but this is a concept that is not limited to the Dublin Core community. Some developers of profiles are aware of and imitate the Dublin Core work; others have developed profiles out of their own data models, proof that this is a wide-felt need, especially in the area of RDF-based vocabularies.

BIBFRAME Profiles

An RDF vocabulary for library bibliographic data is began development in 2012 with the support of the Library of Congress. The vocabulary is call BIBFRAME, for BIBliographic FRAMEwork. In 2014, the project introduced the concept of profiles as a way to accommodate different needs within the cataloging community.(Library of Congress, 2014) These profiles are based on the application profile definition that was developed in the Dublin Core Metadata Community. The BIBFRAME profiles are all derived directly from the BIBFRAME vocabulary, but each includes the data elements needed for a particular audience. The BIBFRAME Lite is the minimal core of RDF classes and properties for general bibliographic description. More specialized profiles are defined for libraries, for archives, and for the cataloging of rare materials.

While not a "mix and match" vocabulary, BIBFRAME illustrates how a single vocabulary can serve different communities by selecting only those specific elements needed by that community. This is an improvement over past practices, such as the MARC21 formats or the Resource Description and Access (RDA) vocabulary, which each have nearly two thousand description elements attempting to cover the needs of all types of libraries and archives. Using a profile, developers and catalogers can work only with those elements that are needed for their specific functionality, and yet retain their compatibility with data-sharing partners.

Schema.org

The vocabulary Schema.org was developed to facilitate the creation of structured data in web pages. Schema.org must attempt to cover anything that can be named on the Internet, which means just about anything one can imagine. Much of Schema.org's vocabulary is used in sites that describe products and services from automobiles to video games. Another large community participating in Schema.org is healthcare, which is adding to the Schema.org vocabulary the terms necessary for medical and healthcare information.

As a large, diverse vocabulary, Schema.org could be quite unwieldy. To mitigate this, Schema.org gathers under each high-level element that describes a thing, such as a movie, a dance event, or a local business type, a page showing the relevant elements from the Schema.org vocabulary that are likely to be useful in describing that thing. Web document creators can focus on the things that are in their purview using the profile provided by Schema.org.

RDF Validation and Shapes

The W3C's RDF standard has many positive attributes, in particular its facilitation of an ever-expanding graph of information. Its use of concepts from the artificial intelligence sciences, such as inferencing, could support sophisticated applications. In addition, RDF describes an "open world" where no assumption can be made regarding the completeness of any ad hoc selection of triples, making the standard highly fault-tolerant as the web of data grows and changes.

This openness has a downside for developers of applications that require stable and predictable data. In most applications, there is a need to perform some quality control over the data such as defining certain elements as required for the application, and controlling the allowed values of elements. The RDF suite of standards, unlike XML, does not yet provide a technology to define and constrain data schemas. There is, however, a recognized need to have functions that are designed to support the validation of individual data elements and the definition of bounded graphs.

These bounded graphs are often described as a kind of "record format" for RDF, in which the content of identified graphs is limited to certain elements. Defining specific graphs in RDF is a kind of profiling; it selects elements based on a profile created by the viewing application.

As use of RDF has increased, especially in the enterprise world, the question of validation has become an issue for the W3C. Individual developers have come up with their own solutions, some have used the RDF query language, SPARQL, to create a validation function for their data. Others, who are using the XML serialization of RDF, have applied XML schema validation to their data. Still others have applied the constraints defined in the Web Ontology Language (OWL) as they would be interpreted in a closed world by reversing the open world assumption of that language. While relatively effective, none of these is a true RDF description and validation method that could be considered part of the suit of RDF standards curated by the W3C.

In September of 2013, the W3C hosted a 2-day workshop with the title "RDF Validation Workshop, Practical Assurances for Quality RDF Data." (World Wide Web Consortium, 2013) Over a dozen developers exhibited their solutions to the RDF quality-control problem, many outlining where the solutions they were using failed in some way, either by not producing the quality of data desired, or by being difficult to share with data partners. These developers represented a range of communities from academia, medical information systems, and traditional information technology companies. Some of the organizations that had developed their own solutions were: IBM, with Open Services for Lifecycle Collaboration (OSLC); Top-Braid, with SPARQL Inferencing Notation (SPIN); and Clark & Parsia's Stardog, which uses OWL constraints.

This show of interest led the W3C to open a Working Group on RDF Data Shapes. (World Wide Web Consortium, 2014) The working group began in September of 2014 and is scheduled to complete its work in 2017. The standard being developed is being called Shapes Constraint Language, or SHACL. SHACL is being developed as an RDF vocabulary and is heavily based on SPARQL functionality. Its basic vocabulary, called SHACL Core, has most of the typical features of data validation such as data type control and cardinality. It includes an extension mechanism that allows for the develop of customized validation functions.

A separate effort called Shapes Expressions (ShEx) also arose out of the W3C workshop and is being developed by a different group as an informal W3C effort. (Boneva, 2016) ShEx is not an RDF vocabulary but is based on a formal definition and has been implemented in Java/Scala, Python, and Javascript. It is approximately equivalent to the validation rules defined in SHACL Core. One difference is that SHACL includes methods to target the nodes in the RDF data that will be subjected to each particular validation process; ShEx defines the validation only, assuming that the data graphs that will be checked for conformance have been previously identified (either through other programs or as an API function).

Either of these validation languages could have a place in the application profile suite of standards, possibly as shown in Figure 3.

These validation standards are powerful members of the application profile stack. They can be used to validation data at the point of input through user interfaces, or to test data received from API queries or searches. Conceivably the validation rules could be transformed into human-readable technical documentation.

Fulfilling the Dublin Core Application Profile Model

By adopting one or more of the emerging validation standards, the Dublin Core model of application profiles becomes nearly complete. Domain models can make use of standard modeling languages like UML. Vocabularies can be defined with RDF/RDFS or the Web Ontology Language (OWL). Validation rules can be written in a validation standard language. One still lacks actual standards for functional requirements and usage guidelines, although these are often provided as texts.

What is still missing, however, is a defined document format that gathers all of these aspects into a coherent application profile that is standardized, machine-readable, and, to the extent possible, machine-actionable. The development of a well-defined standard for application profiles will be motivated through the culture of

Figure 3. Dublin Core Application Profile modified for RDF validation

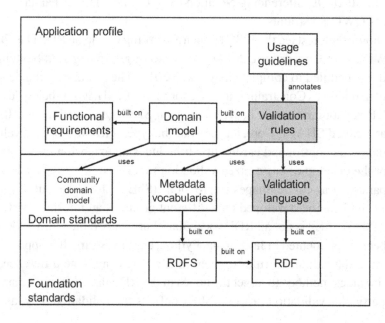

open sharing of data and documents and through the increased re-use of vocabularies and data. The work of the Dublin Core Metadata Initiative has provided a strong theoretical and practical basis for this development, and the community continues to encourage development in this area.

REFERENCES

Boneva, I., & Prud'hommeaux, E. (2016) *Shape Expressions Language*. Retrieved from https://shexspec.github.io/spec

Clark, J., & Makoto, M. (2001) *RELAX NG Specification*. Retrieved from http://relaxing.org/spec-20011203.html

Coyle, K., & Baker, T. *Guidelines for Dublin Core Application Profiles*. (2009) Retrieved 16 from http://dublincore.org/documents/profile-guidelines

Dublin Core Metadata Initiative. *History of the Dublin Core Metadata Initiative*. Retrieved from http://dublincore.org/about/history/

Dublin Core Metadata Initiative Usage Board. (2012) *DCMI Metadata Terms*. Retrieved from http://dublincore.org/documents/dcmi-terms/

Library of Congress. (2014) *BIBFRAME Profiles: Introduction and Specification*. Retrieved from http://www.loc.gov/bibframe/docs/bibframe-profiles.html

Nilsson, M. (2008) *Description Set Profiles: A constraint language for Dublin Core Application Profiles*. Retrieved from http://dublincore.org/documents/dc-dsp/

Nilsson, M., Baker, T., & Johnston, P. (2008) *The Singapore Framework for Dublin Core Application Profiles*. Retrieved from http://dublincore.org/documents/Singapore-framework

Schema.org. (n. d.). XML Schema 1.1.

World Wide Web Consortium. (2013, September 10-11) *RDF Validation Workshop; Practical Assurances for Quality RDF Data*. Washington, DC. Retrieved from https://www.w3.org/2012/12/rdf-val/

World Wide Web Consortium. (2014) *RDF Shapes Working Group Charter*. Retrieved from https://www.w3.org/2014/data-shapes/charterWorldWideWebConsortium

Zepheira. (n. d.). *Bibframe Lite*. Retrieved from http://bibfra.me/view/lite/

Chapter 2
The Development of an Optimised Metadata Application Profile

Paul Walk
EDINA, University of Edinburgh, UK

ABSTRACT

This chapter describes an approach to the development of a metadata application profile. It is particularly concerned with the class of application profile which is optimised for a specific use-case, rather than those which are more concerned with supporting general interoperability in a broader domain. The example of the development of a particular application profile, RIOXX, is used to illustrate some of the methodology discussed. Much of the approach described in the chapter was designed during the course of the development of RIOXX. Issues which are given particular consideration include a focus on the close involvement of 'implementors' (normally software developers), the adoption of ideas from agile software development, continuous testing and open development, and ongoing maintenance and sustainability "on a shoestring".

INTRODUCTION

Application profiles consist of data elements drawn from one or more namespace schemas combined together by implementers and optimised for a particular local application. (Heery & Patel, 2000)

DOI: 10.4018/978-1-5225-2221-8.ch002

This is one of the earliest and, arguably, the best definition of the term application profile. The author prefers this definition because, while mentioning 'data elements', 'namespaces' and 'schemas' (all crucial aspects), it is also careful to emphasise the importance of the involvement of 'implementers' and 'optimisation' for a 'particular local application'.

While this definition suggests that application profiles ought to be focused on meeting particular requirements, the recent history of their varied development places them on a scale, from those which have been developed to enable broad interoperability in a general domain or 'application space', to those which are, indeed, optimised to enable a particular application. The concept of interoperability is intrinsically bound up in the development of metadata standards and profiles. However, interoperability and optimisation do not always complement each other as features, and application profiles tend to emphasise one or the other. For example, the Scholarly Works Application Profile (SWAP) is described as "a DC Application Profile for describing an eprint, or scholarly work" ("Scholarly Works Application Profile", 2009). The documentation for this application profile says nothing about use-cases and it does not identify any 'particular local application'. SWAP, like plenty of other application profiles, is designed to facilitate as-yet-unknown applications by explaining how to describe a particular type of resource to an appropriate level of detail. Essentially, this kind of support for interoperability is about enabling the possibility of future interoperation, rather than being focused on any particular, intended implementation. As such, if SWAP were to be placed on the aforementioned scale, it would be positioned close to the 'interoperability' end of the axis, and some distance away from 'optimisation'.

This chapter is concerned with the other end of that scale, with application profiles which are optimised for particular local applications. The specific example of RIOXX is used to illustrate a methodology for the development of an application profile which focuses on supporting its intended implementation. RIOXX has been developed to address a specific use-case: this use-case together with the application profile itself are briefly introduced, while the bulk of this chapter is concerned with the methodology used in development, deployment and implementation.

BACKGROUND

The Use-Case

In the United Kingdom, research funded by national government is managed by seven Research Councils. With a growing desire to see publicly-funded research made more openly available to those who have funded it through their taxes, a policy for 'open access' to published research papers has been introduced by Research Councils UK (RCUK), the body which represents the Research Councils in such matters.

The RCUK Policy on Open Access1 demands that any organisation which receives Research Council funding should make the outputs from that funding available. RCUK recommends the use of open-access repositories for this purpose. Most research-active institutions in the UK maintain an institutional repository, so this is the *de facto* standard way to make such outputs available. While there is growing interest in other types of research output—in particular data—the focus of this policy is on research *papers*. Publishers often place 'embargoes' on scholarly publications - preventing them from being shared, except through the publisher's own system, for a period (usually between 6-24 months) after publication.

An important detail is that RCUK requires that the institution provide assurance that the policy is being followed. They expect the institution to report that a paper exists, within a short period after it has been accepted for publication, regardless of any embargo. This requires that the institution make available a certain amount of information about the paper. In addition to the common metadata elements such as 'title' and 'author', the institution also needs to supply information about the source of the funding for the paper being described, as well as some indication of the license terms under which it is made available.

Because research-active institutions in the UK already manage papers in institutional repositories, RCUK worked with an organisation called Jisc to fund the development of a metadata application profile designed to enhance the quality of metadata already exposed by those repositories, so that this metadata would satisfy the specific requirement of reporting the existence and funding of papers to RCUK. The author of this chapter was part of a small team (Paul Walk, Sheridan Brown and Ian Stuart) commissioned to undertake this development.

Institutional repositories invariably support a protocol, OAI-PMH, which allows metadata records to be 'harvested'. The agreed solution to the RCUK use-case involved the development of a new metadata application profile, RIOXX, which could be harvested via OAI-PMH. In this way, a given institution could comply with the RCUK policy on open access by creating metadata records, in the RIOXX format, and allowing RCUK to harvest these.

It was quickly established that RIOXX would need to model a fairly common set of properties – those found in a typical metadata record for a scholarly paper, but that certain additional requirements and constraints would need to be introduced to meet the use-case requirements. For example, RCUK would need to verify that a given paper, declared to be 'open access', was indeed publicly available. Given the scale of the problem – the volume of research papers produced under Research Council funding in the UK is considerable – RIOXX would need to support the automated identification of and access to the paper itself. For this reason, RIOXX would need to apply careful constraints to the identification of resources.

Other requirements were less common, and required information not normally found in a typical bibliographic record for a scholarly paper, such as expressions of license for use, and the identification of funders and projects related to the paper. These are described a little more later.

Dublin Core - The Default Starting Point

By their nature, application profiles build upon existing information standards. Having agreed that the development of an application profile was the correct approach to addressing the RCUK open access reporting use-case, the author looked for an appropriate starting point. The default application profile used by the OAI-PMH protocol is called *oai_dc*, where the 'dc' stands for 'Dublin Core'. This reflects the fact that the application profile builds on the Dublin Core Metadata Initiative's DCMI Metadata Terms2. Much of the metadata requirement to support the RCUK use-case is fairly ordinary - a basic bibliographic record with some of the usual elements is required. This is supported by Dublin Core. However, the use-case also demands some information not easily provided by standard Dublin Core or by the *oai_dc* profile. The correct approach to the development of RIOXX suggested, therefore, that it build upon Dublin Core, with properties from the DCMI Metadata Terms making up the bulk of RIOXX - but that it would need to include other namespaces, since Dublin Core does not provide the means to describe all of the information required in the RCUK use-case.

The Lack of Established Development Methodology Appropriate to The Use-Case

One approach to the development of an application profile based on the DCMI Metadata Terms is The Singapore Framework for Dublin Core Application Profiles (Nilsson, Baker, Johnston, 2008). This approach is endorsed by DCMI, and was used to develop the Scholarly Works Application Profile (SWAP). The Singapore Framework asserts that a Dublin Core Application Profile is a "packet of documentation" comprising these components:

- A description of functional requirements (mandatory)
- A domain model, expressed as text or more formally though something like UML, which defines informational entities and relationships in the scope of the application profile (mandatory)

- A Description Set Profile (DSP) - a template for describing the profile in terms of constraints and rules (mandatory)
- Usage guidelines, explaining how the application profile should be implemented (optional)
- Guidelines on syntax and encoding (optional)

It is interesting to note the indicators, given in parentheses, where each comment is labelled as either mandatory or optional. The Singapore Framework appears to emphasise the formal documentation of the application profile at the expense, perhaps, of supporting its implementation. It seems that the Singapore Framework is better suited to those application profiles which are oriented more towards interoperability, and less towards optimisation for a particular application. It is telling that the component which speaks directly to someone implementing the application profile - the 'usage guidelines' - is labelled as an *optional* component.

In considering an approach to the development of RIOXX, the author wished to place a much greater emphasis on supporting its implementation, even at the expense of certain levels of formal documentation. The Singapore Framework does not support this approach well. Because no appropriate, existing methodology presented itself, a new approach was necessary. It was decided to identify and articulate some principles to inform the development, and then to adopt an methodology based upon these principles. The next section describes these principles, and how they may be used to inform development, using the development of RIOXX to illustrate this.

THE CHALLENGE OF DEVELOPING AN OPTIMISED APPLICATION PROFILE

The main thrust of this chapter is to describe an approach to the development of a metadata application profile to support a specific application. The example of RIOXX is used to illustrate this. Because several specific properties of RIOXX are referred to in the chapter, abridged documentation for the application profile is provided as Table 2 in Appendix 1. The reader may consult this as needed but, in summary, the application profile consists of eleven properties from the DCMI Metadata Terms (with the namespace prefixes of 'dc' and 'dcterms'), two properties from NISO's Open Access Metadata and Indicators (with the prefix 'ali') and eight properties created specifically for RIOXX (with the prefix 'rioxxterms').

Supporting Implementation from the Start

For an application profile to have any impact, it must be implemented. Nowadays, this invariably means that the profile must be realised, somehow, in a software system. Therefore, it could be argued that software developers are at least as important as information modelers in the design of a metadata application profile. However, software developers have not necessarily been directly involved in the development of application profiles.

Information modelers and software developers often work in quite different ways. Older methods of software development favoured detailed and precise specifications, prepared and agreed in advance. However, in recent years the practice of software development has taken some interesting turns. The introduction of the 'agile' paradigm in software development, announced with the *Manifesto for Agile Software Development*3, has had significant impact on practices, tools and attitudes in software engineering. Now, a growing number of software projects adopt aspects of the agile approach, with its emphasis on short, iterative development cycles and close collaboration between people, and its preference for working software over detailed specifications.

If an optimised application profile is to be a success, its developers must, to some extent, accommodate the needs and preferred ways of working of those who will implement it. With RIOXX, the author decided to adopt some aspects of agile software development in the process of developing the application profile. For example, rather than preparing detailed documentation in advance, a consultation process with software developers was begun very early in the process. Because RIOXX is clearly intended to be implemented in institutional repository systems, it made absolute sense to involve the developers of the main repository software platforms in use in UK institutions. The RIOXX team consulted very closely with these developers - in some cases even going to visit them in person, in the spirit of the agile approach which emphasises the importance of face-to-face contact.

This approach was found to be very beneficial. For example, the issue of how best to represent the relationship between a publicly funded research paper and its 'funding stream', while being an information modelling problem, also presented a challenge for implementation. The team's analysis of the problem suggested that there were, broadly speaking, five different approaches to this, as outlined in Table 1.

The RIOXX team had initially proposed option 1 (in Table 1). This was a far from perfect approach: because a research paper can have more than one funder, and be associated with more than one project, the RIOXX record would need to accommodate more than one instance of each property. With option 1, those properties would not be directly related within a given record. This was clearly unsatisfying as an information model, interestingly, the use-case did not demand that these

Table 1. Approaches to handling funders and projectIDs in a RIOXX record

#	Option	Description
1	Separate properties for Funder and ProjectID	The version initially proposed. Individual instances of the properties are not related to each other in a given metadata record.
2	Separate properties for Funder and ProjectID, where ordering is significant	Individual instances of the properties are related to each other in a given metadata record by virtue of their order (i.e. the first funder is related to the first project, and so on).
3	Composite property for Funder and ProjectID	An attractive proposition, where a composite property containing information about a funder and a project is used, and may be repeated in a given record.
4	Syntactically rich string containing Funder and ProjectID components	This is the approach used by OpenAIRE, where a text string is syntactically arranged to convey information about funder and project.
5	Globally unique projectID	The ideal approach, where a globally unique identifier is used for the project, and the funder can be extrapolated by resolving that identifier to discover metadata about the project.

properties be closely related. As such, it was a pragmatic approach, proposed because at the time it was 'received wisdom' that repository systems would be unable to cope with a more sophisticated approach, such as described by option 3 in Table 1.

These were documented and discussed with a variety of interested parties - especially systems developers. By presenting options, rather than a finished specification, the RIOXX team was able to gain immediate feedback from software developers, which informed the next iteration of development. In the case of the funder and project properties, the repository system developers agreed that option 3 was viable—with some necessary software development to support it—and that RIOXX should proceed to use that superior model for these properties.

The testing of assumptions, and the discussion of options with implementers at every stage of development is an important activity in the development of an optimised application profile. Furthermore, in keeping with the agile notion of using more, shorter iterations, this testing and discussion must be repeated between each stage of development.

In addition to testing assumptions, the RIOXX team became interested in how to test the actual application profile. This may sound unusual: an application profile is, essentially, a document or a set of documents. Documentation can be tested by humans for accuracy and readability, and formally structured, machine-readable documents can be tested for integrity, but the RIOXX team was interested also in testing implementations of RIOXX. Fortunately, RIOXX is designed to exposed by the systems which support it, via the OAI-PMH protocol. This means that RIOXX records can be harvested and processed. To this end, the RIOXX team developed a testing system which harvests a sample of records from a repository system and checks these for compliance with the application profile's constraints and rules. The results of this testing are made openly available4, with detailed reports showing just where the harvested records do or do not comply with the application profile. All systems which are known to have implemented RIOXX are tested. This information is of use to several different parties. The RIOXX team has been able to analyse which aspects of the application profile are proving difficult to implement, and has been able to advise implementers accordingly. Some of this intelligence may lead to future revisions of the application profile itself - in collaboration with the implementers of course. The administrators of the repository systems being tested are able to see where their management of metadata records in their system might be impacting on compliance with the application profile. And finally, the developers of the software platforms underpinning the institution repositories are able to see the results of testing their implementation of the application profile in software. The testing has already revealed more than one issue with implementations in software, which have then been discussed with the developers with a view to resolving these. In one case, this testing has revealed a fairly fundamental issue with a repository platform itself, which started a significant online discussion.

It is worth saying something about documentation, and the impact this has on implementation. The team chose to document the application profile in three ways: as a structured webpage for the formal documentation, as a machine-readable XML Schema (XSD), and with a user guide (PDF). The structured webpage was written in a style designed to appeal to, and be understood by, software engineers. The application profile is set out in a tabular form (reproduced in Table 2 in Appendix 1), and uses the formal language defined by the Internet Engineering Task Force for this purpose ("Key words for use in RFCs to Indicate Requirement Levels", 1997). The version on the website also includes several examples showing how certain complex properties should be expressed as XML (since XML is the format used by OAI-PMH).

At one stage in development, a request was made by Jisc (the organisation funding the project) to develop a 'crosswalk' between RIOXX and OpenAIRE - a similar metadata application profile used for general interoperability in open access repositories in Europe. The results of this were also delivered through the RIOXX website, using the same approach as for the application profile itself. This Crosswalk has now been implemented in the Open University's open-access papers aggregation system, *CORE*.5

Anecdotally, the RIOXX website has been favourably compared with others in this space, and engineers have reportedly found it easy to use - appreciating the 'showing by example' approach especially.

Being Ruthlessly Pragmatic

The RIOXX team gradually settled on a fairly extreme approach, where the potential for interoperability beyond the immediate RCUK use-case was more or less ignored, and decisions were weighted in favour of the ease of implementation to support the single, narrowly focused application. Even the decision to adopt Dublin Core - itself a great contributor to global interoperability - was taken because implementers are already largely familiar with it and so would find it easier to implement. The team described this approach as 'ruthless pragmatism', where nothing would be allowed to cause the development of RIOXX to deviate from the requirement to satisfy the specific RCUK use-case.

As the development progressed the team encountered an interesting phenomenon, where third parties began to make suggestions about additional features for RIOXX. Typically, this would be a simple request to add a property, so that a RIOXX record might also be used for some other purpose. The team viewed such suggestions as attempts to move RIOXX along the axis from optimisation towards interoperability and, as such, resisted them. Reluctantly, the team made two exceptions to this, and added the *rioxxterms:publication_date* and *ali:free_to_read* properties. Neither of these properties is not strictly necessary for the RCUK use-case, since the important date is the 'date of acceptance', captured by the *dcterms:dateAccepted* property, and the *ali:free_to_read* property is superfluous when the *ali:license_ref* conveys all necessary information about license for use. However, the inclusion of the *rioxxterms:publication_date* property allows a RIOXX record to function as a basic bibliographic record. In itself, this was a decision based on pragmatism, as repository administrators expect to see this property in the metadata records which they manage. The inclusion of the *ali:free_to_read* property was requested by the sponsor of the application profile, RCUK, in order to bring RIOXX into line with what was emerging as a community norm. It was agreed that this would be an optional property - again a pragmatic decision.

Maintaining an unwavering focus on the use-case, the team was able to establish another principle of good design for metadata application profile design: simplicity. The RIOXX profile is small, containing only 21 properties from three namespaces. The majority, eleven of these properties come from the DCMI Metadata Terms, two from NISO's Open Access Metadata and Indicators, with the remaining eight created especially for RIOXX. The reuse of existing namespaces and vocabularies is an important consideration for all application profiles, and RIOXX is no exception to this. By reusing the DCMI Metadata Terms where possible, it is possible to leverage the familiarity and widespread support which already exist for these properties.

In pursuit of the goal of simplicity of implementation, the RIOXX team was confronted with a problem: the domain of describing open access scholarly works is riddled with problematic and ambiguous terms. The phrase 'open access' itself does not have a universally agreed or recognised definition, and attempts to improve the precision of this term by prepending qualifiers such as 'gold' or 'green' have not been completely successful. Furthermore, some common metadata properties are similarly yet, perhaps, surprisingly imprecise. For example, it might be supposed that the date of publication of a paper is a simple fact which can be included in metadata without difficulty. However, often the precise publication date is simply not known. For example, in the RCUK use-case, the RIOXX metadata record must usually be prepared before the paper is published in a journal. And papers in journals are often published in two different ways - 'electronically' and in print. In addition to this, publishers often impose an 'embargo', restricting the rights of authors to make available open access versions of their papers until after a period of time following publication. One of the requirements for RIOXX was to make the expression of embargoes explicit and unambiguous. The RIOXX team established a working principle to constrain the application profile, where possible, to comprise only 'factual' metadata properties, avoiding imprecise terms and values, and avoiding any redundancy in information. The adoption of the *ali:license_ref* property (see Table 2) is an example of this: there had been much discussion about expressing embargo periods directly, but the decision was taken to express licenses information directly instead. This means that the conditions under which the paper may be read are explicit, together with the dates from which these conditions take effect.

Radically Open Development

Metadata application profiles are often developed openly, at least ostensibly. At the heart of many such projects is an email discussion list. This kind of email list brings several benefits. It creates a 'history' for the project, where decisions may be recorded and a kind of 'audit trail' is established and, crucially, it provides the 'place' where the application profile can be developed collaboratively. A typical pattern for such lists is for the project lead to post a message about some aspect of the project, and for a discussion 'thread' to be generated. Normally, any interested person may join such a list by requesting access. However, this technology supports a kind of 'passive openness', where there are no specific barriers to participation, but where the discussion, nonetheless, occurs in a 'walled' environment. In order to participate, a person must make a commitment of sorts - by joining the list - even if they just want to offer a single comment.

From the start of the RIOXX project, the author was keen to adopt a radically open approach to its development. In pursuit of this, it was decided not to use a mailing list at all, but to encourage discussion on the open Web by establishing a blog instead. This approach has proved to be successful for a number of reasons.

Firstly, it has encouraged some valuable discussions, involving a wide range of people such as information specialists, repository managers and software developers. An example of this is the post which described a significant issue discovered (through the systematic RIOXX testing) in the OPAI-PMH implementation of one of the repository platforms6. This post spawned a thread of thirty comments, many of which were from engineers working on that platform. It is unlikely that these engineers would have joined a mailing list dedicated to the development of RIOXX, but to have their contribution here was invaluable. In this way, software engineers have been brought directly into the heart of the project. The obvious limitation in the use of a blog is that only authors may start threads. To mitigate this, when the project team received direct enquiries or comments (by email or through face-to-face contact) which were thought to be of wider interest, the team published these comments or questions (with permission) on the blog.

A related benefit of the use of a blog is that it allowed the project team to do some of their 'thinking' in the open. This is best illustrated by a post which articulated the five options for handling funders and projectIDs in a RIOXX record listed in Table 1. Not only did the blog post allow more people to comment, but even more importantly it provided a freely accessible resource with a link - so that any time this issue needed to be discussed, the link to this post could be provided for easy reference. Again, this is something not easily supported by a mailing list.

Finally, the blog could be used to announce release candidates for the application profile, and to solicit feedback on these. This also proved invaluable, with commenters pointing out potential difficulties in implementation, which could be addressed in the next development iteration. In one case, the blog was also used to announce that an error had been discovered in the XML schema - again, an example of working very openly.

Minimal Maintenance

Funding for the development and hosting aspects of RIOXX ended in 2014. It is quite normal, albeit unfortunate, that projects to develop application profiles receive short-term funding with no prospect of ongoing funding for maintenance (although sometimes an application profile might receive subsequent project funding at a later date to be updated in some way). Anticipating this, the author invested some effort in identifying and implementing the most efficient and sustainable approach to developing, hosting and maintaining a Web-based, documented application profile.

For many years, the standard approach to developing a website to support a project has been to use a Content Management System (CMS) such as Wordpress or Drupal. These systems have several advantages: they are user-friendly, familiar to many users, and provide a good level of functionality, supporting a wide range of features through 'plugins'. However, CMS carry a significant maintenance overhead. They require certain underlying infrastructure components (e.g. a relational database and an application environment) as well as the ubiquitous web server. Furthermore, they do not always support good development practice, such as robust version control.

In recent times, an interesting alternative approach - that of the static site generator - has become viable. The static site generator uses the file-system to store content in simple files, typically formatted using Markdown,7 with metadata sections called front-matter, typically formatted as YAML8. The software (often a simple command-line application) then uses a set of templates to turn this simple content into straightforward 'static' HTML websites, which can then be uploaded to a web server. This approach offers two key advantages: the maintenance requirement for the resulting website is minimal, and the content is easily edited, since it is just a set of simple text files.

The RIOXX team adopted one such static site generator - a program called Hugo9 - to manage the RIOXX website - including all of the blog content, the structured documentation of the application profile and the outputs from the testing software. This approach has proven to be very effective - both in terms of development, but also for ongoing maintenance of the application profile and supporting documentation. The sources for the application profile, the blog posts and the rest of the documentation are stored as Markdown/YAML files and are synchronised with *git* to a repository on GitHub10 - so they are in a world-class version control system (an example of this can be seen in Appendix 2). The templates are stored alongside. Everything which is required to generate the website from scratch is stored in a version-controlled and redundant system.

The RIOXX website, including all documentation, is now maintained with next-to-zero effort. It runs on a completely standard web server, and requires no server-side maintenance whatsoever, since all that is hosted there is HTML, CSS, Javascript and a few binary files such as images. On the client-side, the author makes minor modifications a few times a year, and releases the occasional blog post. This has allowed the RIOXX website to continue to function well with no financial support or dedicated effort.

FUTURE WORK

The use of a static site generator to develop, manage and serve the technical documentation for RIOXX has been interesting, and demands further research and development. The author has begun collaborating with members of the DCMI community to explore how this technology might enable a more sustainable model for the maintenance of the DCMI Metadata Terms themselves.

In addition to this, the author remains interested in finding ways to further improve the likelihood of an application profile such as RIOXX being successfully implemented. Despite the focus on immediate implementation in the RCUK context there have been, nonetheless, expressions of interest in using RIOXX to serve other (albeit similar) use cases in other communities. To this end, some work has already been done to document a less strict version of RIOXX which has been called *Basic RIOXX*11, which retains the syntax but relaxes some of the constraints – notably around the use of certain vocabularies. The intention is to offer this as a re-usable resource, rather than as a supported standard.

The author has been asked if there is any intention to define the rioxxterms vocabulary in formal terms, and perhaps register this in the Linked Open Vocabularies (LOV) database.12 This is not something that was ever considered in the RIOXX project itself, since the sort of interoperability afforded by these steps would not have contributed to addressing the use-case. However, now that there is evidence of interest in the basic version of RIOXX mentioned earlier, this may be considered as worthwhile.

While the documentation was deliberately optimized for developers, the approach taken in using a combination of YAML and Markdown source files with a static site generator offers some options for future work and enhancements. In particular, this approach may be suitable for the simultaneous generation of machine-readable documentation, so the application of, for example, DCMI's Descriptions Set Profiles13 may be possible. While this would offer no particular benefit to RIOXX, this idea is currently being investigated by members of the DCMI community (including this author) in the context of documenting the DCMI Terms themselves.

CONCLUSION

The RIOXX project has provided a great opportunity to develop some ideas around the development, support, implementation and maintenance of an optimised metadata application profile. The radically open development approach, together with the regime of continuously testing implementations, have shown a way in which the wider community - and especially software developers - can actively participate in the development of such a profile.

RIOXX may be considered a success. Since the publication of the final version of the application profile in January 2015, the application profile has been implemented in 67 known institutional repositories in the UK. In addition the profile has been reportedly included in several consuming systems, including SHARE,14 the Open University CORE system and OneRepo.15 RIOXX has gained some reputation beyond the UK, with expressions of interest from Australia and Japan among others, and a review of RIOXX for the Technology Service Quarterly in the latter part of 2015 had this to say:

None of these projects addresses the interoperability problem in a targeted and practical manner as the online RIOxx metadata and application profile, though many refer to and track RIOxx as the current leader in the field.
The RIOxx website is a model for open-source support tool web design. Its simplicity and transparency for current and future implementers is without peer, while it also contains the keys that open doors for further research into the many international agencies that are working to make a bright future for research interoperability and shared information structures for all of us. I recommend this site highly, and I salute the work of the people who make it possible. (Mallory, M 2015)

ACKNOWLEDGMENT

The author would like to acknowledge the contributions of the following:

- The RIOXX team which included Sheridan Brown (Chygrove Ltd) and Ian Stuart (EDINA)
- RCUK, and particularly Ben Ryan, for their excellent sponsorship and support for the development of RIOXX
- EDINA (and the University of Edinburgh) for continuing to host the RIOXX website and technical documentation
- Jisc, for funding the development of RIOXX
- The enthusiastic and knowledgeable community of developers and repository managers for their active engagement with the development of RIOXX

REFERENCES

Bradner, S. (1997). *Key words for use in RFCs to Indicate Requirement Levels.* Harvard University. Retrieved from http://www.ietf.org/rfc/rfc2119.txt

Heery, R., & Patel, M. (2000). Application Profiles: Mixing and Matching Metadata Schemas. *Ariadne*, I25.

Mallory, M. (2015). RIOxx (Research Interoperability Opportunities Extensions) http://www.rioxx.net. Technology Services Quarterly, 32(4).

Nilsson, B.J. (2008). *The Singapore Framework for Dublin Core Application Profiles*. Retrieved from http://dublincore.org/documents/singapore-framework/

Scholarly Works Application Profile. (2009). Retrieved from http://www.ukoln.ac.uk/ repositories/digirep/index/Scholarly_Works_Application_Profile#Introduction

END NOTES

1   RCUK Policy on Open Access http://www.rcuk.ac.uk/research/openaccess/ policy/
2   DCMI Metadata Terms http://dublincore.org/documents/dcmi-terms/
3   Manifesto for Agile Software Development http://agilemanifesto.org
4   RIOXX Implementation http://www.rioxx.net/implementation/
5   CORE https://core.ac.uk
6   RIOXX and OAI PMH http://www.rioxx.net/2015/11/25/rioxx-and-oai-pmh/
7   Markdown https://daringfireball.net/projects/markdown/
8   YAML http://yaml.org
9   Hugo https://gohugo.io
10   GitHub https://github.com
11   RIOXX Basic Application Profile Version 2.0 Final http://www.rioxx.net/ profiles/v2-0-final_basic/
12   Linked Open Vocabularies (LOV) https://lov.okfn.org/dataset/lov/
13   Description Set Profiles http://dublincore.org/documents/dc-dsp/
14   SHARE http://www.share-research.org
15   OneRepo https://onerepo.net
16   RCUK RIOXX Application Profile Version 2.0 Final http://www.rioxx.net/ profiles/v2-0-final/

APPENDIX 1

It is worth describing the application profile itself, since this is used to illustrate the outcome of the methodology described in this chapter. Table 2 lists the complete set of properties in the RIOXX metadata application profile at version 2.0 (the version which is current at the time of writing). This information is adapted from the official RIOXX documentation16.

In Table 2, the terms MUST, MUST NOT, REQUIRED, SHALL, SHALL NOT, SHOULD, SHOULD NOT, RECOMMENDED, MAY, and OPTIONAL should be interpreted according to the Internet Engineering Task Force (IETF) Request for Comments 2119 ("Key words for use in RFCs to Indicate Requirement Levels", 1997).

Table 2. Properties in the RIOXX application profile, version 2.0

Element	Cardinality	Description
ali:free_to_read	Zero or one	This is defined in the NISO Open Access Metadata and Indicators. This element does not take a value - the semantics of *ali:free_to_read* are conveyed by its presence or absence. This element may be modified by two optional attributes, *start_date* and *end_date*. Each of these attributes, if present, takes a date value which MUST be encoded using ISO 8601 (post–2004 versions) which follows the following format: YYYY-MM-DD. The absence of a *start_date* attribute implies that the meaning conveyed by the *ali:free_to_read* element is current and immediate, unless an *end_date* attribute which is a date in the subjective past, is present in the element.
ali:license_ref	One or more	This is defined in the NISO Open Access Metadata and Indicators. This element MUST take an HTTP URI for its value. This HTTP URI MUST point to a resource which expresses the license terms specifying how the resource may be used. This element MUST include the attribute *start_date*. This attribute takes a date value which MUST be encoded using ISO 8601 (post–2004 versions) which follows the following format: YYYY-MM-DD. This attribute is used to indicate the date upon which this license takes effect. Multiple *ali:license_ref* elements may be included. Where several such elements are included, the one with the *start_date* attribute indicating the most recent date takes precedence. This approach allows the expression of 'embargoes', where a particular license takes effect at a date in the subjective future. In the absence of any other license, the copyright holder reserves all rights automatically. As a convenience, RIOXX provides two URLs which may be used to explicitly convey this state: http://www.rioxx.net/licenses/all-rights-reserved and http://www.rioxx.net/licenses/under-embargo-all-rights-reserved
dc:coverage	Zero or more	
dc:description	Zero or more	This field may be indexed and its contents presented to people conducting searches. The goal is to describe the content of the resource using free text. It is RECOMMENDED that an English language abstract be used where available. HTML or other markup tags SHOULD NOT be included in this field.

continued on following page

Table 2. Continued

Element	Cardinality	Description
dc:format	Zero or more	This refers to the format of the resource. The MIME type of the object pointed to by this RIOXX record's *dc:identifier* element MUST be entered here. Note that this element should not be confused with *rioxxterms:type*
dc:identifier	Exactly one	This field MUST contain an HTTP URI which is a persistent identifier for the resource. The purpose of this field is, through direct identification of the resource, to allow access to it, therefore it is RECOMMENDED that this identifier should point to the actual resource being described by the RIOXX record (typically a file in MS Word or PDF format), rather than to an intermediary resource such as a repository web page. Note that RIOXX does not require any require particular file format to be used for the resource. To describe another version of the resource with a different identifier, a completely separate RIOXX record should be created.
dc:language	One or more	This refers to the primary language in which the content of the resource is presented. The element MAY be repeated if the resource contains multiple languages. Values used for this element MUST conform to ISO 639–3. This offers two and three letter tags e.g. "en" or "eng" for English and "en-GB" for English used in the UK.
dc:publisher	Zero or more	This element contains the name of the entity, typically a 'publisher', responsible for making the version of record of the resource available. This could be a person, organisation or service. Where available, the name of the publisher entered here SHOULD be from a controlled list.
dc:relation	Zero or more	The format of this element MUST be an HTTP URI which points to a related resource, e.g. a research data-set which underpins the resource. An exception to this is the DOI identifying the related 'version of record' - this MUST be recorded in the *rioxxterms:version_of_record* element. Each related resource MUST appear as a separate instance of the field.
dc:source	Zero or one	The source label describes a resource from which the resource is derived (in whole or in part). It is RECOMMENDED that the source is referenced using a unique identifier from a recognised system e.g. the unique 8-digit International Standard Serial Numbers (ISSN) assigned to electronic periodicals, or the 13 digit International Standard Book Number (ISBN13) assigned to books. In the latter case, the ISBN13 for the electronic version of the book SHOULD be used if available. Use of this element is applicable where the resource is to be published as part of a larger resource. Examples might include a journal article, a conference paper or a chapter of a book, but not a complete book for example.
dc:subject	Zero or more	
dc:title	Exactly one	This refers to the title, and any sub-titles, of the resource. The title should be represented using the original spelling and wording. The RECOMMENDED format for expressing subtitles is: 'Title:Subtitle'. Note that where the resource is a chapter in a book, the chapter title MUST be entered here, with the ISBN13 of the book being recorded in the *dc:source* element.

continued on following page

Table 2. Continued

Element	Cardinality	Description
dcterms:dateAccepted	Exactly one	The date on which the resource was accepted for publication. The date MUST be encoded using ISO 8601 (post–2004 versions) using the following format: YYYY-MM-DD.
rioxxterms:apc	Zero or one	This element expresses whether or not the resource has an associated 'article processing charge'. The value of this element MUST be one of the following: 'paid', 'partially waived', 'fully waived', 'not charged', 'not required', 'unknown'.
rioxxterms:author	One or more	The author of the resource may be a person, organisation or service, but is most commonly a person. This element SHOULD take an optional attribute called *id*, which MUST contain an HTTP URI which uniquely identifies the author. Where there is more than one author, a separate *rioxxterms:author* element MUST be used for each. As many authors may be entered as required. The ideal use of this element is to include both an HTTP URI in the *id* attribute, and a text string in the body of the element. Where the author is a person, the RECOMMENDED format is to add text in the form Last Name, First Name(s), and to include an ORCID ID, if known, in its HTTP URI form. Where the author is an organisation, the RECOMMENDED format is to add the official name of the organisation, and to include an ISNI ID, if known, in its HTTP URI form. Where the *rioxxterms:author* element appears multiple times for one record, it CAN be assumed that the order is significant, in that the first element describes the 'first named author' of the resource. In order to make this more explicit, an extra attribute, *first-named-author*, SHOULD be used to indicate which of the *rioxxterms:author* elements describes the first named author of the resource.
rioxxterms:contributor	Zero or more	This field is designed to describe an entity – for example the name of a person, organisation or service – responsible for making contributions to the content of the resource. As many *rioxxterms:contributor* elements may be entered as required. This element SHOULD take an optional attribute called *id*, which MUST contain an HTTP URI which uniquely identifies the contributor. The ideal use of this element is to include both an HTTP URI in the *id* attribute, and a text string in the body of the element. Where the contributor is a person, the RECOMMENDED format is to add text in the form Last Name, First Name(s), and to include an ORCID ID, if known, in its HTTP URI form. Where the contributor is an organisation, the RECOMMENDED format is to add the official name of the organisation, and to include an ISNI ID, if known, in its HTTP URI form.

continued on following page

Table 2. Continued

Element	Cardinality	Description
rioxxterms:project	One or more	This is designed to collect the project ID(s), issued by the funder(s), that relate to the resource, together with the name and/or global identifier for the funder(s). The element MUST contain one project ID, an alphanumeric identifier provided by the funder in its original format. In cases where the resource has been funded internally, an appropriate internal code might be used. The element takes two attributes, *funder_name* and *funder_id*. One or both of *funder_name* and *funder_id* MUST be supplied. The canonical name of the entity responsible for funding the resource SHOULD be recorded in the *funder_name* attribute as text. A globally unique identifier for the funder of the resource SHOULD be recorded in the *funder_id* attribute. An HTTP URI MUST be used for this. It is RECOMMENDED that one of the following identifier schemes is used: an ISNI ID, or a DOI (in its HTTP URI form) made available by CrossRef through the FundRef system. Where the resource has been funded by more than one funder a separate *rioxxterms:project* element MUST be added for each. Similarly, where several project IDs provided by the same funder have been attached to the resource, a separate *rioxxterms:project* element MUST be added for each. This means that it is quite normal for a given *funder_name*, *funder_id* or *project_id* to appear in multiple instances of the *rioxxterms:project* element in a single RIOXX metadata record.
rioxxterms:publication_date	Zero or one	This element takes the publication date of the resource in the form in which it would be cited. This element is not used in a RIOXX context but allows for a RIOXX record to become a reasonable bibliographic record for the resource. This is a free-text field. As RIOXX is primarily concerned with such issues as compliance with funders' mandates and licensing of open access publications, the critical dates for the assertion of compliance are those held in the *start_date* attributes of the *ali:license_ref* elements.
rioxxterms:type	One or more	Type refers to the 'type' - the nature or genre of the content of the resource. Take care not to confuse this with *dc:format*. Values recorded here MUST be from the following controlled list of types: 'Book', 'Book chapter', 'Book edited', 'Conference Paper/Proceeding/Abstract', 'Journal Article/Review', 'Manual/Guide', 'Monograph', 'Policy briefing report', 'Technical Report', 'Technical Standard', 'Thesis', 'Other', 'Consultancy Report', 'Working paper'.
rioxxterms:version	Exactly one	This element indicates which 'version' of the resource is being described. The value of this element MUST be one of the following: 'AO', 'SMUR', 'AM', 'P', 'VoR', 'CVoR', 'EVoR', 'NA'. These terms are adopted from the recommendations of the NISO/ALPSP JAV Technical Working Group and have the following meanings: • AO = Author's Original • SMUR = Submitted Manuscript Under Review • AM = Accepted Manuscript • P = Proof • VoR = Version of Record • CVoR = Corrected Version of Record • EVoR = Enhanced Version of Record • NA = Not Applicable (or Unknown)

continued on following page

Table 2. Continued

Element	Cardinality	Description
rioxxterms:version_of_record	Zero or one	This field MUST contain an HTTP URI which is a persistent identifier for the published version of the resource. If a DOI has been issued by the publisher then this MUST be used. Such a DOI MUST be represented in its HTTP form.

APPENDIX 2

An example of the source of the documentation for one property (ali:license_ref) of the RIOXX application profile:

```
---
date: '2016-03-21T10:00:43+00:00'
draft: false
type: metadata_profile_property
title: ali:license_ref
cardinality: One or more
requirement: Mandatory
metadata_profile: v2-0-final
---
```

This is defined in the [NISO Open Access Metadata and Indicators](http://www.niso.org/workrooms/ali/). This element **MUST** take an HTTP URI for its value. This HTTP URI **MUST** point to a resource which expresses the license terms specifying how ***the resource*** may be used.

This element **MUST** include the attribute:

* start_date

This attribute takes a date value which **MUST** be encoded using ISO 8601 (post–2004 versions) which follows the following format: YYYY-MM-DD.

This attribute is used to indicate the date upon which this license takes effect. Multiple *ali:license_ref* elements may be included. Where several such elements are included, the one with the *start_date* attribute indicating the most recent date takes precedence.

Example:

```
    <ali:license_ref start_date="2015-02-17">http://creative-
commons.org/licenses/by/4.0</ali:license_ref>
```

This approach allows the expression of 'embargoes', where a particular license takes effect at a date in the subjective future.

In the absence of any other license, the copyright holder reserves all rights automatically. As a convenience, RIOXX provides two URLs which may be used to explicitly convey this state:

* [http://www.rioxx.net/licenses/all-rights-reserved](/licenses/all-rights-reserved)
* [http://www.rioxx.net/licenses/under-embargo-all-rights-reserved](/licenses/under-embargo-all-rights-reserved)

Chapter 3
The Minimum Mandatory Metadata Sets for the KIM Project and RAIDmap

Alexander Ball
University of Bath, UK

Mansur Darlington
University of Bath, UK

Christopher McMahon
University of Bristol, UK

ABSTRACT

A Minimum Mandatory Metadata Set (M3S) was devised for the KIM (Knowledge and Information Management Through Life) Project to address two challenges. The first was to ensure the project's documents were sufficiently self-documented to allow them to be preserved in the long term. The second was to trial the M3S and supporting templates and tools as a possible approach that might be used by the aerospace, defence and construction industries. A different M3S was devised along similar principles by a later project called REDm-MED (Research Data Management for Mechanical Engineering Departments). The aim this time was to help specify a tool for documenting research data records and the associations between them, in support of both preservation and discovery. In both cases the emphasis was on collecting a minimal set of metadata at the time of object creation, on the understanding that later processes would be able to expand the set into a full metadata record.

DOI: 10.4018/978-1-5225-2221-8.ch003

INTRODUCTION

Between 2005 and 2013 the University of Bath was involved in a series of linked projects aimed at improving knowledge and information management in engineering. The first of these went by the title 'Immortal Information and Through-Life Knowledge Management: Strategies and Tools for the Emerging Product–Service Paradigm', though that was colloquially abbreviated to 'Knowledge and Information Management Through Life' and thence to 'KIM'.

The KIM Project was a Grand Challenge project funded by the Engineering and Physical Sciences Research Council (EPSRC) and the Economic and Social Research Council (ESRC) in the UK (Ball et al., 2006). It ran for three-and-a-half years and involved 11 universities and numerous industrial collaborators. One of the purposes of the KIM Project was to experiment with new ways of working on engineering projects in order to increase efficiency across the lifecycle, and to improve the long-term usability of the project records. This being the case, the project incorporated some of those ways of working into its own governance and processes as both a test and a demonstrator. For example, all project files were given a coded file name that indicated the work unit to which it belonged, the type of document, the initial creator, and the version, but did not reveal the content. Instead, researchers were expected to embed the title in the document properties, and a separate registry was maintained that decoded file names into document titles.

One of the methods used to protect the longevity of the project records was to impose a Minimum Mandatory Metadata Set (M3S) for all project documents. Researchers were required to embed the specified metadata in the documents they created. The intention was to use it, alongside regular file properties and information supplied at the collection level, to generate a complete set of preservation and descriptive metadata for each document. In order to reduce the burden this would place on researchers, document templates were written that used the embedded metadata to fill out content on title pages, headers, footers, and so on. As mentioned above, additional metadata was encoded in the file name convention.

Even though the focus of the KIM Project was on knowledge and information management within industry, some aspects of the work had wider applicability. Therefore, when the Joint Information Systems Committee (JISC) of the UK further and higher education funding councils set up a programme to fund projects tackling various challenges in the area of research data management (RDM), the University of Bath took forward some of the ideas from KIM and applied them to academic research in the course of two much smaller projects.

ERIM (Engineering Research Information Management) developed a set of RDM processes for the Innovative Design and Manufacturing Research Centre at Bath, including a technique for visualizing the inter-relationships between the various records generated by a research project. The latter technique, known as Research Activity Information Development (RAID) modelling, was based on UML activity diagrams and could be used to trace the results published in a paper back to raw data files or further back to project plans (Ball, Darlington, Howard, McMahon, & Culley, 2012).

The follow-on project REDm-MED (Research Data Management for Mechanical Engineering Departments) generalized these processes for use by the Mechanical Engineering Department – in consultation with a parallel project setting up RDM support across the university – and by engineering departments in other universities. The project also developed a software tool called RAIDmap to aid in the creation of RAID diagrams.

In the event the digital RAID diagrams produced by RAIDmap were much richer than the purely graphical diagrams developed by ERIM. They were capable of storing metadata records for each node (file, instrument) in the diagram, populated partly automatically and partly manually. Indeed, the vision for RAIDmap was that it would monitor the user's workspace and automatically add nodes and metadata to the diagram as the user worked; the user would periodically fill in any gaps in the metadata and note relationships between nodes. The question naturally arose of what metadata users should be asked to provide themselves, and what the best practice should be for providing it: embedding it within the document or entering it manually into RAIDmap. To that end, the idea of a Minimum Mandatory Metadata Set was revisited.

This chapter presents the two Minimum Mandatory Metadata Sets and the process by which they were developed and implemented. It explores the rationale and motivation for the respective sets, and reflects on the merits of the approach taken.

BACKGROUND

In discussing the metadata requirements of the various stakeholders involved, the authors found it helpful to use the terminology defined by the Open Archival Information System (OAIS) Reference Model (Consultative Committee for Space Data Systems, 2002). The Information Model presented in that standard defines five types of metadata that have an important role when preserving data objects in an archive:

- **Representation Information:** The information needed by the user to interpret and understand the data object. An archive would be expected to store enough Representation Information to satisfy the needs of a typical member of the Designated Community, that is, the user group that the archive has committed to support. The collective name for the data object and its associated Representation Information is Content Information.

- **Provenance Information:** Information about the source of the Content Information, the chain of custody since its creation and the operations performed on it.
- **Context Information:** Information describing how the Content Information relates to other information resources.
- **Reference Information:** Unique identifiers for the Content Information.
- **Fixity Information:** Checksums or other information that could be used to detect, and possibly reverse, undocumented alterations to the Content Information.

A later version of the standard defines a further class of metadata, Access Rights, consisting of the permissions, licenses and terms of use for accessing, preserving, distributing, and using the Content Information (Consultative Committee for Space Data Systems, 2012). When a data object is packaged together with the above types of metadata, it forms what OAIS calls an Information Package.

While these terms were useful for describing the various metadata that might be of relevance, the OAIS Information Model did not go so far as to enumerate the various metadata elements that would be needed in each category. The authors therefore looked at other work that had been done in the area of preservation metadata.

To serve the needs of its digital collections, the National Library of Australia (1999) proposed a scheme of 25 elements, of which two were complex (i.e., had sub-elements). The starting point for the proposal was a 16-element set recommended by RLG for images generated by digitization projects (Research Libraries Group, Working Group on Preservation Issues of Metadata, 1998). The NLA version was at once more detailed and general: it could be applied to audiovisual material, databases, executables, and text as well as images. The OAIS model was one of the influences for the scheme, as was the data model for PANDORA, Australia's Web archive, along with metadata schemes being developed concurrently by other groups.

One of these was the scheme developed by the Cedars project (CURL Exemplars in Digital Archives, 2000) for university research libraries seeking to preserve archival digital content. This scheme was explicitly based on the OAIS Information Model: it was conceived as a hierarchy of complex elements, with the upper levels reproducing the OAIS model of an Information Package, and the lower levels filling in the details under the above categories. To give an impression of the size of the scheme, the hierarchy terminated in 24 simple elements. Notably, it introduced a detailed tree of elements for rights management that it included under Provenance Information.

Another was developed in the context of the Networked European Deposit Library (NEDLIB) project. Lupovici & Masanès (2000) proposed what they described as a minimal metadata set supporting the preservation of digital publications, aimed at national libraries. It consisted of eight top-level elements: five for Representation Information – one for each of the five layers in the OAIS Layered Information Model – and one each for Reference, Provenance and Fixity Information. The scheme could be said to be minimal in that it excluded rights and Context Information as understood above, but was actually more detailed than the Cedars scheme. The top-level elements were structured with 38 sub-elements, only six of which were themselves grouping further sub-elements.

In response to this flurry of activity, OCLC and RLG convened a Working Group on Preservation Metadata to build a consensus on best practice. They produced two reports in quick succession. The first was a white paper that compared and mapped between the above three schemes, and drew additional insights from an XML schema used by Harvard University's Data Repository Services (OCLC/RLG Working Group on Preservation Metadata, 2001). The second went a step further, using that comparison to merge the NLA, Cedars, and NEDLIB schemes into a unified hierarchy of elements (OCLC/RLG Working Group on Preservation Metadata, 2002). Some elements were added or refined after suggestions by Working Group members, and the elements relating to Fixity Information were taken instead from a scheme used by OCLC for its Digital Archive product. This hierarchy was called a framework rather than a scheme as it was not fully fleshed out: it did not specify how the information should be recorded for each element, for example, but suggested that some elements may need to be decomposed into (further) sub-elements. Also, it did not give much assistance on dealing with complex data objects, where an element from the framework may need a different value depending on which component file was considered.

The OCLC/RLG framework was intended as a foundation for future work rather than an end in itself. When the National Library of New Zealand (NLNZ) came to devise a scheme for its digital holdings, it concurred with the principles behind it, but felt that the NLA proposal was a better starting point for a practical and implementable metadata scheme (National Library of New Zealand, 2003). While the framework had favoured the OAIS Information Model for its basic structure, the NLNZ scheme returned to the NLA's data model of collections, objects, and files, and a more linear sequence of elements. Indeed, it went further and introduced a new four-entity model where elements could apply to objects (simple, complex, or groups), files, processes, or metadata modifications.

OCLC and RLG convened a second working group in 2003 to tackle much the same issue: how to turn the earlier framework into something practical and implementable. The group, Preservation Metadata: Implementation Strategies (PREMIS), came to very similar conclusions to the NLNZ scheme. It developed a five-entity data model of Intellectual Entities (similar to the NLA's idea of a 'work'), Objects (similar to the NLA's idea of a 'manifestation'), Events (similar to the NLNZ's idea of a process), Agents, and Rights. As with the NLNZ scheme, PREMIS recognized three types of object: a file, a bitstream (such as the audio and video streams within a multimedia file), and a representation (a set of files used at once to make a single rendition). Metadata elements were associated directly with these entities instead of being grouped in the OAIS metadata categories. Even more so than earlier schemes, the PREMIS scheme used a hierarchy of sub-elements to allow information to be structured for the benefit of automated tools (OCLC/RLG Preservation Metadata: Implementation Strategies Working Group, 2005).

The PREMIS scheme was warmly welcomed by the digital curation community, and indeed an active user community grew up around it, most conspicuously in the form of the PREMIS Implementors' Group. The Library of Congress agreed to host a Maintenance Activity to support PREMIS and develop it further; it published version 2.0 of the Data Dictionary in 2008 and version 3.0 in 2015. Since the PREMIS activity is focused on implementation, it has produced practical resources including an XML schema, an OWL ontology and a directory of examples of real-world usage (Library of Congress, 2016).

The PREMIS Data Dictionary was in this way the culmination of activity around preservation metadata from a digital repository perspective. There had however been a parallel set of developments among traditional archives (Caplan, 2006; Day, 2004). One strand began with the Functional Requirements for Evidence in Recordkeeping project (University of Pittsburgh, School of Information Sciences, 1996), also known as the Pittsburgh Project. This defined a scheme of elements intended to preserve the evidential value of electronic records over the long term; hence it included concepts, such as the transaction of which the object is a record, that were absent from the repository-based schemes. The scheme had six 'layers' grouping a total of 17 top-level elements and 48 sub-elements, only one of which grouped further sub-elements. About half of the elements and sub-elements were in the structural layer, and related to how the record might be rendered in a computing environment.

This work inspired several other metadata initiatives and was particularly influential in Australia. The *Recordkeeping Metadata Standard for Commonwealth Agencies* (National Archives of Australia, 1999) defined information that the agencies should collect about their records. This scheme was larger in terms of number of elements than the Pittsburgh scheme, but this was due to its having a broader scope. It was shallower in detail, with only four sub-elements dedicated to structural information compared to the 27 in the Pittsburgh scheme, for example. The scheme was fully revised in 2008 and renamed the Australian Government Recordkeeping Metadata Standard; further revisions were made in 2011 and 2015 (National Archives of Australia, 2015). Like the NLNZ scheme and PREMIS, it was reconstructed around a multi-entity model – in this case the five entities of Record, Agent, Business, Mandate and Relationship – with a different subset of the 26 elements applying to each entity.

The Victorian Electronic Records Strategy (Public Record Office Victoria, 2000) defined a self-documenting exchange format for records to permit them to be transferred reliably between systems. The metadata scheme for this format essentially encapsulated the Recordkeeping Metadata Standard with additional fields to aid transfer, such as descriptive metadata and encoding information.

Another strand of work began with the Preservation of the Integrity of Electronic Records project (Duranti, Eastwood, & MacNeil, 1997), which among other things defined a set of metadata attributes for records and dossiers. The emphasis of the project was more on procedures and protocols for the safe and auditable handling of electronic records, rather than on the technical challenges of preserving them, thus preservation metadata does not especially feature in the attribute list. The work was however carried forward by the International Research on Permanent Authentic Records in Electronic Systems project ("InterPARES project," n. d.), which began in 1998. The first phase of InterPARES reviewed the whole notion of what preserving electronic records entails; the second, between 2002 and 2007, performed a survey of relevant metadata standards; the third produced learning materials regarding preservation metadata and an application profile for authenticity metadata (Rogers & Tennis, 2016). As the name suggests, the profile was focused on authenticity and evidential integrity rather than preservation as such, with 10 sub-elements dedicated to structural metadata and upwards of 40 dedicated to provenance and context.

THE KIM MINIMUM MANDATORY METADATA SET

The motivation behind the Minimum Mandatory Metadata Set for the KIM Project was to address a particular issue affecting the construction industry and certain engineering industries such as aerospace and defence. These industries supply products that are expected to have a service life of multiple decades: products such as aircraft carriers or hospitals. The phenomenon addressed by the KIM Project was a movement in these industries towards a product–service paradigm, whereby instead of simply selling the product to the customer, the contractor would lease the implied capability to them. The contractor would therefore retain both the ownership of the product and the responsibility for ensuring it continued to perform to the customer's satisfaction.

Under this regime it is more important than ever that records produced early in the design stage of the product remain accessible and, crucially, reusable all the way through to the eventual disposal of the product. Such records may prove vital for performing maintenance, diagnosing unexpected behaviour, adapting the product to evolving customer needs, and disposing safely of the product once it has reached the end of its service life. The challenge faced by industry was, and is, how to curate digital records over time periods of five decades or more when the organization is likely to change key components of its software environment at intervals of between three and ten years.

Among the proposals for addressing the issue was that companies should systematically collect metadata for the digital records they create: metadata that would assist a digital archivist in preserving the records in the face of technological change. The question that arose naturally from this proposal was what these metadata might be. A literature review conducted in mid-2006 revealed the resources described above, specifically PREMIS version 1.0, the Recordkeeping Metadata Standard for Commonwealth Agencies, and the Victorian Electronic Records Strategy Metadata Scheme. While the first phase of the InterPARES project had concluded by that point it had not produced a workable metadata scheme; that would be a focus of later phases.

The three candidate schemes had a significant degree of overlap, with differences being more a matter of emphasis than of substance. For example, all three recorded information about the digital object, and the chain of processes it has undergone, but PREMIS emphasized the former while the recordkeeping standards emphasized the latter. Similarly, all three provided the means to prioritize the preservation of certain aspects of the digital object. The recordkeeping standards expressed this in terms of a mandate – legal or other requirements that stipulate what must be kept and for how long, or to put it another way, the evidential role or roles that the record would be expected to play. PREMIS used the more abstract and flexible notion of significant properties. The choice was made somewhat harder in that the recordkeeping standards fitted well with the corporate philosophy and environment of the industries with which the project was working, but the interest of the project team was in tackling the preservation challenges of some particularly difficult types of data, for which the PREMIS approach seemed better suited.

The decision was postponed while the next logical question was addressed: how the metadata were to be collected. The project's industrial collaborators were on the whole larger organizations, where there would be a division of labour between those creating the digital objects and those archiving and preserving them. Many had set up dedicated records management systems. A digital archivist in this context would be able to collect a certain amount of information from analysing files as they were ingested into the system, and the system would generate metadata itself as it performed ingest, archiving, and preservation processes on the files. Some information, though, could not be taken for granted: the originator of the file would either have to provide it separately or embed it deliberately within the file for the archivist to extract. This suggested to the project team that a more interesting question to ask was this: what could the archivist not be expected to deduce regardless of the nature of the digital object, and what information, therefore, would the originator be expected to provide in order to plug that gap. There was a tension to address between completeness and effort: if the team recommended that companies require originators to provide too much additional information, the impact on staff workload would make it unlikely that the recommendation would be adopted; or if it were adopted, it may result in staff ignoring or subverting the requirement.

In order to answer the question and test the result, the project team decided to apply the same principles to the digital objects produced within the project itself, and introduce a minimum mandatory metadata set. This would be a set of metadata that each researcher would be required to record for each project document. It would not be a precise analogy for introducing such a requirement in an industrial setting, but there were enough parallels between the two situations to make it an interesting trial. There was again a separation of roles between the researchers originating the digital objects and the repository managers and digital archivists who would eventually preserve them. Within each university, there would be a degree of consistency in the software used by the project team, as one would also expect in a corporate setting. The majority of researchers on the project were looking at issues other than the one in hand, so their tolerance for additional workload would not be extended by an ideological commitment to metadata.

The authors' approach was to derive the Minimum Mandatory Metadata Set (M3S) by taking a full preservation metadata scheme and subtracting the elements that a repository or archive would be able to supply from automated analysis or internal policy. For the remaining elements, they would suggest how authors could provide the information in the most efficient way, so as to reduce the additional effort. Since this would focus on the properties of the documents, rather than processes, it was decided to use PREMIS as the basis for the M3S; it was also felt that this would be more familiar to the repository managers and archivists who would be most likely to receive the documents at the end of the project.

Derivation of the Set

The first stage of the derivation was to work through the top-level metadata elements for each of the entities in the PREMIS data model. Note that in the following discussion, some levels of detail have been omitted for brevity; also, since the M3S relates to properties of a document, the more trivial translations of these properties into relationships with entities have been omitted.

The following elements are associated with *objects*:

- **Object Identifier:** Archives normally assign these for their own purposes, but for the sake of coordination and consistency across project partners (and indeed archives) it was felt important that the project should also provide its own identifiers, to be applied by the document originators.
- **Preservation Level:** This refers to whether the archive will provide bit-level preservation only, or will use techniques such as format migration or emulation to avoid rendering problems as formats become obsolete. This was for archival policy, rather than document originators, to decide.
- **Object Category:** This refers to whether the object in question is a representation (group of files), a single file, or a bitstream within a file. On a practical level, the authors did not expect document originators to provide metadata on a bitstream level, and anticipated that most documents would be represented by a single file.
- **Object Characteristics:** These were considered at the sub-element level:
  - **Composition Level:** This refers to the number of encryption or compression operations that have been applied to an object; it could be supplied implicitly by requiring originators to submit their documents uncompressed and unencrypted.
  - **Fixity:** Checksums could be generated by the archive.
  - **Size:** This could be measured by the archive.
  - **Format:** This could be derived from (a) the filename extension, (b) knowledge of the software environment of the project team members, and (c) information embedded within files by software automatically.
  - **Significant Properties:** This was again a matter of archive policy.
  - **Inhibitors:** This refers to password protection and similar mechanisms, which the project did in fact employ. For obvious reasons, passwords could not be recorded in the document, so the authors resolved to require originators to supply the passwords separately to the archive on ingest.
- **Creating Application:** As for format, this could be derived from (a) the filename extension, (b) knowledge of the software environment of the project team members, and (c) information embedded within files by software automatically.
- **Original Name:** The filename used by the originator, by definition.
- **Storage:** This refers to the location of the object after ingest.
- **Environment:** The authors resolved to collect information about the software and hardware environment for each university's team and record this at the collection level, instead of asking originators to provide it on a per-document basis.

- **Signature Information:** The project had no plans to use digital signatures; if they were applied at all, it was felt likely to be after ingest.
- **Relationships:** There may be various indirect relationships between project documents (e.g., belonging to the same task) but the authors felt that direct relationships should be specified at the point of ingest rather than embedded at the time of document creation.
- **Linking Intellectual Entity Identifier:** This is an artifact of the data model, allowing multiple objects to instantiate the same work. Such relationships could be implied through a file naming convention; for example, the same work in Microsoft Word and Portable Document Format would have the same filename but a different filename extension for each format, and different versions of a file would have the same name apart from the version number.

PREMIS records the processing history of objects as *events*. The important pre-ingest events from the project perspective were the date of creation, date of issue (i.e., when it was last saved before being submitted for approval), date of approval, and date of last modification (typically to record the fact of approval). The following elements are associated with events:

- **Event Identifier:** This is an artifact of the data model and was left to the archive to assign.
- **Event Type, Event Date Time:** Document originators were best placed to provide this information. The authors felt it would be most intuitive for them to do so in the form of key–value pairs, with the type as the key and the date as the value.
- **Event Detail:** By using a standard set of date types, the project hoped to avoid the need for further clarifying text.
- **Event Outcome Information:** This allows archives to record the outcome of a process such as checking a file against its recorded checksum. It did not seem to be applicable to the above four date types.
- **Linking Agent Identifier:** This relationship includes a role, which in the case of the project could be derived from the date type, i.e. 'authorizer' (or similar) for the date of approval, and 'creator' for the others. It was agreed that the originator would provide the identities of the lead author and the person who approved the document.

The intention was for the lead author and authorizer to be recorded in PREMIS as *agents* with agent type 'person'. The project would supply a list of project members and the codes used internally in the project to identify them (corresponding to PREMIS elements "agent name" and "agent identifier") to allow the archive to associate them correctly with its own internal identifiers.

Version 1 of PREMIS acknowledged the importance of recording rights information by including a *rights* entity, but did not specify what would be important to record from a preservation perspective. Meanwhile, the project team had implemented an internal information classification scheme as a way of controlling access to commercially sensitive information:

- **Working:** The document is in draft and only for distribution by and discussion with the lead author.
- **Level 1:** The document is unrestricted and may be disseminated openly.
- **Level 2:** Access to the document is restricted to those registered with the KIM Project (in effect, the project team, the industrial collaborators and other interested academics and researchers).
- **Level 3:** Access to the document is restricted to members of the project team only.
- **Level 4:** Access to the document is restricted to a specified distribution list.

A complete expression of this access control in PREMIS would consist of the following elements:

- **Permission Statement Identifier:** This could be left for the archive to assign.
- **Granting Agent:** It was understood that part of the approval process for documents was to authorize dissemination at the stated access level, so the most appropriate agent to identify here would be the authorizer.
- **Granting Agreement:** This could be generated by the archive.
- **Permission Granted:**
  - **Act:** From the suggested controlled vocabulary in the PREMIS Data Dictionary, the most appropriate term would be 'disseminate'.
  - **Restriction:** For documents at Access Levels 2–4, this should indicate that dissemination would be limited to the given list of individuals. It was agreed that for Access Levels 2–3, this list would be provided by the project, while for Access Level 4, the list would be provided by the originator.
  - **Term of Grant:** The intention was to negotiate this at the time of ingest.

The last entity in PREMIS to consider was the *intellectual entity*. PREMIS does not enumerate metadata elements for this entity, but refers the reader to descriptive metadata schemes such as MARC, MODS and Dublin Core. The authors therefore had to consider which elements would be most useful to enable the discovery and retrieval of project documents. For the project's own purposes, they felt the most useful access points would be as follows:

- **Authors:** The full list of authors, as opposed to just the lead author.
- **Title:** A succinct statement of the subject matter.
- **Keywords:** The major topics of the document.
- **Document Type:** The project had established different series of documents; the most common types were reports and presentations, but there were also agenda, minutes, visit reports, discussion documents, tools (e.g., templates, questionnaires, participant briefings) and internal communications (e.g., procedures, directives, guidance).
- **Task Code:** This could be used as OAIS Context Information, grouping together documents relating to the same strand of research within the project.

After that first pass, the authors were left with four lists of information: that which would be specific to the document, and which the originator should embed within it; that which the originator should provide separately at ingest; that which would be common to all documents, and which the project should provide at the point of ingest; and that which would be generated by the archive. It was the first list that formed the basis of the M3S:

- Document identifier (at the level of intellectual entity and file)
- Filename, including extension and version number
- Title
- Lead author and other authors
- Date created, issued, approved, last modified
- Approved by
- Keywords
- Document type
- Task code
- Access level and, if Level 4, distribution list

The next stage was to rationalize the metadata to enable it to be recorded in the most efficient way. The approach taken was to encode as much information as possible in the identifier, which would also serve as the filename.

In PREMIS terms, the intellectual entity identifier was made up of five elements:

- A code identifying it as a KIM Project document ('kim');
- The task code, represented by two integers (e.g., '12' for Work Package 1, Task 2);

- The document type, represented by a three-letter code (e.g., 'rep' for report);
- A three-digit rank number, with each task code and document type having its own sequence starting at '001' – in order to support this, the project had to set up a central register to allocate the numbers;
- The lead author, represented by a two- or three-letter code.

Filenames were formed by appending two further pieces of information:

- The version number, normally expressed as two integers (e.g. '13' for version 1.3) but in the case of a document edited by someone other than the lead author, extended with a hyphen, the date in YYMMDD format, and the two- or three-letter code for the editor (e.g., '-060312ab');
- The normal filename extension.

In order to make the provision of the remaining information as painless as possible, the project produced a series of templates that made use of embedded metadata or document properties and exposed them as part of the title page information. For example, the Microsoft Word templates used the built-in document properties *Title*, *Author*, and *Keywords*, the custom properties *Access level*, *Approved by*, and *Date approved*, and the built-in metadata for the date and time of creation and last modification. The report template displayed most of these properties on the title page so the author did not have to type them twice. The template also displayed the filename and a generated issue date on the title page, and the title in page headers, using the same mechanism.

Considered thus far, the implementation of the M3S could not be considered a schema or profile. While the conventions in place would allow the metadata to be extracted by an automated script, only those elements taken from built-in document properties could be interpreted by generic tools. The semantics of the remaining elements would have to be inserted by custom scripts.

The opportunity to transform the M3S into an application profile, in the sense defined by Heery and Patel (2000), presented itself when the authors considered how to embed the metadata in PDF files. While the PDF specification did not provide direct support for custom properties, it allowed them to be added indirectly by means of an Extensible Metadata Platform (XMP) packet (Abode Systems, n.d.); XMP packets are XML documents that express properties of the containing document using RDF/XML. The M3S was therefore translated into RDF (see Table 1) so that it could be inserted into PDF files, either at creation time by the LaTeX templates or after the fact using a metadata panel add-on for Adobe Acrobat. Some compromises were made due to a real or perceived lack of entirely suitable predicates (such as

Table 1. KIM M3S expressed using RDF predicates. The namespaces dc, dcterms and owl have their usual meanings; xap refers to Adobe's XMP Basic Schema

Metadata element	RDF predicate	Value
Object identifier	dcterms:isFormatOf	Partial filename
Filename	dc:identifier	Full filename
Task code	xap:Label	'KIM Task *n.m*' or (if *m* = 0) 'KIM Work Package *n*'
Document type	dc:type	'Report, 'Presentation', etc.
Document version	owl:versionInfo	'*n.m*', e.g. '0.1', '1.2'
Date modified	dcterms:modified	Date and time, using W3C profile of ISO 8601 (Wolf & Wicksteed, 1998)
File format	dc:format	Blank node with value of PRONOM Unique Identifier or MIME type, and a label giving name and version as a string
Title	dc:title	String
Author	dc:creator	List of author names as an RDF Sequence or Bag
Approved by	dc:publisher	Name
Date approved	dcterms:dateAccepted	Date and time, using W3C profile of ISO 8601
Access level	dcterms:accessRights	Blank node with value 'Working', '1', '2', etc., and label 'Working draft', 'Public', 'KIM academic members and industrial collaborators', etc.
Keywords	dc:subject	Comma-separated list of keywords
Date created	dcterms:created	Date and time, using W3C profile of ISO 8601
Date issued	dcterms:issued	Date and time, using W3C profile of ISO 8601

for the 'Approved by' property), and the technicalities of how values were handled by available software.

As compared to simply producing documents in the normal way, using the file-name register and templates was a little more work but not significantly more, so it was hoped that compliance rates would be high.

Regarding the file naming convention, the central registry was initially implemented as a set of plain text documents, one for each combination of task code and document type, listing the ranked filenames and corresponding titles. This quickly proved unpopular and unwieldy, since registering a new document meant hunting through 135 different files for the right one, then a cycle of downloading, editing, and uploading the file. The register was then reimplemented as a simple web interface which would take the relevant inputs, generate a filename for the user, and log the result. This was much more successful and a high level of compliance was achieved. The only documents that tended to fall outside the file naming convention and register, as confirmed later when compiling a full list of outputs for the project's final report, were journal submissions.

Regarding the embedded metadata, two sets of Microsoft templates were used: one that enforced the completion of the document properties and one that did not. Some university teams, including the one at the University of Bath, were asked to use the former and the remaining teams used the latter. (The LaTeX templates enforced compliance in that documents would not compile properly if information were missing). The templates that enforced completion were generally successful in collecting the required information, though not necessarily well-liked. With the other templates, a sizeable number of researchers simply added the requested information directly into the document, rather than via the document properties; thus the information was still there, but in a form less amenable to automatic extraction.

One incentive to use the templates as intended was that, if researchers set their file manager to display details of each file, they could add a column to display the document title, as read from the document properties. This would rectify the issue that the file naming convention did not reveal specific details of the content; and since the title could be displayed verbatim was arguably a better solution than having a codified version of the title in the filename. This approach was demonstrated in the display of files in the content management section of the project website, a fact that helped the authors judge levels of compliance. The challenge, however, was that the researchers had to set this up on their own workstations for themselves; the project was not in a position to enforce these settings.

The M3S was therefore a limited success in terms of adoption; it tended to support the team's suspicions that compliance, and quality of compliance, with document and data management protocols would be highest when the effect on the researcher's effort expenditure would be zero or a net decrease. In terms of utility, the planned experiment to extract preservation metadata records from a corpus of project documents did not take place, due to loss of staff towards the end of the project. The central register of filenames did, however, prove enormously helpful in the compilation of the final report and its list of project outputs. When team members were asked for a complete list of their outputs, they had only to fill gaps in an existing list rather than compile a new one from scratch. For those documents conforming to the M3S, the project manager and administrator were able to use information embedded in the filename, along with the title, to judge whether a document should be included and to follow up with the lead author if necessary.

THE RAIDMAP MINIMUM MANDATORY METADATA SET

Five years after the KIM M3S was developed, the authors were engaged on a small, six-month project to design a research data management plan and associated procedures for the Department of Mechanical Engineering at the University of Bath, as an exemplar for similar departments in other institutions (Darlington, 2012). One of the deliverables of this REDm-MED project was RAIDmap (Research Activity Information Development Mapping), a tool to help researchers keep track of their research data outputs. Its primary purpose was to keep a record of the data files produced by a research activity and the associations between them so that, by following the chain of associations, one could see at a glance how a set of published results had been derived from a set of raw data. The motivation was to make it easier to appraise and select data for retention, and to document the data and data processing in such a way as to ensure the reproducibility of the research. A secondary purpose was, once again, to collect enough information about each data file so that, on ingest into a repository, that information could be transformed into standards-compliant preservation and discovery metadata records with minimal effort.

In drawing up the specification for the tool, the question arose of what metadata it should collect about each data file. To answer the question, the authors decided to employ a similar technique to the one they had used in KIM, and to derive an M3S for RAIDmap. It would not have been appropriate to reuse the KIM M3S verbatim as RAIDmap had a quite different set of requirements:

- While the KIM M3S was focused on textual documents, RAIDmap was concerned with data files and databases.
- The KIM approach was intended to be transferable to an industrial context, while RAIDmap was firmly aimed at the academic sector.
- As RAIDmap was intended as a generic tool, not tied to a particular project, it could not rely on a particular file naming convention being used. Neither could a set of project-level common properties be assumed, though a set of common properties might be provided by the user for all files belonging to a given research activity.
- A key part of the RAIDmap proposal was to automate as much of the process of constructing the map as possible. Therefore, some of the metadata extraction that the KIM M3S envisioned happening at the point of ingest into a data archive could and would be performed immediately by the RAIDmap tool.

In addition, in the five years since the KIM M3S was developed, things had moved on in terms of accepted and best practice for preservation and discovery metadata. The DataCite Metadata Schema was achieving acceptance as a cross-discipline standard for research data discovery metadata (Starr et al., 2011), and PREMIS had reached version 2.1 (PREMIS Editorial Committee, 2011). Therefore the authors took these two schemes as their starting point. Once again they worked through each element in turn, and determined whether it should be supplied by the user, extracted by RAIDmap, or deferred until ingest into a repository, and then whether the information should be recorded against the whole map (called a 'data case' by the team), an individual data record (file or database), or an association between two records (called a 'data development process' by the team).

Derivation of the Set

The analysis of the revised PREMIS scheme resulted in many of the same conclusions as before. The differences regarding elements associated with the PREMIS object entity were as follows:

- **Object Identifier:** RAIDmap would generate one of these for its own internal purposes; with appropriate care, it could be made globally unique.
- **Object Characteristics:**
  - **Format:** RAIDmap would extract this information from the file.
  - **Creating Application:** RAIDmap would extract the name and version of the creating application from the file. Similarly, RAIDmap would determine the date of creation and last modification from either the file itself (if embedded as metadata) or the file system.
  - **Size:** RAIDmap would measure this, but as the archive could also measure it without recourse to the user for correction, the authors decided to treat it as optional.
  - **Inhibitors:** RAIDmap would allow users to record technical restrictions by noting their type, what they restricted, and the password to remove the restriction, though this information would itself be encrypted as a security measure. Since this may not apply, or researchers may prefer to handle this information another way, the team decided not to include it as mandatory, but to support it as an optional element.
- **Storage:** Although in PREMIS this refers to the location of the object after ingest, RAIDmap would need to know the location of the object while in active use.
- **Environment:** The authors considered the creating application to be a sufficient indicator of the environment in most circumstances. In order to cover other cases, the authors proposed two optional elements: software dependency (for specialist plugins, addons, libraries, and so on) and hardware dependency (for specialist hardware). They felt that dependencies between re-

cords would be better recorded in RAIDmap as associations rather than in the record's mandatory metadata.

Regarding the PREMIS event entity, the instances of relevance to the M3S were those represented as data development processes in RAIDmap:

- **Event Type:** This would be recorded in RAIDmap as the name of the data development process.
- **Event Date Time:** The user would be expected to supply this, but RAIDmap would supply a sensible fallback value, such as the creation date and time of a resulting data record.
- **Event Detail:** The user would be able to include this as an annotation on a data development process, but the authors did not consider it mandatory.
- **Linking Agent Identifier:** The user would be expected to supply this, with RAIDmap supplying the user's identity as the fallback value.

The authors recognized that other events relevant to preservation may be recorded elsewhere, such as the project's data management plan.

Regarding the PREMIS agent entity, the authors proposed that the user should be able to maintain an 'address book' of agents within the RAIDmap application so they could be associated with data cases, records and development processes by means of an internal identifier. The properties of the agents were considered out of scope for the M3S, but were expected to include names and contact details.

Regarding the PREMIS rights entity, the authors felt that it would not be efficient to deal with this in full within RAIDmap itself. They proposed instead that researchers provide the details of the rights situation in their data management plan. In cases where different data records had different rights regimes, the authors proposed that each regime be assigned a keyword in the data management plan, and that keyword used as the value of a rights element in RAIDmap for all corresponding data records.

As explained above, PREMIS deferred to descriptive metadata standards for elements relating to intellectual entities, so for RAIDmap the REDm-MED team turned to the DataCite Metadata Schema. Not only was it a suitable generic discovery standard for data in its own right, but the metadata could be used to register a Digital Object Identifier (DOI) for the data record should it be published in an archive.

- **Identifier:** For DataCite this means a DOI. RAIDmap would not be using DOIs, for obvious reasons, but would record an identifier.
- **Creator:** RAIDmap would extract this if possible, using the user's identity as a fallback value.
- **Title:** RAIDmap would extract this if possible.

- **Publisher, Publication Year:** These only apply to published datasets, not to working data records.
- **Subject:** RAIDmap would record this at the levels of project and data case. The idea was that, when the user associated a data case with a project, the subject information for the project would be copied to the data case. The user would then be able to adapt it to suit the particular case.
- **Contributor:** For administrative purposes, the team felt it important that RAIDmap should record information about at least three contributors: first, a contact person for the data record, being the person who works or worked with it most frequently, or has the best understanding of it; second, the data manager responsible for it in a curatorial sense; and third, the person or body who holds the rights to the data. RAIDmap would infer the creator as the most likely contact person. For the other two, the user would supply a default value when setting up a given project and their RAIDmap profile respectively.
- **Date:** RAIDmap would record the dates of creation and last modification, as discussed above.
- **Language:** Depending on the nature of the data this may or may not be relevant, so the team decided this should be optional.
- **Resource Type:** RAIDmap would infer general types such as dataset, image, or model, and some specific types such as spreadsheet.
- **Alternate Identifier:** Presumably the RAIDmap identifier would be demoted to this upon the allocation of an archival or publication identifier by a repository or archive.
- **Related Identifier:** This information would be captured by the associations recorded by RAIDmap, rather than as a property of a data record.
- **Size, Format, Rights:** See the respective discussions above.
- **Version:** The user would supply this information.
- **Description:** The user would supply a brief description of the data record.

This process resulted in four lists of elements. Table 2 shows the mandatory elements for data cases. Table 3 shows the mandatory elements for data records. Table 4 shows the mandatory elements for data development processes. Table 5 shows the optional elements for data records. It will be seen that, having set up the RAIDmap tool with a user profile and project information, in the best case scenario the user would only have to supply a description when adding a data record to a data case. Thus, even though it turned out to be quite a large set for something intended as minimal, the team hoped that completing it would not be burdensome for a researcher.

Due to the tight timescales and limited resources of the project it was not practical or desirable to develop the RAIDmap application entirely from scratch. The team therefore used the Open University's Compendium mind-mapping software

Table 2. Mandatory metadata elements for data cases

Metadata element	Collection method
Project	Supplied by the user from suggestion list
Subject	Initially the subject of associated project

Table 3. Mandatory metadata elements for data records

Metadata element	Collection method
Identifier	Generated by RAIDmap
Title	Determined by RAIDmap, falling back to user entry
Version	Default provided by RAIDmap, corrected if necessary by user
Description	Supplied by the user
Type	Inferred by RAIDmap, corrected if necessary by user
File format (*name and version*)	Determined by RAIDmap, corrected if necessary by user
Creating application (*name and version*)	Determined or inferred by RAIDmap, corrected if necessary by user
Date created	Determined by RAIDmap, corrected if necessary by user
Date modified	Determined by RAIDmap, corrected if necessary by user
Creator	Determined or inferred by RAIDmap, corrected if necessary by user
Contact person	Inferred by RAIDmap, corrected if necessary by user
Data manager	Default provided by RAIDmap, corrected if necessary by user
Rights holder	Default provided by RAIDmap, corrected if necessary by user
Rights	Default provided by RAIDmap, corrected if necessary by user
Filename	Determined by RAIDmap
Location	Determined by RAIDmap, corrected if necessary by user

Table 4. Mandatory metadata elements for data development processes

Metadata element	Collection method
Date and time	Default provided by RAIDmap, corrected if necessary by user
Agent	Default provided by RAIDmap, corrected if necessary by user

Table 5. Optional metadata elements for data records

Metadata element	Collection method
File size	Determined by RAIDmap
Software dependency (*plug-in, add-on*)	Supplied by the user
Hardware dependency	Supplied by the user
Technical restriction (*type and subject of restriction, password*)	Determined by RAIDmap, corrected and extended by the user

as a basis; nodes representing digital records were extended to include a metadata table, populated at creation time by the National Library of New Zealand's Metadata Extractor (Ball & Thangarajah, 2012; Darlington, Thangarajah, & Ball, 2012).

While a working prototype was developed, circumstances did not allow the application to be refined into a production-ready state, so the project team was not able to conduct meaningful tests of its usability and utility. Similarly, code for a RAIDwatch application was written that would monitor the files saved to particular directory tree and automatically add them to a RAID data case in the background. This did not progress to a full working prototype within the project timescale. Nevertheless, trials conducted by the project team indicated that the approach showed some promise.

At the time RAIDmap was developed, the University of Bath did not have an institutional data archive; this came later, in 2015. As of this writing, the focus of the archive is on discovery and bit-level preservation, rather than the active preservation envisioned by PREMIS, therefore the M3S has turned out to be more detailed than would be required for deposit. Having said that, the archive also registers DOIs for datasets, for which purpose the DataCite metadata required by the M3S is of direct relevance.

Comparing the M3S with the metadata collected by the archive, it is notable that the information provided by RAIDmap users would also need to be entered into archival records, either directly or via a 'readme' documentation file. Certain other metadata elements generated by RAIDmap, and the RAID diagram itself, would also make welcome additions to the documentation. While further integration work would be necessary, and a refocusing of the M3S desirable, it is potentially the case that the effort spent by researchers on a RAID diagram would be offset by saved effort at the point of deposit.

RECOMMENDATIONS AND FUTURE RESEARCH DIRECTIONS

Even though the two metadata sets were not thoroughly tested for their intended purpose, they were successful inasmuch as they were implemented with a limited amount of development effort and used with minimal additional human effort. This having been done, the result was a consistent set of information that was amenable to extraction, and that could in principle be transformed into a standardized format relevant to the use cases in question.

The method by which the two sets were constructed may be abstracted thus:

1. Establish a clear use case that the metadata set is seeking to address. With KIM, the driver was the long term preservation of project documents; with RAIDmap, it was the archiving and publication of research data. In both cases, the aim was to collect information at the time of object creation that would make tractable the task of transferring a corpus of such objects to an archive some time later.

2. Identify one or more systems from the wider environment with which to inter-operate, and note their metadata requirements. Both the KIM and RAIDmap metadata sets were anticipating the needs of unknown academic sector reposi-tories, and so PREMIS was selected as an appropriate generic target. If the repositories had been known, it would have been better to target their specific requirements. In addition, RAIDmap targeted the DataCite Metadata Schema, being a requirement for obtaining a DOI for a published dataset.

3. Examine the workflow of the user and the environment in which they work, and identify correspondences between the information already in circulation, and the information collected by the target metadata schemes.

4. Identify the most efficient time and place to collect the information. KIM distinguished between information that should be supplied by users when they are actively engaging with the object, by project administrators at the start of the project and at points of change, and by archivists during and after ingest. RAIDmap distinguished between what could be determined automatically, what users should supply once for all their files, and what users should supply about particular files.

5. Find a way to introduce the collection mechanisms into existing workflows and practices such that it either saves the user time and effort, or produces another tangible benefit in exchange for minimal additional effort. The KIM templates were an attempt in this direction, but even the transition to using document properties instead of typing directly into the document seemed to be uncomfortable to the majority of researchers. RAIDmap showed promise for making file organization and data deposit easier, by automatically document-

ing data throughout the active phase of a project. That promise would have been greatly increased had the tool been able to target mature research data management workflows; they were in flux at the time and, while now more settled, they are still evolving.

6. Design application profiles to encode the collected information that both (*a*) make use of and harmonize with metadata structures already in place, and (*b*) match or can be transformed into the format expected by the target metadata schemes. The encoding of the KIM M3S took account of the structures available in common document formats; the encoding of the RAIDmap M3S had more freedom to mimic the requirements and recommendations of PREMIS and DataCite, but still took account of the outputs of the metadata extractor. Had the eventual archives for the outputs been known, it would have been useful to discover their preferred subject terms and suggest them to users as they contributed keywords in the KIM M3S and subjects in the RAIDmap M3S.

The end result is that metadata are recorded in several places with minimal redundancy. This is efficient from the perspective of the Don't Repeat Yourself (DRY) principle: users do not have to duplicate effort providing the same information over and over, and there is less likelihood of inconsistencies being introduced (Hunt & Thomas, 2000). The trade-off is that additional work needs to be performed to assemble a full metadata record from the component sources, and loss of a single source can have a detrimental effect on the whole corpus. This turned out to be an issue in the case of the KIM M3S since, as discussed above, the process of recovering the metadata was not tested, and the matter of encoding the project-level information in a machine-usable form was not addressed.

In hindsight, the KIM work did not go far enough. As well as designing the metadata set and collection mechanisms in tandem, the team should have developed the metadata extraction and transformation mechanisms at the same time, to ensure at the earliest opportunity that the whole workflow would operate as intended. In addition, while some efforts were made to use embedded metadata in project systems, this could have been taken even further to provide greater incentives for compliance.

The avenue explored by RAIDmap warrants further investigation. The prototype tool was able to populate parts of a metadata record automatically for files; there is scope to take that idea further not only for users building an inventory of their own files but to help with uploading that information to repositories. More importantly, the potential of a RAIDwatch-type tool has yet to be fully explored, in particular the ability of a tool to watch changes to a directory and not only add new files to an inventory but also make inferences about the inputs and processes that lead to their creation (McMahon, 2015).

CONCLUSION

Developing a metadata profile for a local application is a task that has many layers. Users must be persuaded to provide the requisite information; the information must be sufficient to support the local application; and it should be possible to transform it such that systems in the wider environment are able to use it as well. The contention of this chapter is that, even if the priorities are in that order, better results may be obtained by tackling the issues in the reverse order. By considering the wider requirements first and then how they compare with local requirements, potential interoperability problems can be avoided and gaps addressed. By allowing the required metadata to be assembled from multiple sources, instead of insisting on a single profile, opportunities open up for highly efficient metadata collection and to reduce the burden on end users. For this to work, though, it is important to design the metadata profiles and supporting systems as a cohesive whole, otherwise the pipeline of metadata from end users to the global infrastructure may break down.

ACKNOWLEDGMENT

The KIM Project was supported by the UK Engineering and Physical Sciences Research Council (EPSRC) and the Economic and Social Research Council (ESRC) under Grant Numbers EP/C534220/1 and RES-331-27-0006. The REDm-MED Project was funded by the Joint Information Systems Committee (JISC) under the Managing Research Data Programme (02) 2011-13.

REFERENCES

Abode Systems. (n.d.). Adobe XMP developer center. Retrieved May 15, 2016, from http://www.adobe.com/devnet/xmp.html

Ball, A., Darlington, M., Howard, T., McMahon, C., & Culley, S. (2012). Visualizing research data records for their better management. *Journal of Digital Information*, *13*(1). Retrieved from https://journals.tdl.org/jodi/article/view/5917/5892

Ball, A., Patel, M., McMahon, C., Green, S., Clarkson, J., & Culley, S. (2006). A grand challenge: Immortal information and through-life knowledge management (KIM). *International Journal of Digital Curation*, *1*(1), 53–59. doi:10.2218/ijdc.v1i1.5

Ball, A., & Thangarajah, U. (2012). *RAIDmap application developer guide*. Retrieved from http://opus.bath.ac.uk/30098

Caplan, P. (2006). Preservation metadata. In S. Ross & M. Day (Eds.), DCC Digital Curation Manual. Edinburgh, UK: Digital Curation Centre. Retrieved from http://www.dcc.ac.uk/resource/curation-manual/chapters/preservation-metadata/

Consultative Committee for Space Data Systems. (2002). *Reference model for an Open Archival Information System (OAIS)* (Blue Book No. CCSDS 650.0-B-1). Retrieved from http://www.ccsds.org/documents/650x0b1.pdf

Consultative Committee for Space Data Systems. (2012). *Reference model for an Open Archival Information System (OAIS)* (Magenta Book No. CCSDS 650.0-M-2). Retrieved from http://www.ccsds.org/documents/650x0m2.pdf

Darlington, M. (2012). *REDm-MED project final report to JISC*. University of Bath. Retrieved from http://www.ukoln.ac.uk/projects/redm-med/reports/redm-med_final_report_v1.pdf

Darlington, M., Thangarajah, U., & Ball, A. (2012). *RAIDmap application user guide*. University of Bath. Retrieved from http://opus.bath.ac.uk/30097

Day, M. (2004). Preservation metadata. In G. E. Gorman & D. G. Dorner (Eds.), *Metadata applications and management* (pp. 253–273). London: Facet Publishing.

Duranti, L., Eastwood, T., & MacNeil, H. (1997). The preservation of the integrity of electronic records. Vancouver, BC: University of British Columbia; Retrieved from http://www.interpares.org/UBCProject/index.htm

C.U.R.L. Exemplars in Digital Archives. (2000). Metadata for digital preservation: The Cedars Project outline specification. Retrieved from http://www.webarchive.org.uk/wayback/archive/20050111120000/http://www.leeds.ac.uk/cedars/colman/metadata/metadataspec.html

Heery, R., & Patel, M. (2000). Application profiles: Mixing and matching metadata schemas. *Ariadne, 25*. Retrieved from http://www.ariadne.ac.uk/issue25/app-profiles/

Hunt, A., & Thomas, D. (2000). *The pragmatic programmer: From journeyman to master*. Reading, MA: Addison-Wesley.

InterPARES project. Project overview. (n. d.). Retrieved from http://www.interpares.org/

Library of Congress. (2016). PREMIS: Preservation metadata maintenance activity. Retrieved from http://www.loc.gov/standards/premis/

Lupovici, C., & Masanès, J. (2000). *Metadata for the long-term preservation of electronic publications.* The Hague, The Netherlands: Koninklijke Bibliotheek. Retrieved from https://www.kb.nl/sites/default/files/docs/NEDLIBmetadata.pdf

McMahon, C. (2015). Design informatics: Supporting engineering design processes with information technology. *Journal of the Indian Institute of Science, 95*(4), 365–378. Retrieved from http://journal.library.iisc.ernet.in/index.php/iisc/article/view/4585

National Archives of Australia. (1999). Recordkeeping metadata standard for commonwealth agencies. Retrieved from http://pandora.nla.gov.au/nph-wb/20000510130000/http://www.naa.gov.au/www.naa.gov.au/recordkeeping/control/rkms/contents.html

National Archives of Australia. (2015). Australian government recordkeeping metadata standard, version 2.2. Retrieved from http://www.naa.gov.au/records-management/publications/agrkms/

National Library of Australia. (1999). Preservation metadata for digital collections. Retrieved from http://pandora.nla.gov.au/pan/25498/20020625-0000/www.nla.gov.au/preserve/pmeta.html

National Library of New Zealand. (2003). *Metadata standards framework – preservation metadata (revised).* Retrieved from http://digitalpreservation.natlib.govt.nz/assets/Uploads/nlnz-data-model-final.pdf

OCLC/RLG Preservation Metadata, & the Implementation Strategies Working Group. (2005). *Data dictionary for preservation metadata.* Retrieved from http://www.loc.gov/standards/premis/v1/premis-dd_1.0_2005_May.pdf

OCLC/RLG Working Group on Preservation Metadata. (2001). *Preservation metadata for digital objects: A review of the state of the art.* Retrieved from http://www.oclc.org/content/dam/research/activities/pmwg/presmeta_wp.pdf

OCLC/RLG Working Group on Preservation Metadata. (2002). *Preservation metadata and the oais information model: A metadata framework to support the preservation of digital objects.* Retrieved from http://www.oclc.org/content/dam/research/activities/pmwg/pm_framework.pdf

PREMIS Editorial Committee. (2011). *PREMIS data dictionary for preservation metadata, version 2.1.* Washington, DC: Library of Congress. Retrieved from http://www.loc.gov/standards/premis/v2/premis-2-1.pdf

Public Record Office Victoria. (2000). PROS 99/007 Standard for the management of electronic records, version 1.2. Retrieved from http://pandora.nla.gov.au/pan/22965/20021222-0000/www.prov.vic.gov.au/vers/standards/pros9907.htm

Research Libraries Group, Working Group on Preservation Issues of Metadata. (1998). *Final report*. Retrieved from https://web.archive.org/web/20040216202156/http://www.rlg.org/preserv/presmeta.html

Rogers, C., & Tennis, J. T. (2016). *General Study 15 – Application profile for authenticity metadata*. InterPARES 3 Project. Retrieved from http://www.interpares.org/ip3/display_file.cfm?doc=ip3_canada_gs15_final_report.pdf

Starr, J., Ashton, J., Brase, J., Bracke, P., Gastl, A., Gillet, J., & Ziedorn, F. (2011). *DataCite metadata schema for the publication and citation of research data, version 2.2*. DataCite Consortium; doi:10.5438/0005

University of Pittsburgh, School of Information Sciences. (1996). Metadata specifications derived from the fundamental requirements: A reference model for business acceptable communications. Retrieved from http://web.archive.org/web/20000302194819/www.sis.pitt.edu/~nhprc/meta96.html

Wolf, M., & Wicksteed, C. (1998). *Date and time formats*. World Wide Web Consortium. Retrieved from http://www.w3.org/TR/1998/NOTE-datetime-19980827

KEY TERMS AND DEFINITIONS

Context Information: Information describing how a data object and its Representation Information (q.v.) relate to other information resources.

Data Case: A set of data records associated with some discrete research activity, such as a project, task, or experiment.

Data Development Process: A process that changes or adds to the research data associated with a research activity or project.

Data Record: An object (usually but not always a digital file) that contains data.

Fixity Information: Checksums or other information that could be used to detect, and possibly reverse, undocumented alterations to a data object.

Provenance Information: Information about the source of a data object and its Representation Information (q.v.), the chain of custody since its creation and the operations performed on it.

Reference Information: Unique identifiers for a data object.

Representation Information: The information needed by a user to interpret and understand a data object.

Research Data: Data pertaining to the object of research, in particular those data used as evidence supporting a research conclusion.

Chapter 4
A Methodology for Effective Metadata Design in Earth Observation

Jean-Christophe Desconnets
IRD, UMR ESPACE-DEV, France

Isabelle Mougenot
UM, UMR ESPACE-DEV, France

Hatim Chahdi
Université de Montpellier, IRD, UMR ESPACE-DEV, France

ABSTRACT

The satellite images have become an essential source of information to address and analyze environmental issues quickly, repeatedly and in a reliable way. The increasing number of remotely sensed images are the first impediments for data discovery, access and processing. In this context, it is critical to simplify efficient multi-sensors image-based data access and query processing to provide accessibility to a variety of users in remote sensing. Describing satellite images through a metadata application profile may leverage capabilities to promote easy use of satellite image for environmental analysis. Accordingly, an application profile conforming to the Dublin Core Application Profile guidelines and designed for Earth observations data have been developed. The aim is to provide insights of key methodological considerations in relation to the design of this profile called EOAP (Earth Observation Application Profile).

DOI: 10.4018/978-1-5225-2221-8.ch004

1. INTRODUCTION

Satellite images have become an essential source of information to address and ana-lyze environmental issues quickly, repeatedly and in a reliable manner. The technical diversity of satellite sensors as well as their increasing number allow satellite images to be considered as unprecedented sources of information, richer and precise enough to deliver new insights or capabilities, such as a novel understanding of ecosystem dynamics or the monitoring of environmental changes at a local scale. However, the ever-increasing number of remotely sensed images as well as their large-scale availability form the first barrier to data discovery, access and processing. In such a context, it is critical to simplify efficient multi-sensor image-based access and processing so that a large variety of users, both experts and non-experts in remote sensing, can draw benefit from them.

To facilitate geospatial data sharing, many initiatives have emerged from the Earth-observation community (space agencies, industry) or from the broader envi-ronmental community, whether they are national (THEIA[1]), European (INSPIRE[2], COPERNICUS[3]) or global (GEOSS[4]). In most cases, access to the images is made possible by the deployment of a spatial data infrastructure that provides access to distributed and heterogeneous data (Maguire & Longley, 2005; Friis-Christensen et al., 2007). This infrastructure provides access to images through web services discovery allowing them to be viewed and downloaded, and, in some cases, pro-cessed online. These facilities require the implementation of an interoperability framework, which relies primarily on the adoption of a specific metadata standard by the user community or of its adaptation. It is the basis for the implementation of image access and processing services.

However, these different distribution hubs are weakly interconnected and do not provide a comprehensive view of available images as end-users would expect. Therefore, users have to expend substantial effort to take advantage of the multiple platforms available for image distribution to identify, select and subsequently process images that meet their needs. Indeed, the design process that led to these develop-ments is domain-specific and produces heterogeneous metadata schemes. This makes it difficult to implement common tools for image discovery. Nevertheless, various interoperability frameworks have been defined in the field of Earth observation. They offer metadata schemes that take the common needs of multiple users from various communities into account. The resulting scheme usually corresponds to the core elements of a standard. It provides general information about the resource to meet the needs only of discovery and localization.

This analysis leads us to propose a new approach to support the interconnection of geospatial resources from various communities in order to manage large sets of heterogeneous and distributed resources and cover critical-use cases for environmental-user practices. In conformance with the Dublin Core application profile (DCAP) guidelines (Coyle & Baker, 2008), the authors have developed a metadata application profile for these purposes. Named EOAP (Earth Observation Application Profile) (Desconnets et al., 2014; Mougenot et al., 2015), this application profile is designed to benefit from the interoperability of metadata standards and linked open-data principles for data sharing on the web. Furthermore, EOAP offers a descriptive framework that is flexible and extensible enough to adapt to numerous environmental-use cases as well as to different user viewpoints. It is currently used as a core component of the national spatial infrastructure GEOSUD[5] (Kazmierski et al., 2014) which aims to promote increased access to and use of satellite imagery to French public stakeholders. In order to make the proposition reusable and thus adaptable to different contexts, it is important to lay out the design approach the authors used for the EOAP application profile, including a description of the many factors that have led to its proposal.

To this end, this chapter's purpose is to revisit the approach used to build the application profile. The functional elements that led to its definition and the specifications that result are therefore explained. First, section 2 explains the specificity of satellite images, and, more generally, of spatial data and metadata that describes them. To complement this perspective, a state of the art describes the relevant metadata standards for describing satellite images. Section 3, which forms the heart of our article, presents the approach followed to construct the EOAP application profile. After a reminder of the building principles proposed by the recommendations of the Singapore framework (Nilsson et al., 2008), the context in which these efforts were undertaken is described: the GEOSUD project. It is subsequently specified how that context, its characteristics and practices of target users helped to define the functional requirements of the GEOSUD spatial data infrastructure. In a third subsection, the path that led to the domain model is also described and discussed. Finally, based on the proposals of Nilsson et al. (2009), the DSP structural model of the EOAP application profile is presented. The vocabularies chosen to define the EOAP properties and the RDF representation are justified and discussed. An example of the use of the EOAP profile is also included. In conclusion, the contribution of the EOAP profile for the GEOSUD spatial data infrastructure, on the one hand, and the design process, on the other, are discussed. Finally, perspectives for strengthening the methodology of constructing an application profile are proposed.

2. BACKGROUND

2.1. Specificity of Spatial Information for the Environment

2.1.1. Nature and Life Cycle

The domain of application for which the EOAP application profile has been implemented pertains to the disciplines and approaches involving the study of the environment. These studies have been made possible through the acquisition and subsequent analysis of spatio-temporal data. A data or an item of information is called "geographic" when it refers to the description of objects or events spatially referenced to the Earth's surface (Livre Blanc, 1998). Figure 1 formalizes the concept and the composite nature of geographical information. It introduces the notion of feature of interest, as an abstraction of a real-world entity. Such an entity can be characterized by a set of properties (see Figure 1):

- A thematic property that corresponds to the nature of the represented object or phenomenon (river system, administrative unit, atmospheric pollution, etc.),
- A spatial property, also known as spatial extent, for defining and positioning the object on the Earth's surface. The data is associated with a spatial reference (e.g., coordinate system, projection system),
- A temporal property that defines the moment at which – or the period during which – an object or phenomenon was observed. The data is thus associated with a specific time reference.

Figure 1. Composite nature of geographical information (UML Class diagram)

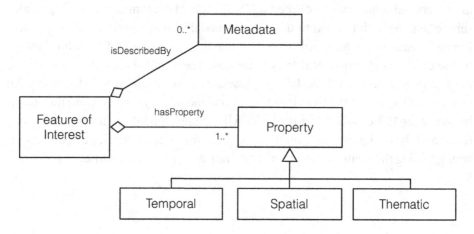

Among these data, there are data called "reference" data that are the basis for the representation of a territory (land registry, administrative unit, hydrography) or the monitoring of natural phenomena. They are usually produced by specialized national or international organizations and are then used by research organizations or civil society to produce new data called "business" data, based on new data acquisitions and/or business-centric processing (Desconnets et al., 2001, Gayte et al., 1997).

Both sets of data always originate from various acquisition protocols (in-situ observation, aerial, satellite) and require complex instrumentation phases (preprocessing, enrichment and validation with *in situ* data) before they can be used for environmental applications. Such is the case for Earth observation data.

Satellite images, for their part, are acquired by observing the ground from artificial satellites. These satellite platforms are equipped with sensors to acquire an image of a portion of the Earth according to an internal acquisition protocol on which depends the nature of the acquired image, such as its spatial resolution or its spectral band. It should be noted that an image is a digital resource that can be large, ranging in size from tens of megabytes to tens of gigabytes. For example, an image at a very high resolution of an area of 20 km × 20 km on the ground will be several gigabytes in size.

2.2. Metadata for Spatial Information

This dual specificity – the composite nature of the information (thematic, spatial and temporal) and the multiplicity of producers – makes it essential to have access to the detailed description of spatial information throughout its life cycle and of all its properties. Although the concept of metadata predates the web, interest in its use is now widespread in the field of environmental applications. Metadata is widely used to discover, share, reuse and manage spatial data. As Lamb (2001) proposes in his classification, at least three categories of metadata elements are helpful to our needs:

- **"Descriptive" Metadata:** describing the content of the resource and its technical characteristics. For example, spatial data require specific elements to describe the mode of representation (raster, vector), the level of representation of objects (scale/resolution) and the coordinate reference system on Earth,
- **"Administrative" Metadata:** providing information on the life cycle of the resource and its long-term conservation. These metadata are specifically dedicated to the management and preservation of resources,
- **"Structural" Metadata:** describing the schemes on which the resources are built and their hierarchical and/or aggregation relationships with each other.

A fourth category, which the authors call "qualitative" metadata, is also necessary to evaluate the quality of information, and therefore its suitability for the intended use. These include information describing the genealogy, accuracy (geometrical or temporal) or even the level of completeness. For example, a very high resolution orthorectified[6] image with a sub-metric geometric accuracy will be useful in mapping built-up areas at the scale of a cadastral plan. Finally, it should be noted that, within geographic information systems, metadata is separate from the original data in most of the cases. That is true for satellite imagery too. This separation allows access to metadata without accessing the data itself (Weibel et al., 1998).

2.3. Metadata Standards for Earth Observation

Different metadata standards[7], general or dedicated to a particular discipline, play essential roles to facilitate the management of distributed resources in decentralized architectures. After specifying the content and the added value of the standard Dublin Core and the DCAT vocabulary (W3C, 2014) originating from the web community, this section presents the relevant standards dedicated to the description of both geospatial resources and Earth observation data originating with the geographical and environmental communities. The state of the art is deliberately limited to the standards that meet, in whole or in part, the functional requirements pertaining to the EOAP application profile.

2.3.1. Dublin Core

The Dublin Core standard has a general scope that extends well beyond the sharing of satellite images. Indeed, it has been proposed to describe generically any type of resource. It thus provides efficient ways to help discovery in the context of the web for any community. For this purpose, the Dublin Core standard lists 15 elements for use in resource description. As the name of the standard suggests, these elements constitute its core. In our context, Dublin Core is used by the OGC CSW Discovery Service (OGC, 2007) to define the queryable elements of the service in a generic way and to also possibly provide a simplified view of the retrieved results.

2.3.2. Data Vocabulary Catalog (DCAT)

The DCAT vocabulary (Data CATalog vocabulary) proposed by the W3C (W3C, 2014), even while not initially designed to manage spatial data, is a seemingly promising initiative for sharing and reusing datasets in the environmental domain. Appropriately, the DCAT vocabulary is a set of terms and recommendations designed to improve interoperability between data catalogs published on the web, and

70

thereby improves data discovery. Consequently, it enables development of efficient applications that are able to benefit from metadata records that document different catalogs. This capability is similar to the one implemented in information systems for distributing spatial data.

Interestingly, the DCAT vocabulary reuses existing vocabularies, such as-but not limited to-dct, dctype, foaf and skos. The vocabulary is designed around a few core classes (see Figure 2), including the *dcat:Catalog* class, which refines the *dctype:Dataset* class and provides the main descriptive characteristics of a catalog, such as its spatial and temporal extents (*dct:spatial* and *dct:temporal*). Additionally, the *dcat:Distribution* class specifies key information about general access to the datasets described in the catalog. As a result the DCAT vocabulary offers a granularity of description that is relevant for a majority of spatial data catalogs, and allows a level of detail that fits well with datasets, such as satellite images.

Recently, the DCAT vocabulary has been the subject of two extensions, DCAT-AP (ISA, 2015) and GEO-DCAT-AP (ISA, 2015b). These extensions are designed to consider domain-specific use cases. For example, GEO-DCAT-AP extends the vocabulary to include the specificities of spatial data and also to consider the functional requirements inherent to data management by incorporating metadata pertaining to the data life cycle.

Figure 2. Simplified DCAT vocabulary abstract model (UML class diagram)
Source: W3C, 2014.

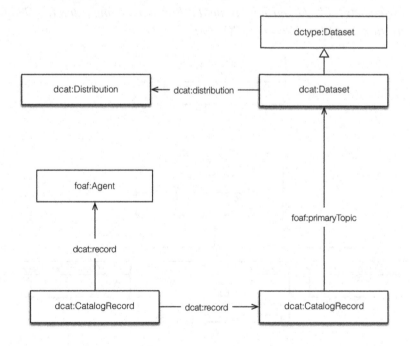

2.3.3. ISO 19115 and ISO 19115-2

The ISO 19115 standard (ISO, 2003) enacted by ISO TC/211, is the metadata standard for geospatial resources. It proposes a conceptual framework for describing these resources and was designed to meet the needs of very large geographic communities, ranging from data management to data processing to data dissemination.

Represented using the UML object formalism, it includes twelve main packages, nine of which are common to all geospatial resources. Many of these packages are dedicated to the description of the spatial dimension of the resources, such as Extent Information, Spatial Representation or Reference System Information. Figure 3 shows an extract of the extent information package of the ISO 19115 standard. The class *EX_GeographicExtent* is refined into three sub-classes which offer three different ways to describe the spatial extent of a resource.

The ISO 19115 standard defines core elements. They are a minimum set of elements considered essential to meet the needs of discovery and localization of a resource. Most of the time, these core elements are used to provide metadata interoperability in information systems that share geospatial resources. The ISO 19115 standard has been extended by the ISO standard 19115-2 (ISO, 2009) to support the description of gridded spatial resources, such as satellite images. It adds new

Figure 3. Extract of a Class diagram of the ISO 19115 extent information package. The sub-class EX_BoundingPolygon describes a spatial extent with a simple or complex geometry, EX_GeographicBoundingBox as a rectangle and Ex_GeographicDescription as a place. Source: ISO, 2003

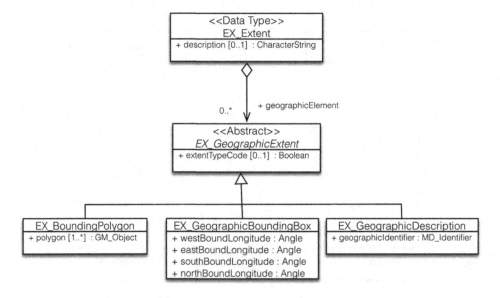

elements of description, such as information about the platform and the acquisition instrument. It also defines a few other elements to complement existing descriptions, for example, to clarify the characteristics of processing (Lineage Information package) performed on a raw image, such as geometric correction or radiometric calibration. Thus, it expands the scope of the ISO 19115 standard to meet the specific needs of image producers. The operationalization of the standards is guided by the ISO 19139 specification (ISO, 2007) which specifies the transformation rules for serialization of metadata in XML format.

2.4. Earth Observation Metadata Profile for Observations and Measurements

To meet the specific needs of the Earth observation community, the Observation and Measurement (O & M) (ISO, 2011) metadata profile was constructed (Gaspéri et al., 2012). It is part of the HMA[8] interoperability framework defined by the ESA[9]. It aims to facilitate the sharing of Earth observation products, irrespective of the mission and the sensor from which they originate. In this context, the concept of the metadata profile is the one proposed by ISO (ISO, 2004) and is quite different in its principles from the one presented in the next section. It describes a metadata scheme[10] and the rules in XML needed to describe the metadata of Earth observation products.

More specifically, the metadata scheme is designed to describe products with different levels of granularity: from a general description of a product to more detailed Earth observation features obtained from a satellite platform (e.g. SENTINEL), such as those concerning the parameters of acquisition of high-resolution images. The metadata profile defines three levels of description (Figure 4) on top of the O & M standard: a "general" level (*General EO Products* level) on the main characteristics of the products, a "thematic" one (*Thematic EO Products* level), which extends the previous level in order to describe the specific characteristics of thematic products, such as optical, radar or atmospheric products. The third one, the "mission" level (*Mission Specific EO Products* level), extends the second level and describes the specific products of a mission, like those of the PLEIADES mission of CNES[11] for the acquisition of very high resolution optical images.

Thus, this metadata scheme provides new metadata descriptions, such as an image's acquisition parameters, for example, the pitch, roll, and yaw of the acquisition platform. These data are essential in order to determine the geometric corrections made to the images after their acquisition.

Figure 4. Three levels of description of a satellite image by the O & M Earth Observation Application Profile. Each level represents a set of metadata elements which address specific purposes of description, shown on the left side (e.g. Thematic EO Products)
Source: Gaspéri et al., 2012.

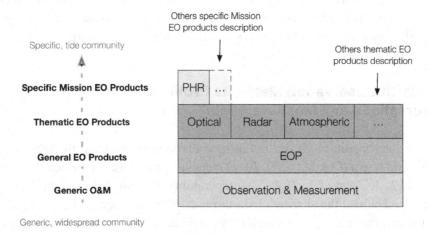

3. METHODOLOGY FOR BUILDING THE EOAP

3.1. Methodological Principles

A potential shortcoming of metadata standards is that they have been designed independently of each other and thus are not able to meet all the information requirements necessary to fulfill a specific application's large functional scope. For this purpose, application profiles reuse metadata standards to respond either to new requirements or to more specific ones. The principle is to take different elements of different metadata standards and combine them to produce a new organization of metadata elements specifically suitable for the target application. This open approach is known as the "mix and match" approach (Heery & Patel, 2000). The construction of an application profile is expected to meet the needs of discovery, characterization and consultation of distributed and heterogeneous resources to meet the application needs of a specific community of practice. It is therefore relevant to define an application profile that can facilitate interoperability between different data sources. Consequently, such an application profile could be considered a model of mediation. Indeed, it ensures semantic interoperability through the use of metadata elements defined in advance in different metadata standards. It also provides structural and syntactic interoperability through compliance with structural and syntactic rules relating to its realization (Nilsson et al., 2008).

The definition of an application profile is subject to different rules: a first principle is to rely on existing metadata standards or to maintain an open and long-term new metadata standard which encompasses the newly introduced metadata elements.

To begin with, the methodology used is based on the model driven architecture approach (Soley, 2000) which is commonly used in software engineering. Two of its main standards are used:

- **The Meta Object Facility (OMG, 2006):** It synthesizes and expands the concepts of classes and metaclasses originating from the object-oriented approach in order to standardize and control the definition of meta-models. This approach embodies the ideas of reflexivity and the meta level. It thus helps to better explain the different levels of representation (meta-metamodel, meta-model and model) needed to build the application profile,
- **UML, Unified Modeling Language (OMG, 2015):** It provides a formalized framework for expressing, during the design phase, different views of our system: use cases (Jacobson & Ng, 2004) and various structural meta-models and models (Rumbaugh et al., 1991).

In addition, the RDF and RDF Schema (RDFS) data formats are used. The primitives around the concepts of *RDFS:Class*, *RDFS:Resource* and *RDFS:Literal* value seem particularly well-suited for the instantiation of metadata in the context of data sharing on the web. Indeed, RDF has two particular features that endow it with distinct advantages: it is self-describing and it plays the role of meta-model in the explanation of structural models associated with the application profile. This set of methods and techniques is part of what Hevner (2007) called the Rigor Cycle, which is useful in eliciting scientific knowledge of the domain.

The construction of the EOAP application profile draws its methodology primarily from the recommendations of the Dublin Core community around the concept of DCAP (Dublin Core Application Profile) and the Singapore framework.

Nilsson et al., 2008 propose a methodological framework based on two conceptual models. They aim to clarify the key concepts on which the application profile is built. A first structural model called DCAM (Dublin Core Abstract Model) (Powell et al., 2007) clarifies the concept of the resource and its specialization as a described resource, which is a set of property-value pairs. The value is sometimes also considered as a resource and the property as a value, as envisaged in the metadata standards and controlled vocabularies. A second structural model called DSP (Description Set Profile) (Nilsson et al., 2009) provides a prescriptive framework for the materialization of the application profile. An application profile is thus envisaged as a profile of a set of descriptions.

Building on the modeling tools described earlier, the methodology presented here takes the path recommended by the Singapore framework (see Figure 5) in order to implement the associated specifications. Finally, the focus is on defining the DSP model. It is especially critical for the realization of the application profile within our platform and its reuse in other contexts.

3.2. Background

The EOAP was constructed in the context of the GEOSUD project (Maurel et al., 2015). The GEOSUD project was triggered by the finding that public stakeholders working in the field of environmental management and public policies underuse satellite images. One of the objectives of this project is to set up an image distribution platform to make high-resolution satellite images accessible to users with heterogeneous skills, ranging from the non-specialist to the remote sensing expert. These images originate from different satellites (e.g., SPOT[12], PLEIADES[13] or RAPID EYE[14]). They are delivered in specific image formats (e.g., GEOTIFF, JPG2000) and the associated metadata formats (DIMAP[15] format from AIRBUS). Furthermore, the GEOSUD image distribution platform is part of the French national data center THEIA (Bagdhadi et al., 2015).

Figure 5. Singapore framework. The application profile layer describes the recommended methodology. The second layer describes the formalized domain knowledge used to build the expected AP specifications. The last one, foundation standards, provides the recommended web standards to be used to build the domain standards
Source: Nilsson et al., 2008.

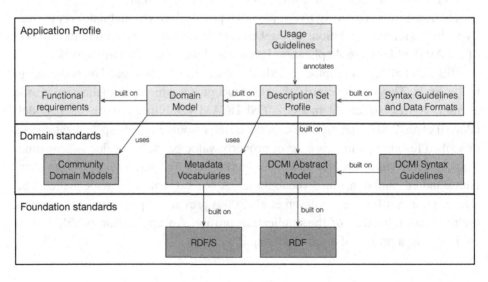

GEOSUD is built around components ensuring harmonization of image metadata, their web-standard visualization services and their archiving. The web user services (discovery, visualization and downloading) are based on an image catalog. This catalog provides the descriptions to search available images, to invoke their visualization and consultation of their detailed characteristics. It also provides information to locate and download images. The application profile is a core element of the platform. It provides descriptions which the metadata harmonization relies on. It plays a central role in the image catalog by structuring stored metadata. Finally, components for image visualization and access build their queries on image metadata. In the near future, it is planned to complement the GEOSUD image distribution platform with an on-demand processing platform. The latter will be designed, for example, to produce environmental indicator maps for the monitoring of natural resources. In this context, the application profile will also be used to provide the descriptions required to set up the processing parameters.

3.3. Defining Functional Requirements

Before the application profile can be constructed, its functional requirements have to be defined. These requirements allow the objectives and limits of the application profile to be precisely defined. To establish them, the aim was to identify and take the variety of target users of the target application into account, particularly with respect to their expertise – or lack of it – in remote sensing. In addition, the nature of the data had to be considered: the syntactic and semantic heterogeneities of metadata, the sizes of images originating from different producers, etc. The functional scope has thus been defined in order to better serve users by improving the process to discover, access and perform processing operations from a large catalog of multi-sensor and multi-resolution images.

3.3.1. Target Users

The GEOSUD image distribution platform is intended primarily for French public stakeholders. In reality, this term encompasses a variety of users who can be separated into two groups:

- Those belonging to academic research and higher education institutions. They undertake studies on environmental issues as well as on image processing. They are in a position to apprehend all or part of the data's complexity in order to extract information relevant to their needs,
- Officials of governmental services and of local or territorial authorities. They have to meet the demands of projects, for example, for the creation of car-

tographic products to track and monitor the implementation of government decisions or ensure local management of the environment (e.g., waste management, biodiversity). The majority of these users have little expertise in remote sensing.

Other types of users have also to be considered:

- The platform administrator. His primary mission is to distribute images received daily from the satellite at the reception station in a timely manner and with consistent quality. He is also responsible for the long-term archiving of the data,
- Other platforms for distribution that want to be interoperable with the GEOSUD platform. To this end, these platforms will access the metadata and images using web standard interfaces, i.e., geographical web services (e.g., OGC web services).

3.3.2. Main Functionalities

Based on the above, three groups of functions are identified:

- Functions for target users,
- Functions for administrators,
- Functions that ensure interoperability with other platforms.

For the first group, the application profile has to meet image discovery requirements for both specialist as well as non-specialist users. In addition to these functions and for the purposes of image selection, functions are necessary to: display the image at its full resolution, consult image characteristics (spectral, temporal, spatial resolution, etc.) and their acquisition parameters. These different functions are necessary for users to accurately assess the suitability of images selected for the intended use. Finally, a download service is required to obtain the selected image. Alternately, the availability of functions to allow online processing of images can replace the download service in order to produce directly a product that can help in decision making. The latter will then require the functions for the discovery of these processing functions, assessing their compatibility with the selected image and an indicator of complexity (computation time) so that the user can be informed about the computing resources necessary for their execution. Administrative functions have also to be implemented. These functions must also allow the insertion of new images to distribute, the management of metadata records and the monitoring of activities of resource-access applications. The UML use case diagram (Figure 6) summarizes these main features.

The specified functional requirements (Desconnets et al., 2014) are relevant to this dual challenge: to make available a large number of multi-sensor and multi-resolution images, heterogeneous both in their format as in the semantics to a community of specialists and non-specialists taking into account the requirements of managing large amounts of heterogeneous data.

For example, the requirement identified as "Solve the heterogeneity of metadata schemes and terminologies to ensure a uniform query of an image catalog" (Desconnets et al., 2014) highlights a need. It is essential to base the description of the images, and the terminology used to annotate them, on a single scheme. This will permit search and visualization operations, as well as those for assessing compatibility or quality, that are uniform regardless of the sensor from which the image originated and, in this way, really make this process simpler for a public actor.

3.4. Construction of the Domain Model

A domain model is a conceptual model. It has the objective of defining the entities that will have to be described by the application profile in conformance with the functional requirements. In fact, it is through this model that the scope of the application profile is defined. The proposed model (Figure 7) is inspired by the concepts of

Figure 6. Main use cases of the GEOSUD platform. UML use case diagram

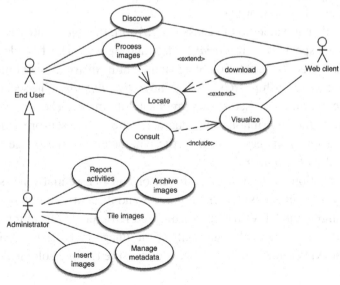

Resource and *Agent* of DCMI and extends them to reflect the specificity of satellite images and their inherent management and processing requirements.

Modeling activities that can meet the GEOSUD requirements have been undertaken in the field of sharing free datasets on the web (see DCAT vocabulary, state of the art section) as well as by the geographic community. The efforts of the latter refer more particularly to the initiative of the Public Geospatial Data Project of the FGDC (OSGEO, 2007) and its variant implemented around the data- and processing-sharing platform for multidisciplinary purposes: GENESI-DEC (Cossu et al., 2010). A domain model has been established to meet these needs: dclite4g (OSGEO, 2008). It is presented in Figure 7. Designed pragmatically, it covers the minimalist requirements for the description of raster and vector datasets. The EOAP profile's domain model is enriched by using the dclite4g model as its skeleton.

The *Resource* core entity refers to the concept of Resource as proposed by the DCAM (Dublin Core Abstract Model). This is an abstract entity that represents all the resources that are shared. It just generalizes the concepts of *dclite4g:DataSet* and *dclite4g:Series*. The specialization of the *Resource* entity helps make explicit the two types of resources that are shared and used within our platform: *EarthImage* and *Process*. The hierarchy of resources is represented by the reflexive relationship *isPartOf* the *Resource* entity. This relationship represents, for an *EarthImage* entity, an aggregation relationship between a collection of images with common properties and an image. This provides flexibility in their management by allowing the performing of batch operations, automatizing the semantic annotation of an entire collection, or associating a rendering style for displaying a set of images. It also allows relationships to be defined between resources of type *Process*. A *Process* can be a processing chain corresponding to a sequence of processes or to a unit process that can be part of a chain or not.

Semantically equivalent to the Class *dcmi:Agent*, the *Agent* entity is an abstract entity which is specialized in *Organization* and *Sensor*. The first describes the institutions involved in the creation of a resource or its distribution within the community through relationships *isCreatedBy* and *isDistributedBy*. The second, *Sensor*, describes the instruments used to acquire a satellite image. The *isAcquiredBy* association allows the description of the characteristics of the sensor used to acquire an image or a set of images as well as the parameters for the image acquisition (association class *Parameter*).

This information is specific to each sensor and is essential for assessing the compatibility of an image with a given process and its configuration before execution. For example, the NDVI index (Normalized Difference Vegetation Index) can be calculated from an optical image only if the image includes the NIR and Red channels. The NDVI index is widely used to measure the physiological activity of

Figure 7. Towards the EOAP domain model: UML Diagram class of the dc4gLite information model and the EOAP domain model (meta-metadata class of EOAP model is omitted for clarity) and their semantic relationships. Sources: OSGEO, 2007; Desconnets et al., 2014

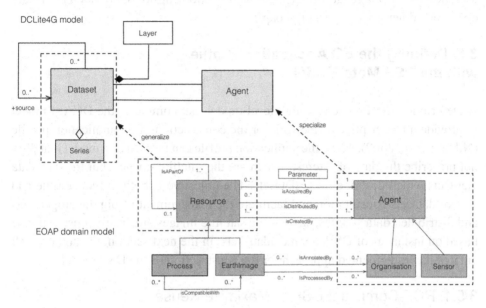

vegetation. It corresponds to the ratio between the difference of the NIR and Red channels and the sum of the two channels (Tucker, 1979).

The *EarthImage* entity represents the Earth observation images the authors wish to make accessible or process. It provides the intrinsic characteristics of the image, including information on the temporal and spatial extent, its spatial and spectral resolutions, and information to help its distribution such as its size and conditions of use. Its characteristics are complemented by semantic annotations pertaining to, for example, administrative entities covered by the image or the land cover classes identified on its spatial extent. These annotations are intended to facilitate the discovery process by non-expert users.

The *Process* entity represents unit processes or processing chains applicable to Earth observation images. They correspond to basic operations that help, for instance, in the extraction of a portion of an image, the calculation of a vegetation index or are used to undertake more complex processing leading to the creation of a new resource, such as a map of indicators of natural resources. The *Process* entity describes the inputs, data and parameters required to run the process and the outputs that will result. The relationship *isCompatibleWith* allows the determination of whether a specific image is suitable for use with a defined process such as the one for deriving the NDVI index. The compatibility depends mainly on the image's spectral and geometrical properties. Finally, the *meta-metadata* entity provides the information required for the management of metadata records (e.g., modification date, description language, etc). Classes and relationships of our domain model are documented here: http://purl.org/eoap/.

3.5. Defining the EO Application Profile with the DSP Meta-Model

A Description Set Profile is a high level model that completes the DCAM model to provide a prescriptive framework for the construction of an application profile (Nilsson et al., 2009). Thus, the application profile can be seen as a model that does not prescribe the data of interest, which are the satellite images, but the metadata elements which describe these datasets. The objective is both to reduce time and cost of datasets consultation and facilitate the management of big, heterogeneous and distributed data sources, such as the satellite images are. Their consultation is based on instances of DSP, i.e. metadata sets. In the next section, the authors will enlarge the implemented approach for the construction of the DSP model.

3.5.1. RDF-Compliant DSP to Maximize Reuse

The authors investigated the potential of the RDF language (Hayes & McBride, 2004) to express the DSP model, as this model has been initially developed as a conceptual meta-model and allows the encoding of resulting conformant models in arbitrary data formats, such as RDF, XML-Schema or DC-Text format. The RDF language is a mature W3C standard for creating and sharing metadata, datasets and vocabularies on the web. And, most relevant, the RDF data model is designed to strike the right balance between expressiveness and simplicity to power efficient data interoperability. As we are giving top priority to release metadata in an open format on the web, we are considering the RDF data model as a far better means of data exchange and sharing within the context of Linked Open Data (LOD) (Warren and Champion, 2014). DCMI provides some guidelines for encoding DSP specification in the RDF/XML concrete syntax (CEN, 2005). Additionally, a significant number of widely used metadata standards including DCTERMS (Dublin Core, 2012) are becoming available in a RDF serialization format, as e.g. RDF/XML or N3. Similarly, controlled vocabularies, as for example Geonames (Ahlers, 2013) or TGN (Getty Thesaurus of Geographic Names), are also made available in RDF formats to facilitate open use.

However, RDF and RDF Schema (RDFS) formalisms are built on a number of language primitives that are not always in line with the requirements for the constraint language DSP. Most importantly, semantics of RDF and RDFS were designed to follow the open world principle and are merely descriptive rather than prescriptive. Therefore, there are no proper mechanisms to add constraints that can aid in detection of inconsistencies and to identify invalid triples. Additionally, RDF only provides a construct for declaring binary properties. Consequently, representing non-binary relations is a well-known problem, since n-ary relations arise frequently during modeling activities.

Modeling activities using the UML profile meta-model, combined with the development of a dedicated RDFS vocabulary, provide a convenient method for approaching these limitations. In our opinion this approach has great ability and potential to provide explicit support for facilities to build metadata models that will conform to the DSP meta-model.

3.5.1.1. Modeling Approach to Build the RDF-Based DSP Vocabulary

A DSP model is intended to represent the overall structure of a metadata description set by means of constraints that apply either on resources described, properties used or values that may be given with respect to the properties. Consequently, a DSP model is built using the notions of description template and statement template that define the valid skeleton of a description and a statement, respectively. A DSP is then a collection of description templates (*DescriptionTemplate*), which in turn are collections of statement templates (*StatementTemplate*). At the same time this notion of collection involves three entities, namely *DescriptionTemplate*, *Property* and *Constraint* and reveals a complex constraint that requires a ternary relation. A UML class diagram for specifying such collections is introduced (Figure 8) and describes the class DescriptionTemplate associated with the classes *Statement-Template*, *Property* and *Constraint* by means of an n-ary relationship. *Statement-Template* is represented as an association class and appears as a class linked to the association with a dashed line. *DescriptionTemplate* contains a reference to *State-mentTemplate*, which in turn contains a first reference to the class Property and a second reference to the class *Constraint*. Consequently, UML class diagram could represent *StatementTemplate* as an association class, whilst the RDF language may define *StatementTemplate* as an auxiliary node. Therefore, in the RDF-based DSP model, *StatementTemplate* is represented as an auxiliary node that does not signify a named resource, i.e. a blank node or anonymous resource. In addition, following the same reasoning, *StatementTemplate* contains a reference to the class *Constraint*. *Constraint* is a nested structure that contains a collection of constraints and is also represented as an anonymous resource.

Blank nodes come with a significant overhead and additionally add unnecessary complexity to the DSP model. As UML leverages the power of modeling effectively, the authors propose an approach coming from MOF (Meta Object Facility)

Figure 8. UML class diagram describing the association class StatementTemplate. Source: Mougenot et al., 2015

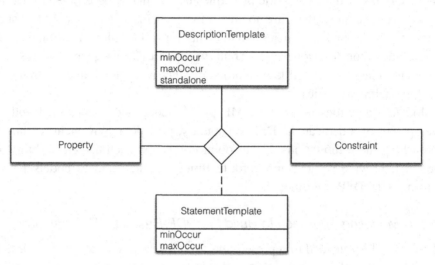

to separate the modeling of the DSP into a three level hierarchy: a model at level 1 (Earth observation domain model), a meta-model at level 2 (DSP meta-representation) and a meta-meta-model at level 3 (RDF and RDFS meta-representations). The authors argue that UML profiling mechanisms could help increase the usefulness of a RDF application profile particularly in a linked open data context. A UML profile (D'Souza et al., 1999) represents a lightweight extension mechanism to the UML language, in particular by defining custom stereotypes. Stereotypes are applied to UML elements to refine their semantics, either as classes or associations. Graphically, stereotypes are rendered by self-explanatory meta-class enclosed by guillemets.

Concerning that point the researchers take advantage of the work carried out on ontology metamodeling (Brockmans et al., 2006) with a corresponding UML profile and a collection of stereotypes that convey the meaning of the semantic web languages primitives (RDF, RDFS and OWL). Some of these stereotypes are illustrated in the simplified diagram of the DSP model depicted in Figure 9.

A meta-class, as an example *RDFSClass, BlankNode* or *RDFProperty*, refines the semantics of each class of the DSP model. For instance, the generic class BlankNode marks appropriate dependencies on the classes *StatementTemplate* and *Constraint* that result from the translation of n-ary properties, respectively.

3.5.1.2 A RDFS Vocabulary for Capturing the Meaning of the DSP Model

The section is intended to present the most important built-in primitives that are used to provide a general model of semantic assertions behind the DSP. The authors use RDFS as a metamodeling architecture to define taxonomies of classes and properties

Figure 9. Simplified DSP diagram qualified with the RDF/RDFS UML profile. Source: Mougenot et al., 2015

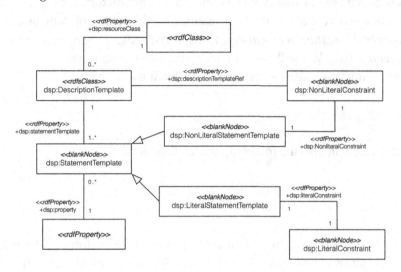

as well as declaring relationships between classes and properties using RDF syntax. There are few classes in the DSP model where *dsp:NonLiteralStatementTemplate* is a *rdfs:subClassOf dsp:StatementTemplate*. Similarly there are few properties declared in DSP where *dsp:statementTemplate* whose *rdfs:domain* is a *dsp:DescriptionTemplate* and *rdfs:range* a *dsp:statementTemplate*. Examples of DSP built-in primitives are provided using N3 concrete syntax in Figure 10.

RDFS is expected to provide simple semantics using positive assertions grounded in the open world assumption. Subsequently there does not exist any possibility to deal with negation and accordingly to benefit from dedicated mechanisms to express constraints. The importance is given rather to derive implicit knowledge

Figure 10. First excerpt of the DSP language

```
dsp:DescriptionTemplate
      a rdfs:Class ;
      rdfs:label "DescriptionTemplate"@en .
dsp:LiteralStatementTemplate
      a rdfs:Class ;
      rdfs:subClassOf dsp:StatementTemplate ;
      rdfs:label LiteralStatementTemplate"@en .
dsp:statementTemplate
      a rdf:Property ;
      rdfs:domain  DescriptionTemplate ;
      rdfs:range   StatementTemplate ;
```

from the statements that are explicitly asserted using entailment rules. These rules are consequently not primarily intended to raise contradictory facts.

To give a concrete example, the semantics for the setting of domain and range of the property *dsp:statementTemplate* to respectively *dsp:DescriptionTemplate* and *dsp:StatementTemplate* will allow to determine two typing rules.

If the authors consider for instance the following statement

```
geosud:ds1 dsp:statementTemplate _:slt1
```

one can derive that also the following triples must hold.

```
 geosud:ds1 rdf:type dsp:DescriptionTemplate
_:slt1 rdf:type dsp:StatementTemplate
```

These typing rules are first of all entailment rules to perform RDFS inferencing but also allow constraints to be expressed. We are therefore able to fix that the resource geosud:ds1 must be *dsp:DescriptionTemplate* and the resource _:slt1 must be a *dsp:StatementTemplate*.

However not all the integrity constraints will be able to be defined in RDFS. Basically integrity constraints are referring to ensuring accuracy and consistency of metadata records. For example a particular resource might be described in an arbitrary manner, using any kind of property. As a result, each description template must be constrained to exhibit some specific statement templates. Additionally cardinality with statements is expected to be specified. To give an example, a description template representing a satellite image may require the defining of at least one and possibly many spatial coverages through the dct:spatial property. Consequently the idea is to express many other well-known constraints as for example cardinality constraints through capabilities of the language of the DSP:

```
dsp:minOccur
        a    rdf:Property ;
        rdfs:domain dsp:DescriptionTemplate,
dsp:StatementTemplate  ;
        rdfs:range   xsd:positiveInteger ;
```

Basically the idea is first to use the elementary properties of RDFS to act mainly as a typing language. Typically the properties under consideration are subclass, subproperty, type, domain and range. Subsequently the DSP language creates a relevant language pattern able to define integrity constraints.

Once class and property primitives are defined in the DSP model, they can be used to build dedicated description sets. Subsequently, the authors focus on a description set for Earth observation that conforms to DSP.

3.5.2. Towards a RDF-Compliant DSP Model for Earth Observations

The authors consider the constraint language DSP as a meta-model, associated with a dedicated UML profile that allows expressing the DSP semantic specifications by means of stereotypes. These stereotypes specialize the stereotypes described within the RDF/RDFS UML profile and provide a specific way of defining typical constraints between DSP languages elements.

Figure 11 gives an excerpt of the DSP instantiation model for EO resources. The classes *EarthImage_T*, *GeographicalExtent_T* and *SpectralBand_T* are annotated by the meta-class *dsp:DescriptionTemplate* that is a kind of *RDFSClass*. *EarthImage_T* refers to the class *EarthImage* through an association annotated with the meta-property *dsp:resourceClass*. Additionally *EarthImage_T* is supported by a number of unnamed classes marked by the meta-class *dsp:NonLiteralStatementTem*

Figure 11. Short of the EOAP model as a DSP meta-model instantiation

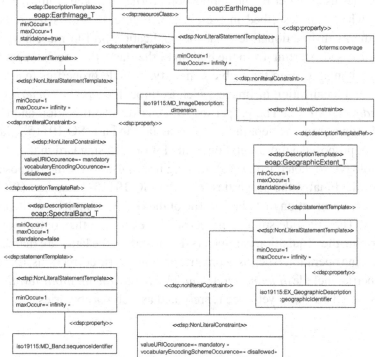

plate. Two of these classes links the Earth Image description template to description template entitled *GeographicalExtent_*T and *SpectralBand_*T entirely dedicated to the spatial location for the first one and dedicated to image content description for the second. An object *SpectralBand_*T is connected through an object typed by *dsp:StatementTemplate* to a property *iso19115:MD_Band:sequenceIdentifier* which corresponds to the different layers with different wavelength when the image is acquired. This kind of property is necessary to distinguish the nature of wavelength available and will greatly facilitate the choice of the image processing that could execute on the image.

The same excerpt of the EOAP model is presented in Figure 12 using N3 syntax. The EOAP model pays particular attention to carefully describing the required level of spatial coverage and image content in relation to real needs for Earth observing and uses relevant metadata standards. The use scenario given in section 3.5.3 illustrates the importance of the spatial and content dimensions by portraying an example of use case of interest. The contribution of the EOAP model together with the provision of multiresolution and multitemporal satellite imagery eases identification of environmental patterns over time and space.

3.5.4. Web and Geospatial Vocabularies for EOAP

The properties used to define the application profile are taken from five metadata standards which are described in section 2.3. Figure 13 shows the relationship between the main functionalities that the application profile must have and the vocabularies used. Starting from the bottom of the stack, the vocabularies dcterms and dcat, originating from the web community, provide properties that allow the discovery and localization of images, such as through properties *dcterms:created* and *dcat:downloadURL*. The properties which cover identification and consultation needs come from the geographical metadata standard ISO 19115. Islam et al. (2004) have proposed a representation of the ISO 19115 standard in the form of an OWL ontology[16] (denoted iso19115), making it thus usable for the purposes of the EOAP profile. Finally, the properties from the ISO 19115-2 standard (ISO, 2007) and the Earth observation metadata profile of the O & M complement the iso19115 vocabulary. They provide suitable properties for exploring the contents of images and describing the acquisition parameters. For instance, the latter are mandatory for pre-processing operations such as geometric or radiometric corrections. Examples of these properties include *illuminationAzimuthAngle* and *illuminationElevationAngle*. These two standards have yet to be represented as web vocabularies.

Figure 12. EOAP RDF excerpt in N3

```
eoap:EarthImage_T
  a dsp:DescriptionTemplate ;
  dsp:maxOccur "1"^^xsd:nonNegativeInteger ;
  dsp:minOccur "1"^^xsd:nonNegativeInteger ;
  dsp:resourceClass eoap:EarthImage ;
  dsp:standalone "true"^^xsd:boolean ;
  [...]
dsp:statementTemplate
[ a dsp:NonLiteralStatementTemplate ;
    dsp:maxOccur "infinity" ;
    dsp:minOccur "1"^^xsd:nonNegativeInteger ;
    dsp:NonliteralConstraint
      [ a dsp:NonLiteralConstraint ;
          dsp:descriptionTemplateRef eoap:GeographicExtent_T;
          dsp:valueStringOccurence "disallowed"^^;
          dsp:vocabularyEncodingSchemeOccurence  "disallowed"^^;
      ] ;
      dsp:property dcterms:coverage
].
dsp:statementTemplate
  [ a dsp:NonLiteralStatementTemplate ;
      dsp:maxOccur "infinity" ;
      dsp:minOccur "1"^^xsd:nonNegativeInteger ;
      dsp:NonliteralConstraint
        [ a dsp:NonLiteralConstraint ;
            dsp:descriptionTemplateRef eoap:SpectralBand_T;
            dsp:valueURIOccurrence  "mandatory"^^<dsp:Occurrence>;
dsp:vocabularyEncodingSchemeOccurrence "disallowed"^^<dsp:Occurrence>;
        ];
        dsp:property iso19115:MD_ImageDescription:dimension
    ].
eoap:GeographicalExtent_T
    a dsp:DescriptionTemplate ;
      dsp:maxOccur "1"^^xsd:nonNegativeInteger ;
      dsp:minOccur "1"^^xsd:nonNegativeInteger ;
      dsp:resourceClass iso19115:EX_GeographicalDescription;
      dsp:standalone "false"^^xsd:boolean .
dsp:statementTemplate
  [ a dsp:NonLiteralStatementTemplate ;
      dsp:maxOccur "infinity" ;
      dsp:minOccur "1"^^xsd:nonNegativeInteger ;
      dsp:NonliteralConstraint
      [ a dsp:NonLiteralConstraint ;
        dsp:valueURIOccurence "mandatory"^^<dsp:Occurrence>;
        dsp:VocabularyEncodingSchemeOccurence "disallowed"^^<dsp:Occurrence>;
      ];
      dsp:property iso19115:EX_GeographicDescription:geographicIdentifier
  ].
  [...]
eoap:SpectralBand_T
  a dsp:DescriptionTemplate ;
    dsp:maxOccur "infinite" ;
    dsp:minOccur "1"^^xsd:nonNegativeInteger ;
    dsp:resourceClass iso19115:MD_Band ;
    dsp:standalone "false"^^xsd:boolean .
    [...]
```

3.5.5. Example of Use for Discovery Purposes

This section provides a brief illustration of the use of the application profile within our platform. For this, the authors assume a base scenario that involves selecting images with properties that will allow the classic vegetation index (NDVI) to be derived from images of the French department of Landes. This index is the starting point to map the clearcuts[17] of a forest (Durrieu & Deshayes, 1994). A GIS special-ist, working in an organization that monitors the forests in the Landes department, wishes to quantify the forest areas that have been clear-cut. For this, he must cal-

Figure 13. Stack of the metadata standard and vocabularies used for the Earth Observation Application Profile. The corresponding functional requirements are shown on the left in relation to the standard and vocabularies used

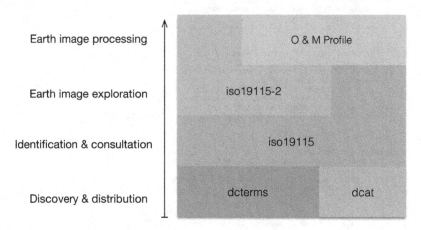

culate the NDVI of optical images acquired on different dates. The authors recall that the NDVI index is calculated from optical images that include a Red channel and a Near Infrared (NIR) channel. In order to select images useful for his mapping requirements, the specialist needs to query the image catalog via the discovery service in this form: "I am searching for images that are located in the Landes department and whose spectral bands contain the 'Red' and 'NIR' channels and that were acquired during spring (March to June)." The querying of the image catalog will be based on the *dcterms:created* property to filter images by creation date and the *iso19115:EX_GeographicalExtent:geographicIdentifier* property to provide the name of the department with which the image is associated. Finally, the selection of images containing the "Red" and "NIR" spectral bands is performed on the values associated with the *iso19115:MD_Band:sequenceIdentifier* property. Figure 14 shows an excerpt of a DSP instance describing one of the selected images. For reasons of clarity, the properties pertaining to the temporal dimension ("March to June") have been omitted.

4. CONCLUSION

This chapter outlines the methodological elements used to define the EOAP application profile. The main objective is to describe satellite images for the purposes of discovery, access and processing for the environmental community. The construction approach also takes into account the different levels of expertise of the target users

Figure 14. Excerpt of EOAP instance in N3

```
geosud:EarthImage_1
      a   eoap:EarthImage_T ;
      dcterms:identifier "2900423f-7aee-478b-ab20-fe932d4adb" ;
      dcterms:created "2015-06-29T12:32:10";
      iso19115:MD_Metadata.hierarchyLevel
              iso19115:MD_Scope.feature ;
      dcterms:coverage eaop:GeographicExtent_1 ;
      iso19115 :MD_ImageDescription.dimension eaop:SpectralBand_1 ;
[..]
dcat:downloadURL http://ids.equipex-geosud.fr/constellation/rest/secured/
download/data/SPOT6_2015_FRANCE-ORTHO_IGN-MS/MD_S6X_2015062937945426CP.tar.gz
[..]
geosud:GeographicExtent_1
      a eoap:GeographicalExtent_T ;
      iso19115:EX_GeographicBoundingBox.geographicIdentifier
              "Ychoux" ;
      iso19115:EX_GeographicBoundingBox.geographicIdentifier
              "Les Landes" .
geosud:SpectralBand_1
      a   eoap:SpectralBand_T ;
      iso19115:MD_Band.sequenceIdentifier "Red" ;
      iso19115:MD_Band.sequenceIdentifier "NIR" .
```

as well as the heterogeneity of metadata associated with the images. For this, the application profile provides a structural and semantic interoperability framework to facilitate the discovery of multi-sensor, multi-resolution images for non-expert users. It also provides for the management and long-term archiving of the volume of images acquired on a daily frequency. Note that it is also designed to ensure the discovery of analytical processing operations for images.

The methodology described is primarily based on the recommendations made by the Dublin Core community around the DCAM and DSP structural models and the Singapore Framework. It is complemented by modeling and meta-modeling tools originating from model-driven engineering (UML, MOF). These tools allow us to formalize the functional requirements and the domain model that results. The constructed models can cover the functional requirements of the target communities and define the domain model. They also allow use of a semi-formal DSP constraints model and help explain better the different levels of representation of the DSP: meta-model, model and instance. These different variants offer a more comprehensive implementation framework for manipulating its RDF representation. Indeed, it allows the operationalization of the DSP in the RDF within a platform with the ability to produce new models that can be validated against the DSP meta-model. It also allows the creation and validation of metadata sets that conform to the DSP model.

Going beyond the methodology used, the question of the RDF representation and the use of the DSP language may arise. Indeed, the RDF representation of the DSP is little used today or not at all. This is mainly due to the complexity of the proposed approach, which draws its representation based on the assumptions of the open world

(RDF/S) and which intends to describe the constraints from the assumptions of the closed world. Other hybrid approaches (Eiter et al., 2008; Hitzler & Parsia, 2009) that are more mature and which meet the requirements of the validation of metadata sets do exist and have been used satisfactorily in domains related to Earth observation (Shu et al., 2016). Still, the authors believe that a constraint language such as DSP has its reasons for existing. For this, the operationalization of the DSP in the RDF continues to be of interest to the authors. To extend this work, the authors therefore plan to make the DSP vocabulary more mature in the RDF in order to facilitate its implementation, particularly within the environmental-data distribution platform.

REFERENCES

Ahlers, D. (2013). Assessment of the accuracy of GeoNames gazetteer data. In C. Jones & R. Purves (Eds.), *Proceedings of the 7th Workshop on Geographic Information Retrieval, GIR '13,* New York, NY, USA (pp. 74-81). doi:10.1145/2533888.2533938

Baghdadi, N., Leroy, M., Maurel, P., Cherchali, S., Stoll, M., Faure, J. F.,... Pacholc-zyk, P. (2015, September). The Theia land Data Centre. *Proceedings of International Society of Photogrammetry and Remote Sensing Conference – RSDI Workshop,* Montpellier, France.

Brockmans, S., Colomb, R. M., Haase, P., Kendall, E. F., Wallace, E. K., Welty, C., & Xie, G. T. (2006, November). A model driven approach for building OWL DL and OWL full ontologies. *Proceedings of the International Semantic Web Conference* (pp. 187-200). Berlin: Springer. doi:10.1007/11926078_14

CEN. (2005). CWA 15248:2005. Guidelines for machine-processable representation of Dublin Core Application Profiles. European Committee of Standardization. Retrieved from http://dublincore.org/moinmoin-wiki-archive/architecturewiki/attachments/cen-cwa15248.pdf

Cossu, R., Pacini, F., Brito, F., Fusco, L., Santi, E. L., & Parrini, A. (2010, October). GENESI-DEC: a federative e-infrastructure for Earth Science data discovery, access, and on-demand processing. *Proceedings of the 24th International Conference on Informatics for Environmental Protection.*

Coyle, K., & Baker, T. (2008). *Guidelines for Dublin Core Application Profiles.* Retrieved from http://dublincore.org/documents/profile-guidelines/index.shtml

D'Souza, D., Aamod, S., & Birchenough, S. (1999). First-class extensibility for UML – packaging of profiles, stereotypes, patterns. In R. France & B. Rumpe (Eds.), *UML'99 – The Unified Modeling Language,*LNCS (Vol. 1723, pp. 265–277). Springer Berlin Heidelberg. doi:10.1007/3-540-46852-8_19

Desconnets, J. C., Chahdi, H., & Mougenot, I. (2014, November). Application profile for Earth Observation images. *Proceedings of theResearch Conference on Metadata and Semantics Research* (pp. 68-82). Springer International Publishing.

Desconnets, J. C., Libourel, T., Maurel, P., Miralles, A., & Passouant, M. (2001, September). Proposition de structuration des métadonnées en géosciences: Spécificité de la communauté scientifique. Proceedings of Journées Cassin 2001: Géomatique et espace rural (pp. 69-82).

Dublin Core. (2012). Dublin Core Metadata Element Set, Version 1.1. (2012). Retrieved from http://www.dublincore.org/documents/dces/

Durrieu, S., & Deshayes, M. (1994). Méthode de comparaison dimages satellitaires pour la détection des changements en milieu forestier. Application aux monts de Lacaune. *Annales des Sciences Forestieres, 51*(2), 147–161. doi:10.1051/forest:19940205

Eiter, T., Ianni, G., Krennwallner, T., & Polleres, A. (2008). Rules and ontologies for the semantic web. In *Reasoning Web* (pp. 1–53). Springer Berlin Heidelberg. doi:10.1007/978-3-540-85658-0_1

Friss-Christensen, A., Ostländer, N., Lutz, M., & Bernard, L. (2007). Designing Service Architectures for Distributed Geoprocessing: Challenges and Future Directions. *Transactions in GIS, 11*(6), 799–818. doi:10.1111/j.1467-9671.2007.01075.x

Gaspéri, J., Houbie, F., Woolf, A., & Smolders, S. (2012). Earth observation metadata profile of Observations & Measurements. Retrieved from https://portal.opengeospatial.org/files/?artifact_id=47040

Gayte, O., Libourel, T., Cheylan, J. P., & Lardon, S. (1997). *Conception des systèmes d'information sur l'environnement. Géomatique*. Paris, France: Edition Hermès.

Hayes, P., & McBride, B. (2004). RDF semantics. Retrieved from http://www.w3.org/TR/2004/REC-rdf-mt-20040210/

Heery, R., & Patel, M. (2000). Application profiles: Mixing and matching metadata schemas. *Ariadne, 25*.

Hevner, A. R. (2007). A three cycle view of design science research. *Scandinavian Journal of Information Systems, 19*(2), 4.

Hitzler, P., & Parsia, B. (2009). Ontologies and rules. In *Handbook on Ontologies* (pp. 111–132). Springer Berlin Heidelberg. doi:10.1007/978-3-540-92673-3_5

ISA. (2015). DCAT Application Profile for data portals in Europe. Version 1.1. Interoperability Solutions for European Public Administration. European Union. Retrieved from https://joinup.ec.europa.eu/node/137964/

ISA. (2015b). GeoDCAT-AP: A geospatial extension for the DCAT application profile for data portals in Europe. Working Group Draft 7. Interoperability Solutions for European Public Administration. European Union. Retrieved from https://joinup.ec.europa.eu/asset/dcat_application_profile/asset_release/geodcat-ap-v10

Islam, A. S., Bermudez, L., Fellah, S., Beran, B. & Piasecki, M. (2004). Implementation of the Geographic Information-Metadata (ISO 19115: 2003) Norm using the Web Ontology Language (OWL). *Transactions in GIS*.

ISO. (2003). *Geographic Information Metadata, ISO 19115*. Geneva, Switzerland: International Organization for Standardization.

ISO. (2004). *ISO 19106:2004. Geographic information — Profiles*. Geneva, Switzerland: International Organization for Standardization.

ISO. (2007). *ISO/TS 19139:2007. Geographic information — Metadata — XML schema implementation*. Geneva, Switzerland: International Organization for Standardization.

ISO. (2009). *ISO19115-2:2009. Geographic information — Metadata — Part 2: Extensions for imagery and gridded data*. Geneva, Switzerland: International Organization for Standardization.

ISO. (2011). *ISO 19156:2011, 2014. Geographic information – Observations and Measurements*. Geneva, Switzerland: International Organization for Standardization.

Jacobson, I., & Ng, P. W. (2004). *Aspect-oriented software development with use cases (addison-wesley object technology series)*. Addison-Wesley Professional.

Kazmierski, M., Desconnets, J. C., Guerrero, B., & Briand, D. (2014, June). Accessing Earth Observation data collections with semantic-based services.*Proceedings of the 17th AGILE Conference on Geographic Information Science, Connecting a Digital Europe through Location and Place*, Castellon, Spain.

Lamb, J. (2001). Sharing best methods and know-how for improving generation and use of metadata. In *New Techniques and Technologies for Statistics and Exchange of Technology and Know-how* (pp. 175-194).

Livre Blanc. (1998). *L'information géographique française dans la société de l'information.* Rapport CNIG/AFIGEO.

Maguire, D. J., & Longley, P. A. (2005). The emergence of geoportals and their role in spatial data infrastructures. *Computers, Environment and Urban Systems, 29*(1), 3–14. doi:10.1016/S0198-9715(04)00045-6

Maurel, P., & Faure, J. F. · Cantou, J.P., Desconnets, J.C., Teisseire, M., Mougenot, I., Martignac, C. & Bappel E. (2015, September). The GEOSUD remote sensing data and services infrastructure. *Proceedings of the International Society of Photogrammetry and Remote Sensing Conference – RSDI Workshop.* Montpellier, France.

Mougenot, I., Desconnets, J. C., & Chahdi, H. (2015). A DCAP to promote easy-to-use data for multiresolution and multitemporal satellite imagery analysis.*Proceedings of the International Conference on Dublin Core and Metadata Applications,* Sao Paulo, Brazil.

Nilsson, M., Baker, T., & Johnston, P. (2008). The Singapore Framework for Dublin Core Application Profiles. Retrieved from http://dublincore.org/documents/singapore-framework/

Nilsson, M., Miles, A. J., Johnston, P., & Enoksson, F. (2009). Formalizing Dublin Core Application Profiles–Description Set Profiles and Graph Constraints. In Metadata and Semantics (pp. 101-111). Springer US. doi:10.1007/978-0-387-77745-0_10

OGC. (2007). OGC Catalogue Services Specification 2.0.2 – ISO Metadata Application Profile (1.0.0). Retrieved from http://portal.opengeospatial.org/files/?artifact_id=21460

OMG. (2006). Meta Object Facility (MOF) Core Specification OMG Available Specification Version 2.0. Retrieved from http://doc.omg.org/formal/2006-01-01.pdf

OMG. (2015). OMG Unified Modeling Language TM (OMG UML). Version 2.5. Retrieved from http://www.omg.org/spec/UML/2.5/PDF

OSGEO. (2007). Geodata metadata model. Retrieved from https://wiki.osgeo.org/wiki/Geodata_Metadata_Model

OSGEO. (2008). DC4GLite, Dublin Core Lightweight Profile for Geospatial. Retrieved from https://wiki.osgeo.org/wiki/DCLite4G

Powell, A., Nilsson, M., Naeve, A., Johnston, P., & Baker, T. (2007). DCMI Abstract Model. DCMI Recommendation. Retrieved from http://dublincore.org/documents/abstract-model/

Rumbaugh, J., Blaha, M., Premerlani, W., Eddy, F., & Lorensen, W. E. (1991). Object-oriented modeling and design, 199 *(1)*. Englewood Cliffs, NJ: Prentice-hall.

Shu, Y., Liu, Q., & Taylor, K. (2016). Semantic validation of environmental observations data. *Environmental Modelling & Software, 79*, 10–21. doi:10.1016/j.envsoft.2016.01.004

Soley, R. (2000). Model driven architecture. OMG white paper.

Tucker, C. J. (1979). Red and photographic infrared linear combinations for monitoring vegetation. *Remote Sensing of Environment, 8*(2), 127–150. doi:10.1016/0034-4257(79)90013-0

W3C. (2014). Data Catalog Vocabulary (DCAT). W3C Recommendation. Retrieved from https://www.w3.org/TR/vocab-dcat/

Warren, R., & Champion, E. (2014). Linked Open Data Driven Game Generation. *In Proceedings of the 13th International Semantic Web Conference – Part II (ISWC '14)* (pp. 358-373). New York: Springer.

Weibel, S., Kunze, J., Lagoze, C. & Wolf, M. (1998). *Dublin core metadata for resource discovery* (No. RFC 2413).

ENDNOTES

[1]   THEIA: French Land Data Center.
[2]   INSPIRE: Infrastructure for Spatial Information in the European Community.
[3]   COPERNICUS: European Earth Observation Program.
[4]   GEOSS: Global Earth Observation System of Systems.
[5]   GEOSUD: GEOInformation for SUstainable Development.
[6]   Orthorectification is a geometric and radiometric correction of aerial or satellite image so that each point can be superimposed on a flat map that corresponds to it.
[7]   A metadata standard explicitly and prescriptively defines metadata elements, their properties, and provides the information necessary for its implementation.
[8]   HMA: Heterogeneous Mission Accessibility (https://earth.esa.int/web/gscb/hma-standards).
[9]   ESA: European Space Agency.
[10]   In this context, the notion of metadata scheme (also called "metadata schema") refers to the notion of the XML schema. This is the W3C-recommended lan-

guage for describing an XML document to define the structure and the content type of an XML document in order to validate it.

[11] CNES: Centre National d'Etudes Spatiales (France's space agency).

[12] SPOT: Satellite for Earth Observation (French acronym: SPOT) is a constellation of satellites with high-resolution sensors with the most recent of them, SPOT 6 and SPOT 7, equipped with very high resolution sensors. The SPOT system is operated by Airbus Defence and Space.

[13] PLEIADES is a constellation of two very high resolution satellites, operated by Airbus Defense and Space

[14] RAPID EYE is a constellation of five high-resolution satellites, operated by RapidEye AG.

[15] DIMAP format specifications: http://www.spotimage.fr/dimap/spec/documentation/refdoc.htm

[16] iso19115: http://loki.cae.drexel.edu/~wbs/ontology/2004/09/iso-19115

[17] Clearcuts: refers to a mode of forestry development through cutting down of all the trees of a parcel.

Chapter 5

The Development Process of a Metadata Application Profile for the Social and Solidarity Economy

Mariana Curado Malta
Polythechnic of Oporto, Portugal & Algoritmi Center, University of Minho, Portugal

Ana Alice Baptista
Algoritmi Center, Universidade do Minho, Portugal

ABSTRACT

This chapter presents the process of developing a Metadata Application Profile for the Social and Solidarity Economy (DCAP-SSE) using Me4MAP, a method for developing Application Profiles that was being put forth by the authors. The DCAP-SSE and Me4MAP were developed iteratively, feeding new developments into each other. This paper presents how the DCAP-SSE was developed showing the steps followed through the development of the activities and the techniques used, and the final deliverables obtained at the end of each activity. It also presents the work-team and how each profile of the team contributed for the DCAP-SSE development process. The DCAP-SSE has been endorsed by the SSE community and new perspectives of SSE activities have been defined for future enlargement of the DCAP-SSE. At the time of writing this chapter, Linked Open SSE Data is being published, they are the first examples of use of the DCAP-SSE.

DOI: 10.4018/978-1-5225-2221-8.ch005

INTRODUCTION

The Social and Solidarity Economy (SSE) can be broadly defined as a type of economy in which the goals are different either from the ones of the market economy or from the state's (Lechat, 2007). Allegedly, these goals are neither centered in profit nor in individualistic needs. It is an economy that presents itself as a material and human alternative to a capitalist economy (Cattani, Laville, Gaiger, & Hespanha, 2009).

SSE organisations work with scarce resources, networking and partnerships appear as a highly relevant way of working, with potential for SSE organisations to gain visibility and attract funding, or to be able to work at scale.

A study by Curado Malta, Baptista, & Parente (2014) revealed that the SSE community is facing a global challenge: this community wants to implement interoperability solutions between their Web Based Information Systems (WIS)—to build a global SSE e-marketplace—and also among their WIS and external ones. This calls for a more universal interoperability solution, like the one provided by Linked Data. Linked Data is structured data that is standardized, reachable, relatable and manageable by Semantic Web tools (W3C, 2015). One key aspect of Linked Data is the relationships among the data. These allow not only relating and inferring relations among different datasets and data sources, as they also provide context to available data. One of the constructs that contributes to maximize the interoperability of linked data is the Metadata Application Profile (MAP) (Nilsson, Baker, & Johnston, 2009).

In the end of 2010 the Intercontinental Network for the promotion of Social and Solidarity Economy (RIPESS)[1] has created a task-force called ESSGlobal for the mapping of SSE organisations and for the development of interoperability among SSE organizations' WIS. After a study of the environment, its requirements and its internal and external constraints, Curado Malta & Baptista (2014) came to the conclusion that there was no Metadata Application Profile (MAP) that could serve the SSE community. Based on this study, in 2012 the ESSGlobal decided to develop a MAP for the Social and Solidarity Economy (DCAP-SSE). The first version of this DCAP-SSE was presented at the DC-2015 conference (Curado Malta & Baptista, 2015). ESSGlobal created a Webpage[2] in order to provide the SSE community with detailed information about the DCAP-SSE adoption. Currently the ESSGlobal task-force is lobbying the world SSE community for a broad adoption of DCAP-SSE. This article presents the development process of this MAP – the DCAP-SSE.

To develop a MAP is a complex task: it depends on many variables as the communities are all different and have very specific particularities and different needs, and the process can start in different stages (e.g. no databases at all, existent local relational databases, existent Web Based Information Systems). It is indeed difficult to systematize all these possibilities and define a path of action depending on them.

99

On the other hand a MAP is something that is not developed often, sometimes only once in a lifetime, there is little documentation on how to develop a metadata application profile (see Curado Malta & Baptista (2013c)) and very little systematization.

This paper has the goal to contribute to enriching the metadata community documentation on how a specific MAP, DCAP-SSE, was developed. This development was based on a method for the development of MAPs (Me4MAP), which was defined by the authors using a Design Science Research (DSR) methodological approach.

This article proceeds as follows: the next section presents the background of the process used to develop the DCAP-SSE; Section 3 presents the DCAP-SSE development process including the activities and techniques, how the activities interact, and the final deliverables at the end of each activity; Section 4 presents future research directions and the last section concludes.

BACKGROUND

The DCAP-SSE development work was framed in a PhD research project (Curado Malta, 2014) that resulted in the definition of a method for the development of Metadata Application Profiles - Me4MAP).

This project was based in a DSR methodological approach, with the framework defined by Hevner & Chatterjee (2010). The DCAP-SSE development work was the "experimental situation" defined by Hevner & Chatterjee (2010) to test the artifact under development - Me4MAP. The DCAP-SSE and Me4MAP were developed iteratively. This iterative development implied that the development of DCAP-SSE did not follow the last version of Me4MAP. Instead, the last version of Me4MAP resulted from this iterative process. The process started with a very preliminary version of Me4MAP based in the results of the state-of-the-art study (see Curado Malta & Baptista (2013c)). The development of the DCAP-SSE along with other inputs then informed the Me4MAP development process, for the first version of Me4MAP that then fed the DCAP-SSE development process and so on in an iterative way. The development of Me4MAP process has produced though, along time, two versions-in-progress and a final version:

- **Version 0.1:** Curado Malta and Baptista (2013b)
- **Version 0.2:** Curado Malta and Baptista (2013a)
- **Version 1.0:** to be published

In the first versions, the method was called Me4DCAP which stands for 'Method for the Development of Dublin Core Application Profiles'. Then the name was changed to Me4MAP – Method for the Development of Metadata Application Profiles in order to make clear in the name the independence from any metadata vocabulary.

With Me4MAP, regardless of the version, a MAP development process should follow the Singapore Stages. The names of the stages come from the seminal document "The Singapore framework for Dublin Core Application Profiles" - see Nilsson et al. (2008). This framework defines the three first Singapore Components: Functional Requirements; Domain Model and Description Set Profile, mandatory, and the last two: Usage Guidelines and Syntax Guidelines, optional.

The following sections will present how the DCAP-SSE was developed: showing the techniques used in the DCAP-SSE activities and the final versions of the deliverables. These deliverables are presented in the document if they are simple to show, otherwise a URL with the information is provided.

DCAP-SSE Development Process

The development of DCAP-SSE followed the Singapore Stages. Each stage was composed by a set of activities:

- In the first stage we developed the Functional Requirements. Activities: (i) definition of the Vision Statement of the project; (ii) definition of the application context; (iii) definition of the high-level requirements; (iv) development of the use-cases model.
- In the second stage we developed the Domain Model. Activities: (i) definition of the Environmental Scan, and; (ii) definition of the Domain Model.
- In the third stage we developed the Description Set Profile. Activities: (i) Development of Pre-Description Set profile (which includes also sub-activities of development of the detailed domain model, development of the vocabulary alignment and definition of the constraints matrix); (ii) Validation in laboratory; (iii) Codification of the Description Set Profile; iv) Validation in Production.

According to Me4MAP, it is important that team members use a common vocabulary of key terms in order to avoid misunderstandings and improve communication (Booch, Jacobson, & Rumbaugh, 1999). For this reason, it is very important to build a Glossary and make it readily available to project team members. A MAP development work-team should be composed of people with different expertise, as defined in Curado Malta & Baptista (2013a); it can happen that one member can have more than one type of expertise, which gives further emphasis to the need of a common Glossary.

The results of the development process as well as the justification of the choices should be recorded. The development of the documentation of each process is fundamental since the documents produced will help some MAP users (such as app designers or programmers) to apply the properties and classes correctly to the specific context. It also ensures that future MAP developers understand the MAP development process that was used. In the DCAP-SSE development process, the work team was geographically dispersed. We used Skype to meet, a logbook on line to write the minutes of the meetings (http://potaopad.me – not available anymore) and a wiki (http://essglobal.org/essglobal/wiki/process) to record information, decision processes, open issues, or thoughts.

Work-Team Structure

The DCAP-SSE development work-team was composed of five members:

- **A SSE Organization Manager and SSE Project Manager:** According to Me4MAP, this work-team member has the profiles of application context expert and of project manager;
- **A SSE Researcher:** According to Me4MAP, this work-team member has the profile of application context expert;
- **A Data Modeler and SSE Manager:** According to Me4MAP, this work-team member has the profiles of system analyst and application context expert;
- **A SSE Expert and Semantic Web Developer:** According to Me4MAP, this work-team member has the profiles of application context expert and semantic developer;
- A System Analyst, Semantic Modeler, Technical Writer and PhD researcher according to Me4MAP, this work-team member has the profiles of system analyst, semantic modeler and of technical editor

The technical writer registered all the information of the process as well the specifications of the final delivery of the DCAP-SSE.

All members of the work-team can be considered final consumers of the SSE economy, thus they are also final users of the SSE Web Portals and/or SSE Informational Web tools.

The team had a person with a management profile; he participated in almost all the meetings and helped to maintain the unity of the work-team. During the process of development some other persons, according to their profile, led the group in meetings depending on the type of activity at stake.

Developing of the Functional Requirements

This activity includes the sub-activities of:

1. Definition of the Vision Statement of the project
2. Definition of the application context
3. Definition of the high-level requirements
4. Development of the use-cases model

Glossary

In multi-disciplinary teams such as the one, just presented it is even more important to build the glossary since there are many visions of the world that have to do with the background of each member.

The DCAP-SSE Glossary is published in the Wiki Page: http://essglobal.org/essglobal/wiki/gloss.

The glossary was developed throughout the DCAP-SSE development process. Each time there were doubts or misunderstandings of ideas or concepts, we introduced a new entry into the Glossary. The technical writer was responsible for the edits.

Vision Statement

As in any other project, it is very important to set boundaries in order to effectively scope the issues the project wants to address. The Vision Statement is published in the Wiki Page at http://essglobal.org/essglobal/wiki/mission:

The Vision Statement was written by the SSE Experts of the work-team, after a brainstorming during the first Skype meeting, where all the other members were present. The Vision Statement was updated later in the development process during the use-case model development. The development of cases made clearer the objectives of the DCAP-SSE.

The Project Manager led the work-team and all members participated.

Application Context

The application context is the Social and Solidarity Economy and the community of organizations that map their activities in Web Information Systems. Those are the users that will implement the MAP in order to publish data as Linked Open Data.

More details about the application context can be found in Curado Malta et al. (2014) and Curado Malta (2014) (in Portuguese).

The application context was defined by one of the system analysts.

High Level Requirements

The elaboration of the High-Level Requirements is the definition of a list of the functional and non-functional requirements expressed by the work team members. The High-Level Requirements are (also published in the Wiki Page http://essglobal. org/essglobal/wiki/high[3]):

- Person searching for SSE organizations
- Researcher looking for aggregate information on SSE
- Person searching for products
- SSE enterprise exchanges local information with the web
- Public Policy Maker makes a public call to buy from or hire SSE enterprises

To define these High Level Requirements the work team brainstormed on the types of things they would like to do with the SSE data. For example, the kinds of searches they would like to do or the kinds of filters they would like to have on the data. There was a period of brainstorming and in the end the ideas were written in the pontaopad.me. Finally, from there, a set of requirements was defined.

The System Analyst led the work-team and all members participated.

Use Cases Model

The process of defining the Use Cases Model had as its starting point the High-Level Requirements deliverable. These requirements are the starting point to thinking about the actions which are needed and the types of actors that will interact with those actions. The goal of this activity was to develop two different things: (i) The definition of the Use-Case Diagram, and (ii) The definition of the Detailed Use-Cases.

The Use Case UML Model summarises the actors and the actions, it is published on the Wiki Page: http://essglobal.org/essglobal/wiki/usecasemodel[4]. The work-team identified two actors:

- A standard final user that could be interested in information about a) SSE Organisations and b) commercial SSE products/services;
- An SSE Researcher interested in aggregated SSE data.

The work-team also identified three types of interactions between the actors and a Website, through three use-cases. Each use case was detailed using the template proposed by Schneider & Winters (2001, pp. 29). The three Use-Cases are [5]:

Case 1: Person searching for SSE Organisation: http://essglobal.org/essglobal/wiki/1
Case 2: Researcher looking for aggregate information on SSE: http://essglobal.org/essglobal/wiki/2
Case 3: Person searching for products: http://essglobal.org/essglobal/wiki/3

The System Analysts led the work-team and all members participated.

Functional Requirements

With the two deliverables previously defined, the work-team identified the Functional Requirements of DCAP-SSE (also published in the Wiki Page http://essglobal.org/essglobal/wiki/functional[6]):

- Facilitate the creation and sharing of consistent metadata
- Support the search of any or all elements: "SSEInitiative," "Network," "Product," "Sale Options" and "Product-Input" (Use Cases 1, 2 and 3).
- Search for any property of each element mentioned in the previous paragraph and also "Cost Composition" of any Product-Input (Use Cases 1, 2 and 3).

The System Analyst led the work-team and all members participated.

Developing the Domain Model

The work-team continued its work with two different activities that were done simultaneously: (i) the Environmental Scan, and; (ii) the definition of the Domain Model.

Environmental Scan

The Environmental Scan is a report that contains a review of the metadata schemas, RDF vocabularies or Ontologies (from now on referred to as vocabularies) that are available in any serialization of the Semantic Web (e.g. RDF/XML, turtle) and that may serve the needs of the Detailed Domain Model (see below). The environmental scan was one of the outputs of the study of the state-of-the-art presented in Curado Malta & Baptista (2014). The Environmental Scan is available as MatrixII and MatrixIII stored in the institutional repository of the University of Minho, accessible through the handle http://hdl.handle.net/1822/23412[7].
This activity was developed by the semantic modelers.

Domain Model

According to Baker & Coyle (2009) "a domain model is a description of what things your metadata will describe, and the relationships between those things". It identifies the entities and their relationships, while attributes (e.g., datatypes and other attributes with literal values) are detailed further in the development process.

The work team decided to use the UML class diagram notation to represent the domain model.

The system analysts led the team discussion on what kind of things the team would need to capture in order to be able to respond to the Functional Requirements previously defined. The process is similar to the one of modeling a relational database: entities that have attributes and participate in relationships. After defining the entities, the team defined the relationships between the entities. It was an iterative process and it took more than one meeting to arrive at a stable model. The Domain Model is published in the Wiki Page: http://essglobal.org/essglobal/wiki/uml[8]

The system analysts led the work-team and all members participated.

Developing the Description Set

The work-team continued its work with three different main activities that were done sequentially. Since the activities were complex the work-team broke them in sets of sub-activities:

1. Development of Pre-Description Set profile: this sub-activity is also complex therefore Me4MAP breaks it in another set of sub-activities (see below)
2. Validation in laboratory
3. Codification of the Description Set Profile

The following paragraphs will detail each of these activities.

Development of Pre-Description Set Profile

This work is divided in:

1. The development of the Detailed Domain Model: it is the deepening of the Domain Model, where the whole team defines the attributes of the entities of the Domain Model and some constraints over the attributes;
2. The development of the vocabulary alignment: it is a sub-activity where the semantic modelers look for terms (of vocabularies) that describe each entity and related attributes that are defined in the Detailed Domain Model;

3.   The definition of the Constraints Matrix: it is a sub-activity where the semantic modeler has to define, for each entity, and for each attribute of the Detailed Domain Model, which term of the vocabulary alignment is the one that best describes the entity or attribute; the semantic modeler also has to define the possible constraints over the attributes. The Constraints Matrix of the DCAP-SSE format is a simple worksheet.

These sub-activities are detailed bellow.

Detailed Domain Model

This sub-activity deepens the Domain Model defining the attributes of the entities and also the constraints on the model's entities and attributes. A Detailed Domain Model is also known as Data Model. The work team used the ORM technique (Halpin & Morgan, 2008) to represent the data model.

The "semantic modeling approach views the world simply in terms of objects (things) playing roles (parts in relationships)" (Halpin & Morgan, 2008, pp.9). Semantic modeling is made of triples, very close to the natural language structure where sentences are as "subject verb and object"; a triple is defined as a statement of the kind "subject predicate and object". ORM is ideal to transform the informal description in natural language into a more formal one. ORM has a great advantage over UML or ER, it offers greater semantic stability. The System Analysts concluded that ORM is in fact the best way to model data that will be defined as triples.

The data model is published in the Wiki Page: http://essglobal.org/essglobal/wiki/dm[9]

The activity was led by the system analysts and all the work-team participated.

Vocabulary Alignment

The Vocabulary alignment defines the vocabularies that will be used by the DCAP-SSE, having as its basis of work the data model. The sub-activity consists of identifying which existent terms in the vocabularies of the Environmental Scan can describe the attributes of each entity of the data model. At the end of this process a table with names of the vocabularies and namespaces was defined (also published in the Wiki Webpage http://essglobal.org/essglobal/wiki/vocab_align[10]):

RDF vocabularies, metadata schemes, ontologies
        DCMI Terms: http://www,purl.org/dcterms/
        The friend of a friend: http://xmlns.com/foaf/0.1/
        Good Relations: http://purl.org/goodrelations/v1

    VCARD: http://www.w3.org/2006/vcard/ns

    Organisation Ontology: http://www.w3.org/ns/org

Syntax Enconding Schemes (SES)

    ISO 3166: http://purl.org/dc/terms/ISO3166

Vocabulary Encoding Schemes (VES)

    TGN: http://purl.org/dc/terms/TGN

Every time a term from a vocabulary that conveniently expressed the semantics of a given attribute of the data model was not found, a new term was declared in a new vocabulary.

The new vocabulary is called ESSGlobal RDF vocabulary and is openly available through the IRI: http://purl.org/essglobal/vocab/[11]. The ESSGlobal RDF vocabulary technical documentation is available at http://essglobal.org/essglobal/vocabs/html/[12].

The Vocabulary Alignment was developed by the semantic modelers.

Constraints Matrix

The DCAP-SSE Constraints Matrix is published in the Wiki Page: http://essglobal. org/essglobal/wiki/_media/constraintsmatrixv1.0-final.pdf[13] This matrix is based in the table presented by Baker & Coyle (2009).

The terms "entities" and "attributes" are used when modeling the application context. The terminology changes to "classes" and "properties" in the implementation phase. The entities of the data model correspond to the classes of the implementation, and the attributes to the properties of the implementation.

The Constrains Matrix has two tables:

1.   **Definition of Namespaces Used:** Identifies the Namespaces of the vocabularies used in DCAP-SSE;
2.   **Definition of Description Templates:** Is comprised of a set of sub-tables defining the Description Templates of DCAP-SSE. Each Description Table corresponds to an entity of the data model – now class -, and each row of a Description Template corresponds to an attribute of that entity – now property. The subsequent rows of each Description Template define the properties of a specific class. There are data properties[14] (that relate an instance of a class to a literal) and object properties[15] (that relate two instances of different classes) on the Description Template. In order to simplify the process of creating the tables and their reference downstream, the work-team filled first the data properties followed by the object properties.

Every time there was the need to constraint a property to a set of terms and there was no Vocabulary Encoding Scheme (VES) on the Environmental Scan Report that could answer that specific need, the work-team decided to define a new VES. For every new VES it was necessary to brainstorm all the possibilities the term could have as value, and register it. The work-team defined the following five VES[16]:

- Economic Activities/Sectors: http://purl.org/essglobal/standard/activities
- Macro-themes: http://purl.org/essglobal/standard/themes
- Qualifiers: http://purl.org/essglobal/standard/qualifiers
- Type of Labour: http://purl.org/essglobal/standard/type-of-labour
- Legal form: http://purl.org/essglobal/standard/legal-form

ESSGlobal's VES technical documentation is available at http://essglobal.org/essglobal/vocabs/html/[17].

The sub-activity was led by the semantic modelers and all application context experts participated. The application context experts are key to the development of this sub-activity since they are the ones that have the knowledge of the application. The application context experts knew precisely what properties should be constrained, and how. The semantic modelers knew how to technically define the constraints but could not know how to define those constraints in terms of content. These two different roles interacted deeply during this activity.

Validation in Laboratory

Some tests were made after defining the Constrains Matrix. The idea was to understand if the work was correctly done, that is, if the data model could respond to the informational needs real users would have. The work-team identified a set of resources, from SSE Web Based Information Systems in Brazil, Italy, Spain and USA, that constituted a trustworthy sample of the application domain of the DCAP-SSE. These SSW WIS were the ones identified by the SSE Experts as being the ones with better mappings of the SSE Economy in the World. These mappings have been developed over the last seven years. Others may exist but do not have mappings so advanced and organized, or are not, in fact, the core of the SSE[18]. The SSE WIS are[19]:

- **Brazil – Cirandas:** http://cirandas.net_
- **Italy - GoFair:** http://go-fair.eu_
- **Spain - Mercado Social:** http://mercadosocial.konsumoresponsable.coop_
- **Spain - Mercado Social Madrid:** https://madrid.mercadosocial.net/_
- **USA - Solidarity Economy US:** http://solidarityeconomy.us_

The work-team identified one to four resources per SSE WIS. The identification of resources had the concern of choosing resources that had enough information to be described, the more detailed the better. There was also the concern to choose resources that were different from each other in order to explore the most of the data model that was being tested. In total seventeen resources were chosen.

The work-team defined a worksheet template[20], based on the Constraints Matrix in order to collect and organize the data. It proceeded as follows:

1.   For each resource the worksheet was filled with the specific information of the resource;
2.   For each worksheet, the work-team encoded the information in turtle and in RDF/XML and created the graphs with the W3C RDF validator[21];
3.   If there was information on the resource that could not be expressed with the properties or encoding schemes defined on the Constraints Matrix, the process would iterate, i.e, the work-team had to go back to the definition of the Domain Model or the definition of the Detailed Domain Model, or even to the definition of the Functional Requirements. That, in fact, never happened as all the resources could be fully described with the information defined on the Constraints Matrix.

The validation in laboratory is published in http://www.essglobal.org/essglobal/howto[22].

This activity was developed by the semantic modelers with some help from final users since they were the ones that have chosen the resources for the validation.

Codification of the Description Set Profile

The Codification of the Description Set Profile (DSP) was straightforward having as basis the Constraints Matrix and the primer of DSP (see Nilsson (2008)). The DSP file is available at http://purl.org/essglobal/dsp-xml[23].

This activity was developed by the semantic modelers.

Validation in Production

A very simple first implementation of DCAP-SSE was set. This implementation only uses the "SSE Organization" and "Address" classes of the Go Fair[24] SSE WIS. The implementation was straight forward and had no issues. GoFair is implemented as follows:

1. An SSE Organization is identified with an ID in the SSE WIS as follows: http://www.go-fair.eu/#/organisation/ID[25]
2. The server has the organization data available in Turtle via the IRI http://app-gofair.rhcloud.com/api/app/negozi/ID/rdf[26]

The programmer of the SSE WIS implemented the DCAP-SSE with the support of the project manager and semantic modelers.

Since the RIPESS-ESSGlobal task-force expects to have many top SSE world organizations interested in the implementation of the DCAP-SSE, they asked the work-team to work on a "How To" Webpage in order to help future DCAP-SSE implementers. This "How To" Webpage[27] uses the seventeen cases of the Validation in Laboratory. Every case is detailed as follows:

1. Presentation of the resource in natural language;
2. Building of a table with the triples;
3. Presentation of the detailed explanation of the Turtle code, step by step;
4. Presentation of the detailed information in graphs, also step by step;
5. At the end of the page the whole code is provided in a Turtle file, as well as an image file with the whole graph, both openly available for download.

The RIPESS task-force expects to monitor and support more validations in production in the future as the SSE community is willing to use the DCAP-SSE.

FUTURE RESEARCH DIRECTIONS

The development of DCAP-SSE was the experimental situation of a DSR project aimed at putting forth a method for developing MAPs: Me4MAP. The DCAP-SSE and Me4MAP were developed iteratively.

In terms of DCAP-SSE future work:

1. The RIPESS-ESSGlobal task-force wants to continue the tests in the future with more resources, especially the ones that are not the core of SSE.
2. The RIPESS-ESSGlobal task-force hopes to enlarge the scope of DCAP-SSE without losing the first original purpose of serving the SSE Community. The idea is to develop extensions to the first DCAP-SSE version to integrate all activities in the same model. By doing so the SSE LOD cloud would be of an interesting dimension to empower the local, regional, national and transnational SSE communities.

In terms of Me4MAP future work:

1. Study and integrate in Me4MAP other software development approaches, such as the ones related to "agile methods". We want to study what is being done in this area (e.g. Ochiai, Nagamori, & Sugimoto (2014)) in order to propose a future version of Me4MAP that integrates these approaches. This future version will not necessarily replace the current version of Me4MAP; the two approaches may stand side-by-side for use in different settings.
2. Me4MAP is in the validation phase - we want to continue to validate the method in different settings in order to address the question of its generalizability. In fact, we think that Me4MAP may be adequate in a context similar to the one used in the SSE community. However, it's important to determine the conditions of its generalizability and the limits of its applicability.

CONCLUSION

This chapter presents the process of developing a Metadata Application Profile for the Social and Solidarity Economy (DCAP-SSE). The Social and Solidarity Economy (SSE) is a type of economy that is different from the one of the market economy or state. Although having similarities with these two types of economy, the SSE has very specific characteristics. Examples are:

1. The SSE networks that exist that produce common goals, products or services, and
2. The need to present an open price that explains how the final price of a product or service is build.

This community wants to publish the data that is trapped in silos of information on the Web of Documents (the common Web that we, as humans, access every day) as Linked Open Data, and then be able to use each other's data, or to build more sophisticated software in order to show actually the dimension of the SSE economy in the world. This was the motivation for the development of a metadata application profile.

This MAP development was integrated in a PhD project that had as main goal to define a method for the development of metadata application profile (Me4MAP). The development of the DCAP-SSE was used as test for Me4MAP definition, in an intensive iterative process.

This chapter shows the steps undertaken to build the MAP. Since Me4MAP defines a set of activities and the flow of these activities, and the deliverables that should be developed along the process, the chapter presents how the flow happened, and describes how the deliverables were developed.

The authors continue to undertake activities of research to improve Me4MAP. At the time of writing this chapter there is one important activity of validation occurring within the context of a research project[28] that is developing a MAP for European poetry (see Curado Malta, Centenera, & Gonzalez-Blanco (2016)), a completely different context, in terms of content and starting point, then the context of the SSE.

ACKNOWLEDGMENT

We would like to thank:

- Some members of the RIPESS task-force Alan Tygel, Daniel Tygel, Craig Borowiak and Jason Nardi because without them the design science research work would have never taken place.
- Marina Popesku from the University Politehnica of Bucharest for the work she did on the Validation in Laboratory activity, first as a student with a scholarship, later for free, always with the eager to learn. She started the work in 2015 as an Engineering student and finished it in 2016 as a graduated Engineer! Congratulations!

The DCAP-SSE development had the support of:

- Réseaux Intercontinental de Promotion de l'Économie Social Solidaire;
- FCT - Fundação para a Ciência e Tecnologia within the Project Scope UID/ CEC/00319/2013
- Erasmus+ Program.

REFERENCES

Baker, T., & Coyle, K. (2009). Guidelines for Dublin Core Application Profiles. Retrieved April 12, 2016, from http://dublincore.org/documents/profile-guidelines/

Booch, G., Jacobson, I., & Rumbaugh, J. (1999). *The unified software development process* (1st ed.). Addison-Wesley Professional.

Cattani, A. D., Laville, J.-L., Gaiger, L. I., & Hespanha, P. (2009). *Dicionário Internacional da Outra Economia*. CES.

Curado Malta, M. (2014). *Contributo metodológico para o desenvolvimento de perfis de aplicação no contexto da Web Semântica.* University of Minho. Retrieved from http://hdl.handle.net/1822/30262

Curado Malta, M., & Baptista, A. A. (2012). State of the Art on Methodologies for the Development of a Metadata Application Profile. *Metadata and Semantics Research, 343*(July), 61–73. doi:10.1007/978-3-642-35233-1_6

Curado Malta, M., & Baptista, A. A. (2013a). A method for the development of Dublin Core Application Profiles (Me4DCAP V0.2): detailed description. In M. Foulonneau & K. Eckert (Eds.), Proc. Int'l Conf. on Dublin Core and Metadata Applications 2013 (pp. 90–103). Lisbon: Dublin Core Metadata Initiative; Retrieved from http://dcevents.dublincore.org/IntConf/dc-2013/paper/view/178/81

Curado Malta, M., & Baptista, A. A. (2013b). Me4DCAP V0. 1: A method for the development of Dublin Core Application Profiles. *Information Services & Use, 33*(2), 161–171. doi:10.3233/ISU-130706

Curado Malta, M., & Baptista, A. A. (2013c). State of the Art on Methodologies for the Development of Dublin Core Application Profiles. *International Journal of Metadata, Semantics and Ontologies, 8*(4), 332–341.

Curado Malta, M., & Baptista, A. A. (2014). A panoramic view on metadata application profiles of the last decade. *International Journal of Metadata. Semantics and Ontologies, 9*(1), 58. doi:10.1504/IJMSO.2014.059124

Curado Malta, M., & Baptista, A. A. (2015). A DCAP for the Social and Solidarity Economy. In M. Curado Malta & S. A. B. G. Vidotti (Eds.), *2015 Proceedings of the International Conference on Dublin Core and Metadata Applications* (pp. 20–29). S. Paulo, Brazil: DCMI.

Curado Malta, M., Baptista, A. A., & Parente, C. (2014). Social and Solidarity Economy Web Information Systems: State of the Art and an Interoperability Framework. *Journal of Electronic Commerce in Organizations, 12*(1), 35–52. doi:10.4018/jeco.2014010103

Curado Malta, M., Centenera, P., & Gonzalez-Blanco, E. (2016). POSTDATA – Towards publishing European Poetry as Linked Open Data. In V. Charles & L. G. Svensson (Eds.), *International Conference on Dublin Core and Metadata Applications*. North America: Dublin Core Metadata Initiative. Retrieved from http://dcevents.dublincore.org/IntConf/dc-2016/paper/view/440

Halpin, T., & Morgan, T. (2008). *Information Modeling and Relational Databases* (2nd ed.). Burlington: Morgan Kaufman.

Hevner, A., & Chatterjee, S. (2010). Design Research in Information Systems - Theory and Practice. (R. Sharda & S. Voß, Eds.) (Integrated). Springer.

Lechat, M. P. (2007). Economia social, economia solidária, terceiro setor: do que se trata? *Civitas- Revista de Ciências Sociais, 2*(1), 123–140.

Nilsson, M. (2008). Description Set Profiles: A constraint language for Dublin Core Application Profiles [misc]. Retrieved April 6, 2016, from http://dublincore.org/documents/2008/03/31/dc-dsp/

Nilsson, M., Baker, T., & Johnston, P. (2008). The Singapore Framework for Dublin Core Application Profiles. Retrieved February 10, 2015, from http://dublincore.org/documents/singapore-framework/

Nilsson, M., Baker, T., & Johnston, P. (2009). Interoperability Levels for Dublin Core Metadata. Retrieved October 10, 2016, from http://dublincore.org/documents/interoperability-levels/

Ochiai, K., Nagamori, M., & Sugimoto, S. (2014). A Metadata Schema Design Model and Support System Based on an Agile Development Model. In M. Kindling & E. Greifeneder (Eds.), iConference 2014 Proceedings (pp. 921–927). article, Illinois: iSchools. http://doi.org/ doi:<ALIGNMENT.qj></ALIGNMENT>10.9776/14314

Schneider, G., & Winters, J. P. (2001). *Applying use cases: a practical guide (Second Edi). book.* Boston: Addison-Wesley.

W3C. (2015). W3C - Linked Data. Retrieved November 19, 2016, from https://www.w3.org/standards/semanticweb/data

KEY TERMS AND DEFINITIONS

Data Model: The same as Domain Model.

Domain Model: A conceptual model that describes certain aspects of a domain of knowledge. The model has concepts of the aspects of the real world that need to be modeled. These concepts include the data to be modeled and business rules in relation to the data. Conceptual models can be represented in different notations like Entity-Relationship Model or Unified Modeling Language, among others.

Entity: The conceptual model captures concepts in a domain. Concepts are called Entities when using the notation of Entity-Relationship Model. Entities are types of things that are part of a same group and that have the same characteristics, like "client" in a business that sells products or services, or "student" in a School, or "book" in a library.

Functional Requirements: A function of the system that will be modeled, the type of "things" the user or machine will do with the system.

Me4MAP: A method for the development of metadata application profiles, it establishes which activities to develop, when these activities may take place, how they are interconnected and which artifacts these activities produce.

Property: The common things of an entity, like "address," "name," "surname," "date of birth" of an entity "client," or "number of student" of an entity "student" or "title" of an entity "book".

ENDNOTES

[1] See http://www.ripess.org – accessed May 25, 2016

[2] See http://essglobal.org/dcap-sse/ - accessed May 25, 2016)

[3] Accessed November 20, 2016

[4] Accessed November 20, 2016

[5] Accessed November 20, 2016

[6] Accessed November 20, 2016

[7] Accessed November 20, 2016

[8] Accessed November 20, 2016

[9] Accessed November 20, 2016

[10] Accessed November 20, 2016

[11] Accessed November 20, 2016

[12] Accessed November 20, 2016

[13] Accessed November 20, 2016

[14] See https://www.w3.org/2007/OWL/wiki/Syntax#Data_Properties - accessed November 20, 2016

[15] See https://www.w3.org/2007/OWL/wiki/Syntax#Object_Properties - accessed November 20, 2016

[16] Accessed November 20, 2016

[17] Accessed November 20, 2016

[18] In fact some talks are in place in order for other project to use the DCAP-SSE. See http://www.essglobal.org/essglobal/howto/index.php?title=LOD_Activity - accessed November 20, 2016 - on the topic "Talking to" for a more refresh version of the progress of the work.

[19] Accessed November 20, 2016

[20] Access http://www.essglobal.org/essglobal/howto/turtle/ESSGlobal-template.zip - accessed November 20, 2016 - to download the zip file with the worksheet template

[21] See https://www.w3.org/RDF/Validator/ - accessed November 20, 2016

[22]   Accessed November 20, 2016

[23]   Accessed November 20, 2016

[24]   See http://go-fair.eu - accessed November 20, 2016

[25]   Accessed November 20, 2016

[26]   E.g. the organization http://www.go-fair.eu/#/organisation/920 - accessed November 20, 2016has data available in turtle via the IRI http://app-gofair.rhcloud.com/api/app/negozi/920/rdf - accessed November 20, 2016

[27]   See http://www.essgobal.org/essglobal/howto/ - accessed November 20, 2016

[28]   See http://postdata.linhd.es - accessed November 20, 2016

Chapter 6
Developing Metadata Application Profiles for Open Educational Resources Federated Repositories:
The Case of the Open Discovery Space Metadata Application Profile

Panagiotis Zervas
Centre for Research and Technology Hellas, Greece

Demetrios G Sampson
Curtin University, Australia

ABSTRACT

With many Learning Object Repositories (LORs) implemented and maintained independently from different organizations or communities, valuable Learning Objects (LOs) are scattered over different LORs and making it difficult for end-users (namely, instructional designers, teachers and students) to easily find and access them. A suggested solution towards addressing this issue is to create federated LORs, which aim to harvest and aggregate LOs' metadata from different LORs towards facilitating LOs' discovery across these LORs through a single infrastructure. However, a challenging issue during the development of federated LORs is the design of appropriate metadata application profile (AP) which supports harvesting heterogeneous

DOI: 10.4018/978-1-5225-2221-8.ch006

metadata records from the aggregated LORs. Thus, the aim of this book chapter is twofold, namely (a) to present a methodology for developing metadata APs that can be used in building federated LORs and (b) to present a case study from the implementation of the proposed methodology for the development of the metadata AP used by the OpenDiscoverySpace federated LOR.

INTRODUCTION

Opening up education is an emerging and global movement that aims to facilitate innovative and flexible ways of learning and teaching by exploring the potential of ICT (Conole, 2013; Iiyoshi & Kumar, 2008). Open educational resources (OERs) have been attributed as a key element of the opening up education movement (The William and Flora Hewlett Foundation, 2013; UNESCO, 2012) and several OER initiatives have been developed worldwide by large organizations/institutions such as UNESCO OER Community (UNESCO, 2012), Open Education Europa, Carnegie Mellon Open Learning Initiative, MIT's OpenCourseWare (OCW), Stanford's iTunes and Rice University's Connexions or by communities/ consortia such as MERLOT and OER Commons (Zervas et al., 2014a). The main aim of such initiatives is to support the process of organizing, classifying, storing and sharing OERs in the form of Learning Objects (LOs) and their associated metadata in web-based repositories which are referred to as Learning Object Repositories (LORs) (McGreal, 2008).

These efforts have led to the development and operation of a rich variety of LORs hosting collections of LOs for different subject domains, educational levels, as well as languages (Zervas et al., 2014b; Ehlers, 2011). A key factor, in order to facilitate access to

(and efficient retrieval of) these LOs, is by incorporating appropriate educational metadata associated with them. For this purpose, existing LORs are using widely accepted metadata specifications such as ISO MLR (ISO/IEC, 2011), LRMI (Barker & Campbell, 2014), IEEE LOM (IEEE LTSC, 2005), Dublin Core (Dublin Core, 2004) or application profiles of these specifications that have been developed to accommodate specific needs such as characterizing LOs that address specific subject areas (i.e. science education, business education etc.) or different grade levels (i.e. school education, higher education, vocational training etc.) (Sampson et al., 2012).

On the other hand, with many LORs implemented and maintained independently from different organizations and/or communities/consortia, valuable LOs are scattered over different LORs and it is difficult for end-users (namely, instructional designers, teachers and students) to easily find and access them (Klerkx et al., 2010). A suggested solution towards addressing this issue is to create federated LORs, which aim to harvest and aggregate LOs' metadata from different LORs towards facilitating LOs' discovery across these LORs from one single infrastructure. Examples of widely known federated LORs are GLOBE alliance (GLOBE, 2011), ARIADNE foundation (Ternier et al., 2009), MACE (Prause et al., 2007), iCOPER (Totschnig, 2007), Organic.Edunet (Manouselis et al., 2009) and OpenScout (Kalz et al., 2010). Nevertheless, a challenging issue during the development of federated LORs is the design of their metadata application profile. More specifically, aggregating hetero-geneous metadata records to a single metadata application profile might (Yamada, 2013; De la Prieta et al., 2011; Ha et al., 2011):

- Lead to loss of information richness due to incompatibilities between the metadata application profile of the federated repository and the metadata application profiles of the harvested repositories
- Hinder the LOs retrieval because the selected search elements of the feder-ated LOR search engine could correspond to incomplete harvested metadata records from the aggregated LORs. Within this context, the aim of this book chapter is twofold, namely:
  ○ To present a methodology for developing metadata application profiles for federated LORs that aim to harvest metadata records from existing LORs. The methodology will be described in terms of its procedure and statistical metrics for the systematic analysis of the metadata application profiles and metadata records of the different LORs that will constitute the federated LOR.
  ○ To present a case study from the implementation of the proposed meth-odology, namely the development of the metadata application profile of the Open Discovery Space (ODS) federated LOR[1]. ODS is a major European Initiative, which aims to build a federated LOR on top of six-teen (16) existing LORs (Athanasiadis et al., 2014).

The chapter is structured as follows. Following this introduction, Section 2 provides an overview of the key issues that constitute the background of this work, namely open educational resources, learning objects, metadata schemas, learning object repositories and application profiles. In Section 3, a review of the metadata application profiles of existing federated LORs is performed towards summarizing the modification types performed to these metadata application profiles. Section 4 presents the proposed methodology for designing metadata application profiles for federated LORs. Section 5 presents a case study of the implementation of the proposed methodology for the development of a metadata application profile for the ODS federated LOR. Finally, main conclusions and directions for future work are discussed.

BACKGROUND

Open Educational Resources and Learning Objects

A popular definition of the OER term has been provided by UNESCO (2002) defining OER as the "technology-enabled, open provision of educational resources for consultation, use and adaptation by a community of users for non-commercial purposes". Another widely used definition of OERs has been provided by OECD (2007) defining OERs as: "digitized materials offered freely and openly for educators, students and self-learners to use and reuse for teaching, learning and research". According to Geser (2007), and deriving from the aforementioned definitions, OERs have three core features:

1. They are available for open and free of charge access by educational institutions and end-users such as instructional designers, teachers and students
2. They are licensed for re-use, free from restrictions to modify, combine and repurpose, as well as they are designed for easy re-use in open content schemas and formats
3. With regard to software tools, their source code is open and licensed for re-use

On the other hand, Learning Objects (LOs) are a common format for developing and sharing educational content and they have been defined by Wiley (2002) as: "any type of digital resource that can be reused to support learning". More specifically, LOs include: "video and audio lectures (podcasts), references and readings, workbooks and textbooks, multimedia animations, simulations, experiments and demonstrations, as well as teachers' guides and lesson plans" (McGreal, 2008). Thus, one can claim that OERs are related to LOs assuming open access licensing (Friesen, 2009; Lane & McAndrew, 2010).

OERs' definitions do not explicitly include the notion of modular design, whereas LOs do not include notions of openness (Friesen, 2009). Both consider sharing and re-use but LOs appear to acknowledge the intellectual property rights of the content developers, whereas many OERs are explicitly released under a non-commercial use license (Lane & McAndrew, 2010). In the context of this work, the authors adopt LOs' definition provided by Wiley (2002) by considering also the open access licensing paradigm proposed by OERs.

Metadata Standards and Specifications for Learning Objects

Metadata are simply defined as "data about data" or "information about information" (Sen 2004; Steinacker et al., 2001). Metadata describe the different characteristics and attributes of an information source, e.g. the title, the author, the date and the subject domain. They consist of data elements that are associated with the information sources, which are called metadata elements. Metadata schemas are structured sets of metadata elements designed for a specific purpose, such as describing a particular type of information source (NISO, 2004). Metadata specifications are well-defined and widely agreed metadata schemas usually developed and promoted by individual organizations or consortia of partners from industry and/or academia. When a specification is widely recognized and adopted by some standardization organization, it then becomes a metadata standard. Existing metadata standards or specifications for characterizing LOs include:

- **The Dublin Core Metadata Element Set (DCMES):** An official standard for describing general information resources available on the web (Dublin Core, 2004). This standard has been developed by Dublin Core Metadata Initiative (DCMI) and it has been also used for describing LOs. An indicative example of using DCEMS for characterizing LOs is the Education Network Australia (EdNA) initiative (Education Network Australia, 2006).
- **The IEEE Learning Object Metadata (IEEE LOM):** A widely used official standard developed by IEEE Learning Technology Standards Committee (LTSC) particularly for describing LOs (IEEE LTSC, 2005).
- **The ISO/IEC 19788-2 Metadata for Learning Resources (MLR):** Aimed at harmonizing IEEE LOM and DCMES. This official standard has been developed by ISO/IEC JTC1/SC36 (Joint Technical Committee Information Technology for Learning, Education and Training) and it provides an extensible and modular framework for specifying new metadata elements while maintaining compatibility with both IEEE LOM and DCMES (ISO/IEC, 2011).
- **The Learning Resources Metadata Initiative (LRMI):** A metadata specification for describing LOs on the web with embedded metadata. LRMI is promoted by popular search engines such as Google, Bing, and Yahoo and it is led by Creative Commons and the Association of Educational Publishers. LRMI has extended the schema.org metadata elements with elements that are specifically relevant towards facilitating discovery of LOs via search engines (Barker & Campbell, 2014).

However, despite the fact that the goal of the ISO MLR and LRMI has been put forward as a complement or alternative to IEEE LOM and DCMES, wide adoption of these metadata schemas is still rather low. This is evident by the fact that of the majority of existing LORs still use IEEE LOM or DCMES as their base metadata schema (Malta & Baptista, 2014).

Learning Object Repositories

LOs and their associated metadata are typically organized, classified and stored in web-based repositories which are referred to as Learning Object Repositories (LORs). McGreal (2004) has defined LORs as systems that "enable users to locate, evaluate and manage learning objects through the use of "metadata," namely, descriptors or tags that systematically describe many aspects of a given learning object, from its technical to its pedagogical characteristics". McGreal (2008) classifies LORs into two basic types, namely:

- LORs that store both LOs as well as the LOs descriptions in the form of meta-data. These LORs are used for both searching and accessing LOs.
- LORs that store only the metadata descriptions. In this case, the LOs them-selves are located elsewhere and the LOR is used only as a mean to facilitate searching towards accessing LOs from their original location. This category includes also LORs that harvest and aggregate metadata from different LORs. This specific type of LORs is called "federated LORs" (McGreal, 2004)

When a new LOR is developed, an initial step includes the definition of the metadata schema that will be used for characterizing the LOs to be stored in this LOR. Despite the existence of widely accepted metadata schemas (as previously mentioned), it has been identified that it is not possible for generic standards/ specifications to fully meet specific requirements and thoroughly accommodate the particular needs of different educational communities requiring local extensions or modifications to these standards/specifications (Sampson et al., 2012; Duval et al., 2002). As a result, a common practice of generating LOs' metadata application profiles (APs) has emerged as a means of addressing this problem (Mason & Ellis, 2009; Currier, 2008; Mason & Galatis, 2007).

Guidelines for Developing LOs' Metadata Application Profiles

Metadata APs consist of metadata elements selected by one or more base metadata schemas with additional restrictions applied to these elements (Malta & Baptista, 2012). International Organizations such as IMS GLC and European Committee for Standardization (CEN/ISSS) have published guidelines for the development of APs with specific focus on the IEEE LOM (Smith et al., 2006; IMS GLC, 2005). These guidelines include the steps that are depicted in Table 1.

The aforementioned steps (except from step 9) constitute the type of modifica-tion that can be applied when developing a metadata AP. Next, the authors discuss

Table 1. Guidelines for developing LOs' metadata application profiles (Smith et al., 2006; IMS GLC, 2005)

Steps	Main Actions Performed per Step
1. Selection of data elements	Data elements for the new metadata AP are selected from a base metadata schema
2. Size & smallest permitted maximum	The size that a data element is allowed to have at a metadata record is defined., the size can be equal to one (when the data element is allowed only one value at the metadata record) or more than one (when the data element is allowed multiple values at the metadata record)
3. Data elements from multiple namespaces	Data elements from different namespaces, which are part of different metadata schemas are defined
4. Adding local data elements	New local data elements, which are not contained to the base metadata schema, are added to the new metadata AP
5. Obligation of data elements	Mandatory, recommended and the optional data elements are defined
6. Value space	The value space of the data elements is defined. The value space defines the set of values that the data element shall derive its value from
7. Relationship & dependency	Inter-relationships and dependencies between data elements are defined
8. Data type profiling	Data type profiling of the metadata elements of the new metadata AP is performed
9. Application profile binding	The AP binding is defined, which is the conceptual data schema of the AP and could be represented in XML schema, RDF format or other technical representations for data sharing

metadata APs of existing federated LORs and identify common modification types in accordance with these steps.

Related Work: Federated Learning Object Repositories and their Application Profiles

In this section, the authors analyze and discuss the metadata APs of existing federated LORs. More specifically, initially the authors provide an overview of these metadata APs (as depicted in Table 2) by presenting the following information:

- Metadata AP's title and relevant reference where the metadata AP has been reported
- The organization or the initiative that has developed the metadata AP
- The base metadata schema
- The URL of the federated LOR that use the metadata AP

Table 2. Overview of metadata APs of existing federated LORs

No	Title	Reference	Developed by	Base Metadata Schema	Federated LOR URL
1	GLOBE	GLOBE (2011)	GLOBE Alliance	IEEE LOM	http://globe-info.org/_
2	ARIADNE	Ternier et al. (2009)	ARIADNE Foundation	IEEE LOM	http://ariadne.grnet.gr/ariadne_ finder/_
3	MACE	Prause et al. (2007)	MACE Project (EU funded)	IEEE LOM	Not Available
4	OpenScout	Kalz et al. (2010)	OpenScout Project (EU funded)	IEEE LOM	http://learn.openscout.net/_
5	iCOPER	Totschnig (2007)	iCOPER Project (EU funded)	IEEE LOM	Not Available
6	Organic. Edunet	Manouselis et al. (2009)	Organic. Edunet Project (EU funded)	IEEE LOM	http://organic-edunet.eu/_
7	Photodentro	Megalou & Kaklamanis (2014)	Digital School Project (Nationally funded)	IEEE LOM	http://photodentro.edu.gr/lor/_

Next, in Table 3 the authors summarize the modifications of the aforementioned metadata APs in accordance with the steps of the guidelines summarized in Table 1. It is worth mentioning that step 9 of these guidelines does not correspond to a modification type and for this reason it has been excluded from Table 3. This analysis (as depicted in Table 3) can help us to extract useful conclusions about the most common types of modifications typically made in popular metadata APs utilized at existing federated LORs.

As it can be noticed from Table 3 all metadata APs of the existing federated LORs:

- Select the full set or the subset of data elements from the base metadata schema (according to Table 2 all metadata APs use IEEE LOM as the base metadata schema)
- Define mandatory, recommended and optional data elements (step 5)
- Define the value space of the data elements (step 6)

Moreover, only one (1) of them (namely, MACE) defines new local data elements which are not included at the base metadata schema (step 4), which in this

Table 3. Types of modifications at metadata APs from existing federated LORs

Modification Types	GLOBE	ARIADNE	MACE	OpenScout	iCOPER	Organic.Edunet	Photodentro
1. Selection of data elements	✓	✓	✓	✓	✓	✓	✓
2. Size & smallest permitted maximum	-	-	-	-	-	-	-
3. Data elements from multiple namespaces	-	-	-	-	-	-	-
4. Adding local data elements	-	-	✓	-	-	-	-
5. Obligation of data elements	✓	✓	✓	✓	✓	✓	✓
6. Value space	✓	✓	✓	✓	✓	✓	✓
7. Relationship & dependency	-	-	-	-	-	-	-
8. Data type profiling	-	-	-	-	-	-	-

case is the IEEE LOM. On the other hand, none of the metadata APs from existing federated LORs:

- Define the size that a data element is allowed to have at a metadata instance (step 2)
- Define data elements from multiple namespaces (step 3)
- Define inter-relationships and dependencies between data elements (step 7)
- New data types for specific metadata elements (step 8)

A closer look to all examined metadata APs reveals that these modifications are not performed due to the fact that all examined metadata APs are adopting the default values proposed by IEEE LOM regarding these types of modifications. As a result, the selected base metadata schema (namely, IEEE LOM) can address the need for these modifications and no further changes are needed when developing metadata APs for federated LORs. The aforementioned analysis of the modification types of the metadata APs from existing federated LORs and their comparison highlights the important modifications that should be addressed when developing a metadata AP for a federated LOR. The outcomes of this analysis set the ground for the methodology presented in the next section.

A Methodology for Designing Metadata Application Profiles for Federated Learning Object Repositories

In this section the authors present their proposed methodology for designing metadata APs for federated LORs. This methodology has been based on:

- The outcomes from the analysis of the modification at metadata APs of existing federated LORs (as discussed in previous section)
- The methodology that has been utilized for the development of the metadata AP of the GLOBE federated LOR (GLOBE, 2011), which constitutes the only similar work identified by the literature

However, GLOBE methodology implements only a small fraction of the authors' proposed methodology (namely, only step 3 described below). More specifically, GLOBE methodology has proposed an analysis of the metadata records of each aggregated LOR of the GLOBE federated LOR. This analysis included identification of occurrence frequency (OF) for each metadata element that was present in the metadata records of each aggregated LOR. The results from the OF was used by representatives of the GLOBE alliance members to decide mandatory, recommended and optional elements but this was done without clearly presented criteria. To this end, the methodology includes four (4) main steps, which are in accordance with the most common types of modifications identified in previous section and it extends the GLOBE methodology by introducing new steps, as well as by extending the step proposed by GLOBE methodology. More specifically, the authors' methodology includes the following steps:

Step 1 - Select Base Metadata Schema and Metadata Elements: During this step the base metadata schema for developing the metadata AP for the federated LOR should be selected. This requires an analysis of the base metadata schemas of the metadata APs that are used by the aggregated LORs. In case that there are different base metadata schemas utilized by the analyzed metadata APs, then the richer base metadata schema should be selected and all other schemas should be mapped to this one. This is important for harmonizing the metadata records of the aggregated LORs and avoiding information loss during metadata harvesting. When the base metadata schema has been selected, an in depth analysis of the percentage of appearance of each metadata element should be performed, so as to identify the master set of elements that are used at least once. Following this process, it can be identified whether there are elements from the base metadata schema that have not been selected to be included in none of the metadata APs of the aggregated LORs and as a result these elements can be excluded from the metadata AP of the federated LOR.

Step 2 - Select Local Data Elements: During this step it should be indentified whether local metadata elements (namely, metadata elements that are not part of the selected base metadata schema of the federated LOR metadata AP) should be included to the federated LOR metadata AP. This decision should be taken by analyzing the metadata APs of the aggregated LORs, so as to indentify whether they have introduced local metadata elements (namely, metadata elements that are not part of the selected base metadata schema of each metadata AP from the aggregated LORs) in their metadata APs. If this is the case, then these local metadata elements should be included to the metadata AP of the federated LOR only if there are no semantic overlaps between them. In case of semantic overlap, a mapping should be performed between the local elements of each metadata AP from the aggregated LORs and the local elements that have been added to the federated LOR metadata AP.

Step 3 - Set Obligation Status: This step includes selection of the obligation status for the metadata elements of the federated LOR metadata AP. This requires an analysis of the metadata records that will be harvested by the federated LOR, so as to identify metadata elements that are present in the metadata records of the aggregated LORs. In order to perform this analysis the metadata records from all aggregated LORs should be collected following a technical binding (i.e. XML binding). Afterwards, the *OF* of each metadata element for all aggregated LORs should be calculated according to the following formula:

$$OF_i = \sum_{j=1}^{N} OF_{ij} * w_j \qquad (1)$$

where OF_{ij} is the *OF* of the ith metadata element at the jth aggregated LOR, which is calculated as the percentage of the times that the ith metadata element was completed to the total metadata records of the jth aggregated LOR. N is the total number of aggregated LORs and w_j is the weighting factor, which is calculated as the ratio between the number of available metadata records of the jth aggregated LOR and the total number of metadata records of the federated LOR, at the time of designing the metadata AP. It is worth mentioning that weighting factor has not been considered to the GLOBE methodology (GLOBE, 2011). However, the weighting factor is important because the decisions about the obligation status should be influenced by the calculated *OF* of metadata elements to specific LORs that contribute the largest portion of metadata records to the federated LOR. An indicative way of interpreting the calculated OF_i could be as follows: (a) if OF_i is higher than 75% then the element can be considered as mandatory, (b) if OF_i is between 50% and 75% the element can be considered as recommended and (c) if OF_i is less than 50% the element can be considered as optional.

Step 4 - Value Space of Data Elements: This step includes the identification of metadata elements for which their value space needs to be modified compared with the base metadata schema initial value spaces. This requires an analysis of the modification types that has been performed to the vocabularies of the metadata elements of each aggregated LORs. More specifically, the following cases are identified:

- ◦ **Restricted:** This means that the vocabulary of a metadata element has been restricted to fewer values than the initial vocabulary of the base metadata schema
- ◦ **Identical:** This means that the vocabulary of a metadata element is the same with the vocabulary of the base metadata schema
- ◦ **Extended:** This means that the values of a metadata element vocabulary has been extended with additional values that are not included in the vocabulary of the base metadata schema.
- ◦ **Differentiated:** This means that the values of a metadata element vocabulary are totally different from the values that are not included in the vocabulary of the base metadata schema

For each metadata element which has a vocabulary data type, the modification types (as previously described) are counted in all metadata APs of the aggregated LORs. Afterwards, a total score is calculated per metadata element as follows:

- • Each differentiated vocabulary is weighted with 1.5 points
- • Each extended vocabulary is weighted with 1 point
- • Each restricted or identical vocabulary is weighted with zero points

In case that the final score of a metadata element is zero, this means that the specific metadata element either follows the vocabulary of the base metadata schema or a subset of this vocabulary. For this case, it can be safely considered that the value space for this specific metadata element could be the same with one at the base metadata schema and this will not create incompatibilities during the metadata harvesting process. In case that the final score of a metadata element is higher than zero, this means that the vocabulary of the specific metadata element has been extended or differentiated. For this case, a closer look is needed to the semantics of the specific values that has been added to the vocabularies utilized in the different metadata APs for the specific metadata element. Possible solutions for defining the vocabulary of these metadata elements could be by considering supersets of the values used in the vocabularies of the metadata APs of the aggregated LORs or by creating mapping rules of the values of these vocabularies and the master vocabularies of the federated LOR metadata AP (Otón et al, 2012; Woodley, 2008). For instance, in case of different vocabularies used by the metadata APs of the aggregating LORs for describing the LOs' subject domain, a master vocabulary could be created by the federated LOR metadata AP and all individual vocabularies from each metadata AP could be mapped to the master vocabulary.

Applying the Proposed Methodology for the Open Discovery Space Federated Learning Object Repository

In this section, the authors present the implementation of the proposed methodology for the development of the Open Discovery Space (ODS) federated LOR metadata AP. ODS federated LOR has being developed in the context of a major European initiative referred to as "Open Discovery Space: A socially-powered and multilingual open learning infrastructure to boost the adoption of eLearning Resources". The Open Discovery Space Project (http://opendiscoveryspace.eu/) aims to include more than 750.000 LOs by aggregating open licensed LOs from a federated network of LORs in Europe. The main outcome of Open Discovery Space project is a community-oriented social platform for school education where teachers and students from all around Europe will be able to search and retrieve LOs on their topics of interest.

List of Aggregated LORs

Table 4 presents the list of LORs that constitute the ODS federated network of LORs. More specifically, for each LOR the following information is presented:

- LOR's title and URL
- The base metadata schema of LOR's metadata AP
- The regional coverage of the community that the LOR targets
- The number of LOs that was included in the LOR at the time of the ODS metadata AP development (namely, November 2012)
- The calculated weighting factor based on formula (1) that was described in previous section towards analyzing the occurrence frequency of the metadata elements at LOR's metadata records

Overall, there are sixteen (16) LORs. From these LORs, thirteen (13) are using IEEE LOM compatible metadata and three (3) are using DCMES compatible meta-

Table 4. List of aggregated LORs

No	LOR Name	LOR URL	Coverage	Base Metadata Schema	Number of LOs[2]	Weighting Factor
1	Open Science Resources Repository (OSR)	http://www.osrportal.eu_	European	IEEE LOM	1862	0,002
2	Photodentro / Digital School LOR	http://photodentro.edu.gr/lor_	National (Greece)	IEEE LOM	6340	0,008
3	Photodentro / Educational Video Repository	http://photodentro.edu.gr/video_	National (Greece)	IEEE LOM	679	0,001
4	Discover the COSMOS	http://portal.discoverthecosmos.eu_	European	IEEE LOM	81000	0,108
5	I2G Intergeo	http://i2geo.net_	European	IEEE LOM	3635	0,005
6	Dryades	http://www.dryades.eu_	European	DCMES	200465	0,267
7	LMS.at	https://lms.at_	National (Austria)	IEEE LOM	13224	0,018
8	Bildungspool	http://bildungspool.bildung.at_	National (Austria)	IEEE LOM	385	0,001
9	SIVECO LRE Repository	http://www.siveco.ro/en_	European	IEEE LOM	794	0,001
10	Znam.bg	http://znam.bg_	National (Bulgaria)	DCMES	96000	0,128
11	Bulgarian National Educational Repository	http://resursi.e-edu.bg_	National (Bulgaria)	DCMES	1050	0,001
12	Moodle for CARNet's Users	http://moodle.carnet.hr_	National (Croatia)	IEEE LOM	44000	0,059
13	OpenScout	http://learn.openscout.net/search.html_	European	IEEE LOM	52958	0,070
14	Organic.Edunet	http://portal.organic-edunet.eu/_	European	IEEE LOM	12360	0,016
15	LAFLOR	http://laflor.laclo.org_	European	IEEE LOM	51000	0,068
16	Learning Resource Exchange (LRE)	http://lreforschools.eun.org_	European	IEEE LOM	185940	0,247
Total Number of LOs					**751692**	**1,00**

data. Moreover, nine (9) of them have a European coverage, whereas seven (7) of them have national coverage targeting four (4) different European Countries, namely Greece, Austria, Bulgaria and Croatia. The total number of LOs included in these LORs was more than 750.000 LOs at November 2012.

Analysis of Metadata Application Profiles of Aggregated LORs

Following the proposed methodology described in the previous section, the first step includes the selection of the base metadata schema for the developing the ODS metadata AP. According to Table 4, it is evident that the dominant metadata schema among the list of aggregated LORs is the IEEE LOM (it is used in 13 out 16 aggregated LORs), which is also richer than DCMES. For these reasons, IEEE LOM was selected as the base metadata schema of the ODS metadata AP (as explained in step 1 of the proposed methodology). For those LORs that are using metadata APs based on DCMES, a mapping proposed by the IEEE LOM standard (IEEE LTSC, 2005) was adopted.

The next step included a further analysis of the metadata APs to identify whether the metadata APs have introduced local data elements. Based on the authors' analysis, none of the metadata APs defined new local data elements which were not included at the base metadata schema (namely, IEEE LOM). As a result, no further action was needed regarding the set of data elements that the ODS metadata AP was built on.

After that, the authors calculated the number of times that a LOM metadata element appears in the metadata APs of the aggregated LOs. Table 5 gives an overview of the percentage of appearance of elements. The presentation of elements follows the IEEE LOM categories but the elements in each category have been sorted based on their appearance to the examined metadata APs.

As Table 5 depicts, all IEEE LOM metadata elements appear at least once in all examined metadata APs. Moreover, all metadata APs are using an element to store the identifier of the LO. This identifier is captured by the element "1.1.2 Entry" (inferior element of 1.1 Identifier). Additionally, all metadata APs are using an element to capture the title of the LO. This title is captured by the element "1.2 Title" of the "General" LOM category. These are initial indications that these elements can be considered as mandatory. However, these indications should be complemented with the occurrence frequency of these elements to the metadata records of the aggregated LORs. This analysis is described in the next section.

Analysis of Metadata Records of Aggregated LORs

The metadata records from the different aggregated LORs was obtained through a metadata aggregation visualization tool that has been developed in the framework of

Table 5. LOM Elements Percentage of Appearance in Metadata APs of the Aggregated LORs

Metadata Element	Times of Appearance	Percentage of Appearance (%)	Metadata Element	Times of Appearance	Percentage of Appearance (%)
1. General			**5. Educational**		
1.1.2 Entry	16	**100,00%**	**5.5 Intended End User Role**	13	**81,25%**
1.2 Title	16	**100,00%**	**5.6 Context**	13	**81,25%**
1.3 Language	15	**93,75%**	**5.1 Interactivity Type**	12	**75,00%**
1.4 Description	15	**93,75%**	**5.2 Learning Resource Type**	12	**75,00%**
1.1 Identifier	14	**87,50%**	**5.3 Interactivity Level**	12	**75,00%**
1.1.1 Catalog	14	**87,50%**	**5.8 Difficulty**	12	**75,00%**
1.5 Keyword	13	**81,25%**	**5.7 Typical Age Range**	11	**68,75%**
1.7 Structure	10	**62,50%**	**5.9 Typical Learning Time**	10	**62,50%**
1.8 Aggregation Level	10	**62,50%**	**5.11 Language**	9	**56,25%**
1.6 Coverage	6	**37,50%**	**5.4 Semantic Density**	8	**50,00%**
2. Lifecycle			**5.10 Description**	8	**50,00%**
2.3.2 Entity	15	**93,75%**	**6. Rights**		
2.3.3 Date	14	**87,50%**	**6.2 Copyright and Other Restrictions**	15	**93,75%**
2.3 Contribute	13	**81,25%**	**6.1 Cost**	13	**81,25%**
2.3.1 Role	13	**81,25%**	**6.3 Description**	11	**68,75%**
2.2 Status	12	**75,00%**	**7. Relation**		
2.1 Version	11	**68,75%**	**7.1 Kind**	11	**68,75%**
3. Meta-Metadata			**7.2 Resource**	11	**68,75%**
3.1.2 Entry	12	**75,00%**	7.2.1 Identifier	11	**68,75%**
3.2.3 Date	12	**75,00%**	7.2.1.1 Catalog	11	**68,75%**
3.4 Language	12	**75,00%**	7.2.2 Description	10	**62,50%**
3.1 Identifier	11	**68,75%**	7.2.1.2 Entry	9	**50,00%**
3.1.1 Catalog	11	**68,75%**	**8. Annotation**		
3.2 Contribute	11	**68,75%**	**8.1 Entity**	7	**43,75%**

continued on following page

Table 5. Continued

Metadata Element	Times of Appearance	Percentage of Appearance (%)	Metadata Element	Times of Appearance	Percentage of Appearance (%)
3.2.1 Role	11	**68,75%**	**8.2 Date**	7	43,75%
3.2.2 Entity	11	**68,75%**	**8.3 Description**	7	43,75%
3.3 Metadata Schema	10	**62,50%**	**9. Classification**		
4. Technical			**9.2 Taxon Path**	13	**81,25%**
4.1 Format	11	**68,75%**	9.2.2.1 Id	13	**81,25%**
4.3 Location	11	**68,75%**	9.2.1 Source	12	**75,00%**
4.2 Size	9	**56,25%**	9.2.2 Taxon	12	**75,00%**
4.6 Other Platform Requirements	6	**37,50%**	9.2.2.2 Entry	12	**75,00%**
4.4 Requirement	5	**31,25%**	**9.1 Purpose**	10	**62,50%**
4.4.1 OrComposite	5	**31,25%**	**9.3. Description**	5	**31,25%**
4.7 Duration	5	**31,25%**	**9.4 Keyword**	5	**31,25%**
4.5 Installation Remarks	2	**12,50%**			

the ODS Project (Athanasiadis et al., 2014). This system harvest metadata records from the aggregated LORs by using the Open Archives Initiative Protocol for Metadata Harvesting (OAI-PMH). Once the occurrence frequencies for each individual LOR were obtained from each metadata record, the authors used formula (1) to calculate the overall occurrence frequency, so as to identify the metadata elements that are present in the metadata records of the aggregated LORs.

As Table 6 depicts, title and identifier (including its superior elements "1.1.1 Catalog" and "1.1.2 Entry") of the LO are used in almost all metadata records of the aggregated LORs. This is evident from the calculated OF for these elements which is higher than 75%. As result, the authors can consider them as mandatory elements for the ODS Metadata AP.

Moreover, based on the calculated OF for the other elements the authors can consider 28 metadata elements (with OF more than 50% and less than 75%) as recommended for the ODS Metadata AP. These elements include:

- 4 elements from the "General" category
- 3 elements from the "Lifecycle" category
- 7 elements from the "Meta-metadata" category

Table 6. LOM Elements Value Space Modifications in Metadata APs of the Aggregated LORs

Metadata Element	Occurrence Frequency (OF)	Suggested Obligation Status	Metadata Element	Occurrence Frequency (OF)	Suggested Obligation Status
1. General			**5. Educational**		
1.1.2 Entry	**100,00%**	Mandatory	**5.7 Typical Age Range**	**62,11%**	Recommended
1.2 Title	**100,00%**	Mandatory	**5.9 Typical Learning Time**	**62,02%**	Recommended
1.1 Identifier	**88,42%**	Mandatory	**5.8 Difficulty**	**58,60%**	Recommended
1.1.1 Catalog	**78,50%**	Mandatory	**5.2 Learning Resource Type**	**56,14%**	Recommended
1.3 Language	**71,44%**	Recommended	**5.6 Context**	**51,58%**	Recommended
1.4 Description	**61,40%**	Recommended	**5.5 Intended End User Role**	**47,37%**	Optional
1.5 Keyword	**55,61%**	Recommended	**5.3 Interactivity Level**	**40,35%**	Optional
1.8 Aggregation Level	**53,33%**	Recommended	**5.1 Interactivity Type**	**36,84%**	Optional
1.7 Structure	**31,33%**	Optional	**5.11 Language**	**29,82%**	Optional
1.6 Coverage	**24,56%**	Optional	**5.10 Description**	**22,81%**	Optional
2. Lifecycle			**5.4 Semantic Density**	**21,05%**	Optional
2.3.2 Entity	**66,67%**	Recommended	**6. Rights**		
2.3.1 Role	**61,40%**	Recommended	**6.2 Copyright and Other Restrictions**	**74,19%**	Recommended
2.3 Contribute	**59,12%**	Recommended	**6.1 Cost**	**66,67%**	Recommended
2.3.3 Date	**42,11%**	Optional	**6.3 Description**	**47,89%**	Optional
2.2 Status	**36,84%**	Optional	**7. Relation**		
2.1 Version	**35,09%**	Optional	**7.1 Kind**	**43,33%**	Optional
3. Meta-Metadata			**7.2 Resource**	**37,82%**	Optional
3.1.2 Entry	**68,42%**	Recommended	7.2.1 Identifier	**28,82%**	Optional
3.1.1 Catalog	**63,16%**	Recommended	7.2.1.1 Catalog	**27,62%**	Optional
3.2.1 Role	**59,65%**	Recommended	7.2.2 Description	**25,07%**	Optional
3.2.2 Entity	**58,35%**	Recommended	7.2.1.2 Entry	**24,32%**	Optional
3.1 Identifier	**54,39%**	Recommended	**8. Annotation**		
3.2 Contribute	**51,88%**	Recommended	**8.1 Entity**	**26,32%**	Optional
3.2.3 Date	**50,38%**	Recommended	**8.2 Date**	**24,56%**	Optional
3.4 Language	**48,88%**	Optional	**8.3 Description**	**21,05%**	Optional
3.3 Metadata Schema	**47,37%**	Optional	**9. Classification**		

continued on following page

Table 6. Continued

Metadata Element	Occurrence Frequency (OF)	Suggested Obligation Status	Metadata Element	Occurrence Frequency (OF)	Suggested Obligation Status
4. Technical			**9.2 Taxon Path**	**61,40%**	Recommended
4.3 Location	**73,65%**	Recommended	9.2.2.1 Id	**61,40%**	Recommended
4.1 Format	**45,61%**	Optional	9.2.2.2 Entry	**61,40%**	Recommended
4.2 Size	**31,58%**	Optional	9.2.1 Source	**56,14%**	Recommended
4.4.1 OrComposite	**21,05%**	Optional	9.2.2 Taxon	**56,14%**	Recommended
4.4 Requirement	**17,54%**	Optional	**9.1 Purpose**	**55,61%**	Recommended
4.7 Duration	**16,24%**	Optional	**9.3. Description**	**25,59%**	Optional
4.6 Other Platform Requirements	**15,79%**	Optional	**9.4 Keyword**	**15,79%**	Optional
4.5 Installation Remarks	**8,77%**	Optional			

- 1 element from the "Technical" category
- 5 elements from the "Educational" category
- 2 elements from the "Rights" category
- None element from the "Relation" and "Annotation" categories
- 6 elements from the "Classification" category.

Based on these results, it seems that 50% of all IEEE LOM elements can be considered either mandatory or recommended. Moreover, these elements cover 7 out of the 9 main IEEE LOM categories and as a result they constitute an adequate metadata set for describing the LOs that are harvested by the ODS federated LOR. Finally, all other elements with calculated OF less than 50% (namely 32 elements) can be considered as optional for the ODS Metadata AP.

Analysis of Metadata Elements Value Space

For all metadata elements of the IEEE LOM, which have a vocabulary data type (namely, 18 elements), the authors studied the modifications that have been performed by the metadata APs of the aggregated LORs to the LOM vocabularies of these elements. In order to capture the different types of modifications, the authors identified four types of modifications, namely (Duval et al., 2006):

- **LOM Restricted:** When the values of the initial LOM vocabulary have been restricted to fewer values
- **Same with LOM:** When the vocabulary has not changed and it follows the initial LOM vocabulary
- **LOM Extended:** When the values of the initial LOM vocabulary have been extended with more values that are not included in the initial LOM vocabulary
- **Different than LOM:** When a different vocabulary has been used, which is not related with the initial LOM vocabulary

Table 7 depicts the results of the authors' analysis. More specifically, for each element the authors studied the type of modification per metadata AP of the aggregated LORs. For each element, the authors calculated also the total score following the rules described in step 4 of the proposed methodology. Finally, the elements were sorted based on the calculated score.

As it can be noticed from Table 7, 7 out of 18 elements mainly use the same vocabulary with LOM or they restrict the values of the LOM vocabulary (score 0). As a result, no actions were needed regarding the value space of these elements to the ODS metadata AP and the authors considered that these elements can safely use the LOM vocabulary. On the other hand, there is a significant number of 11 out of 18 elements for which their vocabulary has been extended or differentiated from the value space of the IEEE LOM. For each one of these elements close collaboration with LORs' owners was needed, so as to indentify the semantics of each value and either map them to the value space of the IEEE LOM vocabularies or consider extensions/differentiations for the ODS metadata AP. This is very important for maintaining consistency between the vocabularies of the metadata APs of the aggregated LORs and the ODS metadata AP towards avoiding LOs retrieval problems from the federated LOR search engine. For instance, regarding the metadata element "5.2 Learning Resource Type" a master vocabulary was compiled by considering the different (semantically) values that were identified from the metadata APs of the aggregated LORs. Afterwards, the individual vocabularies of this element per each metadata AP was mapped to the master vocabulary in collaboration with each LOR owner. This mapping was performed by using an open source mapping tool, namely MINT[3], which generated technical representations of the mapping of ODS metadata AP with the individual metadata APs as Xtensible Stylesheet Language (XSL) transformations. This process was repeated for all metadata elements (namely, 11 elements) for which their vocabulary has been extended or differentiated from the value space of the IEEE LOM. Finally, all vocabularies produced for the ODS metadata AP were uploaded to a vocabulary bank[4], so as to be available for any interested LOR owner, who wants to perform similar mappings and connect his/her LOR with the ODS federated LOR.

Table 7. LOM elements value space modifications in metadata APs of the aggregated LORs

No	Metadata Element	LOM Restricted	Same with LOM	LOM Extended	Different than LOM	Score
1	5.2 Educational. Learning Resource Type	0	4	3	9	16,5
2	5.5 Educational. Intended End User Role	1	6	9	0	9
3	2.3.1 LifeCycle. Contribute. Role	2	8	2	4	8
4	5.6 Educational. Context	1	10	0	5	7,5
5	7.1 Relation. Kind	0	9	7	0	7
6	3.2.1 Meta-Metadata. Contribute. Role	2	9	5	0	5
7	2.2 Lifecycle. Status	0	13	0	3	4,5
8	5.1 Educational. Interactivity Type	1	12	0	3	4,5
9	9.1 Classification. Purpose	3	11	0	2	3
10	6.2 Rights. Copyright and Other Restrictions	2	12	1	1	2,5
11	6.1 Rights. Cost	2	13	0	1	1,5
12	1.7 General. Structure	1	15	0	0	0
13	1.8 General. Aggregation Level	4	12	0	0	0
14	4.1 Technical. Format	2	14	0	0	0
15	4.4.1.1 Technical. Requirement Or Composite Type	0	16	0	0	0
16	5.3 Educational. Interactivity Level	1	15	0	0	0
17	5.4 Educational. Semantic Density	1	15	0	0	0
18	5.8 Educational. Difficulty	1	15	0	0	0

FUTURE RESEARCH DIRECTIONS

In this work, the authors presented a methodology for developing metadata APs for federated LORs taking into consideration the pre-existing metadata APs of the aggregated LORs. This is important for ensuring consistency with the metadata APs and the already populated metadata records of the aggregated LORs. However, this is only an initial step towards supporting OER providers to set up metadata APs for federated LORs. To this end, future research directions in this field could include:

- The enhancement of the proposed methodology by considering the growth rate (which indicates the addition over time of the number of the LOs added to a specific LOR along with their educational metadata records) of the aggregated LORs instead of the proposed weighting factor $\left(w_j \right)$, which is rather biased towards existing mature LORs. This enhancement could offer a more accurate way of defining the obligation status for the metadata elements of the federated LOR metadata AP by capturing the trend of fast developing aggregating LORs compared to slower developing aggregating LORs. Additionally, the enhancement of the proposed methodology could include also additional steps for the alignment and harvesting of paradata (i.e., system and user generated use data, transaction data, and feedback) from different LORs to a federated LOR.
- The development of tools that can:
  - Import the technical bindings of metadata APs from different LORs and automatically analyze them following the methodology described in this book chapter
  - Import populated metadata records from different LORs and automatically analyze them following the methodology and metrics presented in this book chapter
- This kind of tools can be very helpful for OER providers when developing federated LORs because they can support them in the process of:
  - Selecting which existing LORs can be connected to the federated LOR and under which conditions
  - Defining what type of search services can be developed for the end-users (namely instructional designers, teachers and students) for example browsing by categories, free text search, as well as faceted browsing and search with specific values.

CONCLUSION

Within the landscape of setting up federated networks of interconnected LORs, it seems that there are limited previous studies that discuss and propose guidelines and best practices that can be used by OER providers to develop metadata APs for federated LORs.

Thus, in this chapter a methodology for developing metadata APs for federated LORs was proposed and described in terms of its procedure and statistical metrics for the systematic analysis of the metadata APs and metadata records of the different LORs that will constitute the federated LOR. Moreover, it was demonstrated the implementation of the proposed methodology for the development of a metadata AP utilized by the ODS federated LOR. It is worth mentioning that ODS federated LOR after its initial start by interconnecting sixteen (16) LORs, it has managed to interconnect twenty-five (25) LORs providing access to more than 1 million LOs available worldwide. This fact provides an indicator of the capacity of the methodology presented in this book chapter for effectively setting up and expanding a federator LOR.

ACKNOWLEDGMENT

The work presented in this chapter has been partly supported by the Open Discovery Space Project that is funded by the European Commission's CIP-ICT Policy Support Programme (Project Number: 297229). This document does not represent the opinion of the European Commission, and the European Commission is not responsible for any use that might be made of its content.

REFERENCES

Athanasiadis, N., Sotiriou, S., Zervas, P., & Sampson, D. G. (2014). The Open Discovery Space Portal: A Socially-Powered and Open Federated Infrastructure. In D. G. Sampson, D. Ifenthaler, J. M. Spector, & P. Isaias (Eds.), *Digital Systems for Open Access to Formal and Informal Learning* (pp. 11–23). USA: Springer International Publishing.

Barker, P., & Campbell, L. (2014, April 23-25). Learning Resource Metadata Initiative: Using Schema.org to Describe Open Educational Resources. Proc. of the Open-CourseWare Consortium Global 2014 (OCWC Global 2014), Ljubljana, Slovenia.

Conole, G. (2013). *Open Educational Resources. In Designing for Learning in an Open World* (pp. 225–243). NY, USA: Springer International Publishing. doi:10.1007/978-1-4419-8517-0

Currier, S. (2008). Metadata for Learning Resources: An Update on Standards Activity for 2008. *Ariadne, 55*(2).

De la Prieta, F., Gil, A., Rodríguez, S., & Martín, B. (2011). BRENHET2, A MAS to Facilitate the Reutilization of LOs through Federated Search. In J. M. Corchado, J. B. Pérez, K. Hallenborg, P. Golinska, & R. Corchuelo (Eds.), *Trends in Practical Applications of Agents and Multiagent Systems. AISC* (Vol. 90, pp. 177–184). Heidelberg: Springer. doi:10.1007/978-3-642-19931-8_22

Dublin Core Metadata Element Set (DCMES). Version 1.1 (2004). Reference description. Retrieved from http://dublincore.org/documents/2004/12/20/dces/

Duval, E., Hodgins, W., Sutton, S., & Weibel, S. L. (2002). Metadata Principles and Practicalities. *D-Lib Magazine*, 8.

Duval, E., Smith, N., & Van Coillie, M. (2006, July 5-7). Application profiles for learning. *Proc. of theIEEE International Conference on Advanced Learning Technologies (ICALT)*, Kerkrade, The Netherlands (pp. 242–246). doi:10.1109/ICALT.2006.1652415

Education Network Australia. (2006). EdNA resources metadata application profile 1.0. Retrieved from http://edna.wikispaces.com/EdNA+Metadata+Standard+1.1

Ehlers, U. D. (2011). Extending the Territory: From Open Educational Resources to Open Educational Practices. *Journal of Open, Flexible, and Distance Learning*, *15*(2), 1–10.

Friesen, N. (2009). Open educational resources: New possibilities for change and sustainability. *International Review of Research in Open and Distance Learning*, *10*(5). doi:10.19173/irrodl.v10i5.664

GLOBE. (2011). *GLOBE metadata application profile specification document. Version 1*. Retrieved from http://www.globe-info.org/images/ap/globe_lom_ap_v1.0.pdf

Ha, K. H., Niemann, K., Schwertel, U., Holtkamp, P., Pirkkalainen, H., & Boerner, D. et al.. (2011). A novel approach towards skill-based search and services of open educational resources. *Proc. of Metadata and Semantic Research* (pp. 312–323). Berlin: Springer. doi:10.1007/978-3-642-24731-6_32

IEEE Learning Technology Standards Committee (LTSC). (2005). Final Standard for Learning Object Metadata. Retrieved from http://ltsc.ieee.org/wg12/files/IEEE_1484_12_03_d8_submitted.pdf

Iiyoshi, T., & Kumar, M. V. (Eds.). (2008). *Opening up education: The collective advancement of education through open technology, open content, and open knowledge*. London, UK: MIT Press.

IMS Global Learning Consortium (GLC). (2005). IMS Application Profile Guidelines Technical Manual. Retrieved from http://www.imsglobal.org/ap/apv1p0/imsap_techv1p0.html

ISO/IEC. (2011). *ISO/IEC 19788-1:2011 Information technology – Learning, education and training – Metadata for learning resources - Part 1: Framework*. International Organization for Standardization.

Kalz, M., Specht, M., Nadolski, R., Bastiaens, Y., Leirs, N., & Pawlowski, J. (2010). OpenScout: Competence based management education with community-improved open educational resources. In S. Halley, C. Birch, D.T. Tempelaar, M. McCuddy, N. Hernández Nanclares, S. Reeb-Gruber, W.H. Gijselaers, B. Rienties, and E. Nelissen, (Eds.), *Proc. of the 17th Conference on Education Innovation in Economics and Business (EDiNEB '11)* (pp. 137-146). Maastricht, The Netherlands: FEBA ERD Press.

Klerkx, J., Vandeputte, B., Parra Chico, G., Santos Odriozola, J. L., Van Assche, F., & Duval, E. (2010). How to share and reuse learning resources: the Ariadne experience. *Proc. of the 5th European Conference on Technology Enhanced Learning (EC-TEL '10)* (pp. 183–196). Heidelberg: Springer. doi:10.1007/978-3-642-16020-2_13

Lane, A. & McAndrew, P. (2010). Are open educational resources systematic or systemic change agents for teaching practice? *British Journal of Educational Technology*, *41*(6), 952-962.

Malta, M. C., & Baptista, A. A. (2012). State of the art on methodologies for the development of a metadata application profile. *International Journal of Metadata. Semantics and Ontologies*, *8*(4), 332–341. doi:10.1504/IJMSO.2013.058416

Malta, M. C., & Baptista, A. A. (2014). A panoramic view on metadata application profiles of the last decade. *International Journal of Metadata. Semantics and Ontologies*, *9*(1), 58–73. doi:10.1504/IJMSO.2014.059124

Manouselis, N., Kastrantas, K., Sanchez-Alonso, S., Cáceres, J., Ebner, H., Palmer, M., & Naeve, A. (2009). Architecture of the Organic.Edunet Web Portal. *International Journal of Web Portals*, *1*(1), 71–91. doi:10.4018/jwp.2009092105

Mason, J., & Galatis, H. (2007). Theory and practice of application profile development in Australian education and training. *Proc. of the 2007 International Conference on Dublin Core and Metadata Applications: application profiles: theory and practice (DCMI '07)*, Singapore (pp. 43-52).

Mason R.T., & Ellis T. J. (2009). Extending SCORM LOM. *Issues in Informing Science and Information Technology*, 6.

McGreal, R. (2004). *Online Education Using Learning Objects*. Washington, D.C.: Falmer Press.

McGreal, R. (2008). A typology of learning object repositories. In: H. H. Adelsberger, Kinshuk, J. M. Pawlovski & D. Sampson, (Eds.), International Handbook on Information Technologies for Education and Training (2nd ed., pp. 5-18). New York: Springer. doi:10.1007/978-3-540-74155-8_1

Megalou, E., & Kaklamanis, C. (2014). Photodentro LOR, The Greek National Learning Object Repository.*Proc. of the 8th International Technology, Education and Development Conference (INTED '14)* (pp. 309-319).

NISO. (2004). *Understanding Metadata. National Information Standards Organisation*. Baltimore, USA: NISO Press.

OECD. (2007). Giving knowledge for free: The emergence of open educational resources. Retrieved from http://www.oecd.org/dataoecd/35/7/38654317.pdf

Otón, S., Ortiz, A., de-Marcos, L., de Dios, S. M., García, A., García, E., & Barchino, R. et al. (2012). *Developing Distributed Repositories of Learning Objects*. INTECH Open Access Publisher. doi:10.5772/29447

Prause, C., Ternier, S., de Jong, T., Apelt, S., Scholten, M., Wolpers, M., & Duval, E. et al. (2007, September 18). Unifying learning object repositories in mace.*Proc. of the 1st International Workshop on Learning Object Discovery & Exchange (LODE '07)*, Lassithi, Greece.

Sampson, D. G., & Zervas, P. (2013). Learning object repositories as knowledge management systems. *Knowledge Management & E-Learning: An International Journal, 5*(2), 117-136.

Sampson, D. G., Zervas, P., & Chloros, G. (2012). Supporting the process of developing and managing LOM application profiles: The ASK-LOM-AP tool. *IEEE Transactions on Learning Technologies, 5*(3), 238–250. doi:10.1109/TLT.2011.39

Sen, A. (2004). Metadata Management: Past, present and future. *Decision Support Systems, 37*(1), 151–173. doi:10.1016/S0167-9236(02)00208-7

Smith, N., Van Coillie, M., & Duval, E. (2006). Guidelines and support for building Application profiles in e-learning. *Proc. of the CEN/ISSS WS/LT Learning Technologies Workshop on Availability of alternative language versions of a learning resource in IEEE LOM* (pp. 1-26). Brussels: CEN Workshop Agreements.

Steinacker, A., Ghavam, A., & Steinmetz, R. (2001). Metadata standards for web-based resources. *IEEE MultiMedia, 8*(1), 70–76. doi:10.1109/93.923956

Ternier, S., Verbert, K., Parra, G., Vandeputte, B., Klerkx, J., Duval, E., & Ochoa, X. et al. (2009). The Ariadne Infrastructure for Managing and Storing Metadata. *IEEE Internet Computing, 13*(4), 18–25. doi:10.1109/MIC.2009.90

The William and Flora Hewlett Foundation. (2013). White Paper: Open Educational Resources. Breaking the Lockbox on Education. Retrieved from http://tinyurl.com/oerhewlett

Totschnig, M. (2007). Open ICOPER Content Space Implementation of 2nd Generation of Open ICOPER Content Space including Integration Mini Case Studies.

UNESCO. (2002). *Forum on the Impact of Open Courseware for Higher Education in Developing Countries-Final Report.* Retrieved from http://goo.gl/eOkgdD

UNESCO. (2012, June 20-22). 2012 World Open Educational Resources (OER) Congress. UNESCO, Paris. Retrieved from http://tinyurl.com/unescoparis2012

Walsh, T. (2010). *Unlocking the gates: How and why leading universities are opening up access to their courses.* Princeton, NJ: Princeton University.

Wiley, D. A. (2002). The instructional use of learning objects. Bloomington, USA: Association for Educational Communications and Technology (AECT) Press.

Woodley, M. S. (2008). Crosswalks, metadata harvesting, federated searching, metasearching: Using metadata to connect users and information. In M. Baca (Ed.), *Introduction to metadata* (3rd ed., pp. 38–62). Los Angeles, CA: Getty Research Institute.

Yamada, T. (2013). Open educational resources in Japan. In G. Dhanarajan & D. Porter (Eds.), Open educational resources: An Asian perspective (pp. 85-105). Vancouver: Commonwealth of Learning and OER Asia

Zervas, P., Alifragkis, C., & Sampson, D. G. (2014a). A quantitative analysis of learning object repositories as knowledge management systems. *Knowledge Management & E-Learning: An International Journal, 6*(2), pp. 156-170.

Zervas, P., Kalamatianos, A., & Sampson, D. G. (2014b). A Systematic Analysis of Metadata Application Profiles of Learning Object Repositories in Europe. In R. Huang & N. S. Chen (Eds.), *The New Development of Technology Enhanced Learning* (pp. 75–91). Berlin: Springer. doi:10.1007/978-3-642-38291-8_5

KEY TERMS AND DEFINITIONS

Application Profile: It consists of elements selected by one or more base standards or specifications by applying additional restrictions or modifications to these elements.

Educational Metadata: Data elements, which are associated with educational resources to describe their characteristics.

Federated Learning Object Repository: A web-based application that provides access to LOs through an interconnected federated network of LORs.

Learning Object (LO): A modular digital resource that can be used to support teaching or learning.

Learning Object Repository (LOR): A web-based application that provides access to LOs, so end-users (namely, instructional designers teachers and learners) can search for, find and make use of these LOs.

Metadata Harvesting: the process of aggregating metadata records from multiple LORs into a single database (namely, the database of the federated LOR).

Open Educational Resource (OER): A digital resource offered by its creator under open licenses (such as Creative Commons) to be used for supporting teaching and learning.

ENDNOTES

[1]   http://portal.opendiscoveryspace.eu/

[2]   Data retrieved on 9 November 2012 (namely, the time of the ODS metadata AP development)

[3]   http://mint.image.ece.ntua.gr/redmine/projects/mint/wiki/Mapping_Tool

[4]   http://vocbank.opendiscoveryspace.eu/vocab/

Chapter 7
Using Reverse Engineering to Define a Domain Model:
The Case of the Development of a Metadata Application Profile for European Poetry

Mariana Curado Malta
Polytechnic of Oporto, Portugal & LINHD-UNED, Spain

Paloma Centenera
LINHD-UNED, Spain

Elena Gonzalez-Blanco
LINHD-UNED, Spain

ABSTRACT

This chapter presents the early stages of a metadata application profile (MAP) development that uses a process of reverse engineering. The context of this development is the European poetry, more specifically the poetry metrics and all dimensions that exist around this context. This community of practice has a certain number of digital repertoires that store this information and that are not interoperable. This chapter presents some steps of the definition of the MAP Domain Model. It shows how the developers having as starting point these repertoires, and by means of a reverse engineering process are modeling the functional requirements of each repertoire using the use-case modeling technique and are analyzing every database

DOI: 10.4018/978-1-5225-2221-8.ch007

logical models to extract the conceptual model of each repertoire. The final goal is to develop a common conceptual model in order to use it as basis, together with other sources of information, for the definition of the Domain Model.

INTRODUCTION

Comparative literary studies have always been a source of new discoveries which enlighten the perspectives of other related disciplines, such as history, archaeology or sociology. It is sometimes difficult, however, to get results in the philological field, as the sources to compare are uneven, follow different historical, linguistic and literary traditions and do not have many elements in common to take them as a reference or starting point.

Poetry studies have suffered from this reality, as each different cultural tradition has followed an independent way, where no standards were adopted for terminology or classification. Each literary school has modelled a different system that looked to be the most suitable for its own problems. Communication between different languages and literatures has been almost scarce, even from the critical point of view. The result is a fragmentary puzzle which includes different traditions, languages, literary and poetic schools not possible to analyze using the same methods and straightforward paths to compare poetic forms.

From the point of view of literary analysis, the studies on metrics and poetry were first linked to grammar and rhetoric, and were not considered independent as "ars metrica" or "ars poetica" until the 14th century (Gómez Redondo, 2001). During the Middle Ages and the Renaissance, the powerful influence of Latin as the language of culture made scholars inherit the terminology of Classical treaties and apply it to Romance languages, regardless of their different way of structuring. When vernacular theories start to arise, each particular school makes up its own terminology and classification system. This multiplicity leads to paradoxical and complex situations, such as the creation of conceptual genres that only exist in some literatures.

A special case to illustrate this problem is the phenomenon of metrical repertoires, catalogues which aimed at gathering all poetic and metrical features in any of the different literary tradition. They show the way in which researchers measure and classify poems, counting syllables, accents, rhythm and rhymes to define the essential elements of the poem structure, its musicality and the type of contents that it shapes. A digital poetry metrics repertoire is a tool that gives account of metrical and rhythmical schemes of either a poetical tradition or school gathering a long corpus of poems, which are defined and classified by their main characteristics.

The first poetic repertoires appeared as books at the end of the 19th century with the works of Gaston Raynaud (1884), Gotthold Naetebus (1891), and Pillet and Carstens (1933), followed by some other important books after the Second World War, as the classic work of Frank (1953-1957) on Provencal troubadours' poetry, and with the editions of printed metrical repertoires in Old French lyrics Mölk and Wolfzettel (1972), in Italian Antonelli (1984), Solimena (2000), Zenari (1999), Pagnotta (1995), and Gorni (2008), in the Hispanic philology Tavani (1967), Parramon i Blasco (1992), and Gómez Bravo (1999), in the German, Touber (1975) and Brunner et al. (1986-2007).

The evolution of technologies in the last decades had a strong impact in all disciplines. Humanities were also transformed by these changes after Padre Busa in 1949 published the first digital database: the *Corpus Thomisticum* supported by IBM technology. After that date, many projects —especially related with philology and linguistic studies- tried to combine the technological innovations with their data building digital databases and resources which would make life easier for researchers and future users. Although they did not consider themselves "digital humanists," those researchers were the pioneers of the creation of a new research area.

Technological advances made possible to create a new generation of repertoires, in which time of research is considerably reduced and the user experience much better than in the previous paper books. The first digital poetic repertoire online was the *RPHA:* Répertoire de la Poésie hongroise ancienne jusqu'à 1600[1]. Galician researchers created MedDB: Base de datos da Lírica profana galego-portuguesa[2]; Italian researchers digitalized BEdT: Bibliografia Elettronica dei Trovatori[3]; the Nouveau Naetebus for French narrative poetry[4], the Oxford Cantigas de Santa María Database[5] the Analecta Hymnica Digitalia[6], the Dutch Song Database[7], the Corpus Rhythmorum Musicum[8], the Repertorio della tradizione poetica italiana dai Siciliani a Petrarca[9], the Digital Edition of the Index of Middle English Verse[10], The Last Song of the Troubadours[11], the Czech Versification Research Group[12], and finally "Repertório Métrico Digital de la poesia medieval castellana" (ReMetCa)[13] started in 2011 by the POSTDATA research group, which is the last piece of this poetic multilingual Babel-like puzzle.

The latest mentioned projects were created as web-based resources and databases and interoperability among poetic repertoires is not simple, as there are not only technical issues involved, but also conceptual and terminological problems: each repertoire belongs to its own poetical tradition and each tradition has developed an idiosyncratic analytical terminology in a different and independent way for years. The result of this uncoordinated evolution is a bunch of varied terminologies to explain analogous metrical phenomena through the different poetic systems, whose correspondences have been hardly studied.

The approaches to digital poetic repertoires have been always linked to a philological purpose, following traditional research methodologies which have been considered a "close reading" approach to texts and corpora (Moretti 2013), even though the advanced in digital repertoires have been great in the last decades. The POSTDATA project is presented in this chapter as a Digital Humanities frame in which "distant reading" is the approach to compare hundreds of results at the same time, the research questions and the ways of representing knowledge becomes different[14]. This Digital Humanities approach is what POSTDATA team aims at achieving by publishing the data of the digital repertoires as linked open data (LOD).

To achieve this goal of publishing the data of the digital repertoires as LOD there is the need to have a common model for the data. POSTDATA is now developing a metadata application profile for the European Poetry, and this chapter presents the process and techniques used to define a common domain model. This chapter proceeds as follows: Section 2 presents the motivation for the development of a metadata application profile for the European Poetry, Section 3 shows how developers used a reverse engineering process 1) to model Functional Requirements and; 2) to analyze existent databases to build conceptual models as a process to develop the Domain Model. Section 4 presents recommendations and Section 5 concludes and presents future work.

Motivation

The POSTDATA project focus in the interoperability issue between the digital poetry metrics repertoires in Europe. These digital repertoires are mainly in the Web of Documents[15], but there are also some stored locally. The repertoires were developed in a specific technology along time, and store the data in their own silos. This data is at the moment locked in the silos of information of each repertoire, not available freely to be compared and to be used by intelligent machines that could infer over data. In fact the interoperability problem exists because the technological solutions used for building each digital repertoire and data model is very different from each other.

POSTDATA is a project that aims to provide the means to open this data stored in many databases of the Web of Documents publishing it as Linked Open Data (LOD). All the data trapped in the silos of information of each digital repertoire needs to be mapped to a common semantic model. This semantic model is in fact a metadata application profile (MAP), a construct that enhances interoperability (Nilsson, Baker, & Johnston, 2009)þþ.

POSTDATA is now, at the time of writing this chapter, developing a MAP for the European Poetry. Next chapter will show in detail how the first steps of this development are being implemented.

Developing Functional Requirements and Domain Model

Introduction

As mentioned previously the context of POSTDATA is the digital repertoires of poetry. This kind of repertoires may sometimes contain the text of the poem and information related to authors, manuscripts and editions all of them related to the poems. They also have other dimensions that are related to the poems depending on the mission of the repertoire and context. They have distinct corpus of poems and information that are, as example:

- Relations between poems and songs, and metrics of the songs,
- Relations between poems and miracles that are described in poems,
- Relations between poems and places that are referred in poems,
- Relations between poems and people, real persons that existed and other that are imaginary like for example, Don Quijote de la Mancha.

The development of a MAP is a crucial task for a community of practice. This development should be structured, and integrate, since the early phases of development, elements of all representative members of the community. Commonly the organizations differ in organization-type, location, culture and in the language they speak. To find a common ground of understanding in such an environment becomes a huge challenge. Adding to this, a MAP development is often done in complex settings that are very open, in contrast with the development of software that serves a certain organization that is protected inside its walls of context, culture and language, where requirements can be elicit more easily using very well known techniques. In a MAP development, designers will never know in fact the total reach of the MAP, the community of practice that the MAP serves can be very well defined but there will be always a degree of uncertainty - to elicit requirements is not easy in such uncertainty.

The POSTDATA team thinks that the existence of a method for the development of a MAP may help to address all the referred challenges. Recent studies say that there is no method for the development of MAPs (see Curado Malta & Baptista (2013c)), in order to address this issue Curado Malta and Baptista (2013a, 2013b) have been working on the definition of a method for the development of metadata application profiles (Me4MAP). The POSTDATA team is using Me4MAP16 to develop the referred MAP.

MeMAP defines the need to develop a set of deliverables in order to define a MAP of quality. These deliverables are the output of a set of activities that are globally organized by the Singapore Stages. This name comes after the seminal document "Singapore Framework for the development of dublin core application profiles - see Nilsson, Baker, and Johnston (2008)þ. S1, the Singapore Stage 1, develops the functional requirements of the MAP and S2, the Singapore Stage 2, defines the Domain Model. Every stage includes a certain number of activities to achieve the main deliverable of every Singapore Stage. Other Stages exist but it is not the aim of this chapter to explain in detail Me4MAP rather than to address the way POSTDATA defined the Functional Requirements and the Domain Model, main deliverables of S1 and S2, respectively.

POSTDATA knows the existence of twenty-two digital repertoires, twenty-one are in the Web of Documents and one is local. The owners of the repertoires were contacted and documentation from seventeen repertoires was received. The following sources of information were used to develop the Functional Requirements and the Domain Model:

- Study of the functionalities of the Web interfaces of the twenty-one repertoires;
- Study of the seventeen data models:
  - Eleven of the repertoires implemented the database in a relational database management system
  - Four of the repertoires are implemented in a XML database system
  - One of the repertoires uses Perl objects to store data
  - The local repertoire is implemented in a stylesheet
- Survey to final users of the repertoires to know what kind of things they would like to do in an interface (e.g. Webpage, App, SPARQL endpoint) that deals with information about poems
- Two case studies of digital repertoires that are being built at the same time the MAP is being developed. These case studies also provide information on how to model the data that needs to be captured

Next sections will present in detail the techniques used to develop the Functional Requirements and the Domain Model deliverables.

Modeling Functional Requirements

A MAP development process is guided by data since data is the essential part of a MAP. The main objective to define functional requirements is to identify the data and relationships between the data that support the identified functionalities during the functionalities analysis. This section explains how the analysis of the Websites of the repertoires was implemented in order to model the functional requirements of the MAP.

In the case of the MAP for the European Poetry, the functional requirements definition was developed using a reverse engineering process (Müller et al., 2000) (Pressman, 2015). Chikofsky and Cross wrote in the 90's about reverse engineering and design recovery taxonomies. They defined reverse engineering as "the process of analysing a subject system to identify the system's components, their interrelationships, and create representations of the system in another form or at a higher level of abstraction" (Chikofsky and Cross, 1990, pp.15). This process reconstructs abstract models from implementation, the abstract models help to understand the different aspects of the system to be analysed.

The reverse engineering process was very important in the past for the maintenance of legacy systems (Bianchi, Caivano, Marengo & Visaggio, 2003) (Hassan, Qamar, Hassan & Waqas, 2015) (Sneed, 1995). Nowadays this process is very useful in domain engineering processes that aim to define the commonality and the variability of the software product line (Linden Schmid and Rommes, 2007) (Pohl, Blöckle & van Der Linden, 2005). Software product lines reduce the cost of customized applications, building them by assembling reused components. These components are previously built in a domain engineering process. The aim of domain engineering processes is that the final products are highly reusable. This aim is aligned with our objective because a MAP serves a wide range of users, all very different. A MAP is in fact highly reused. This is the reason why the authors decided to use reverse engineering in the process of developing the Domain Model.

This reverse engineering process has three steps:

Step 1: Identification of the functionalities that exist in the Websites of the repertories
Step 2: Use-case model development
Step 3: Identification and description of the data elements of the use-case model

In Step 1 developers navigated through the Webpages of the repertoires and analyse the functionalities these pages have. The Oxford Advanced Learner's Dictionary[17] defines functionality as "the range of functions that a computer or other electronic system can perform." In fact, a functionality is the set of functions executed by the system that transform input data in output data in a way that the user obtains a useful result. The aim of Step 1 is the rebuilding of the model of the requirements of the Website. When the Webpages are simple, this work can be done with no tools, just analyzing the Webpages and taking notes in a structured text document. In more complex Websites the analysis can be made resorting to tools that help to automatize the process (Bouillon, Vanderdonckt & Chow, 2004).

In Step 2 the use-case modeling technique is used to express the functional requirements (Jacobson, Booch, Rumbaugh, & Booch, 1999). This is also the technique suggested by Me4MAP. A use case is "a unit of functionality expressed as a transaction among actors and the subject" (Rumbaugh, Jacobson, & Booch, 2004). Actors are entities outside the system that interact with it. A use-case model "characterizes the kinds of behavior provided by an entity, such as a system, subsystem, or class, in its interactions with outside entities. Outside entities are actors of the entity" (Rumbaugh et al., 2004). The use-case model is expressed in a UML use case diagram. Such a diagram is built by doing the description of the actor interaction with the system in the different use-case scenarios. This description allows more or less formal methods of representation and formulations (Rumbaugh et al., 2004) of UML interactions. Satechart diagrams, sequence diagrams, collaboration diagrams, or informal text descriptions can be used. In the present case, the POSTDATA team has used informal text descriptions (Somé, 2009) because the functionalities identified in the Websites are simple, and with this representation the use case model is easy to understand.

Table 1 presents a template for the description of use-cases. Each use-case is identified by a number and a name. Then the actor that performs the Use-Case is identified and a short description of the use-case function is defined. The main flow is set by enumerating the interactions between the actor and the system in the main scenario. The main scenario is the most used, alternative flows can exist at any moment of the flow, they should be described in the second column (Alternative flow) and only if a specific action is very different compared to the main flow. There may exist more than one alternative flow. All alternative flows should be numbered. Each interaction should have a number, and the alternative flow of a specific action should have the same number one level up (e.g See Table 1: Main flow - 1, Alternative flow(1) - 1.1.; Main flow - 2, Main flow - 3).

In Step 3 data elements identified in the navigation of the repertoire's Webpages are documented (see the activity defined in Step 1). Table 2 shows a template of the documentation, it consists in a description of the characteristics of the data elements such as:

Table 1. Template for a textual description of a Use-Case

Main flow	Alternative flow (1)
Number: The number assigned to the Use Case **Use Case Name:** The name of the Use Case **Actor:** The main actor of the Use Case. It is the actor who launches the Use Case **Description:** Short description of the Use Case function	
1. Description of interactions between user and system in the main scenario 2. 3.	1.1 Description of the interaction in a alternative scenario. Only if a specific step is very different compared to the main flow

Table 2. Template of the data elements documentation

Window number/name: Number or name of the window that is being described. Data elements			
Label	**Cardinality**	**Searchable**	**Link**
The label of the data element in the window	e.g 1; 0 - *; 1 – *	Yes/No	Yes/No

- **Cardinality**: If the data element is or not repeatable, is or not optional
- **Searchable**: If the data element is in a search filter
- **Linkable**: If the data element is or not a link to navigate to another window

The content of Table 2 helps to understand the functionalities of the Webpages. This information will feed activity S2 – developing the Domain Model, since it defines data elements to integrate this model.

Each repertoire case has its own model of functional requirements. To finalise S1 – Developing the Functional Requirements the POSTDATA team has to analyse all models and define a common model for the Functional Requirements of the MAP. This model integrates the requirements of all repertoires and new requirements that come from the survey and the case studies already mentioned. Also, since the MAP is going to be used by LOD technologies which are different from the ones of the Web of Documents, all the requirements should be submitted to a reengineering process to be adapted to this new reality and to take advantage of the potential of the available technology. This adaption is under study in order to understand the implications of the new reality.

Next paragraphs will present a real case by using the ReMetCa[18] repertoire as example to show this reverse engineering process.

Step 1: Functionalities Identification

A user accesses the Website of the ReMetCA to look for metrical information about a certain poem. To be able to access the repertoire the user clicks in the "repertoire" menu option on the top menu. The Webpage presents all poems of the repertoire (see Figure 1) by showing a list of title poems. By default they are ordered by title (also called "incipit"). The user has the possibility to search a poem, or group of poems, by "Fórmula Rimática," by "Title" or by "all fields" (it is not clear the meaning of "all fields" since later in the process there are other fields displayed in the result of a search and it is not clear if those fields were object of the search too). The Webpage also has a functionality that allows to filter the list of titles of poems

Figure 1. Front page of the ReMetCa repertoire

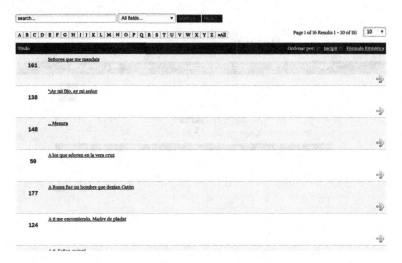

by letter. For this functionality, the Webpage presents a list of letters (all letters of the alphabet) where the user can click on the required letter to activate the filter.

In order for the user to do a search there is the need of doing three actions (see Figure 2):

1. Insert a string in the search text box
2. Choose a field
3. Press the search button

The result of the search is a list of poem titles that correspond to the criteria of the search. This information is displayed in the same window where the search is performed. If the user clicks in a title of a poem of the list, the system displays all the metrical information about that specific poem (see result in Figure 3). If the user clicks the print button (see (1) in Figure 3) the system prints the metrical information of the selected poem (see Figure 4).

Step 2: Requirements Modeling

There are three main use-cases in ReMetCa (see Figure 5).

The use-cases' description is displayed in Table 3, 4 and 5.

Each use-case presents a function of the system. The Functional Requirements are explicit in those use-case descriptions. Step 3 shows what data elements are needed to support these functionalities.

Figure 2. Window 1: REMETCA front page with the actions identified by numbers (1), (2) and (3)

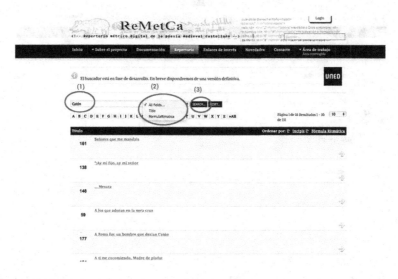

Figure 3. Window 2: Detailed metrical information about a poem

Step 3: Describing Data Elements

Each use-case explicits a certain number of data elements, the task here is to extract that information using the template of Table 2. The description of the data elements identified in the use-cases of Step 2 is presented in Tables 6, 7 and 8.

Figure 4. Window 3: Detailed metrical information about a poem to be printed

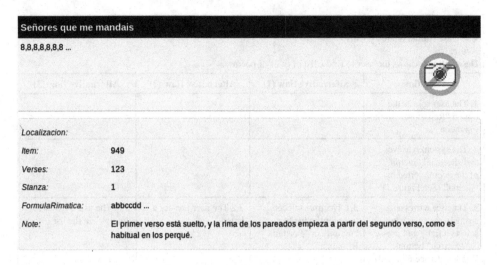

Figure 5. UML use-case diagram for ReMetCa

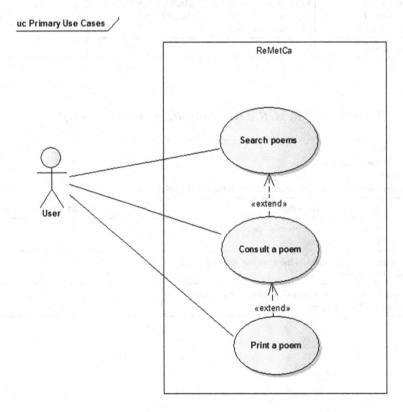

Table 3. Description of ReMetCa Use-case 001 (Search poems)

Number: 001			
Use Case Name: Search poems			
Actor: User			
Description: Allows the user to find a list of titles of poems			
Main flow	**Alternative flow (1)**	**Alternative flow (2)**	**Alternative flow (3)**
1. The user selects the option "Repertorio" in the top menu			
2. The system retrieves and shows all "incipit" of the poems sorted by "incipit" (See Figure 1)			
3. The user writes a string in the search box, selects a field, and presses the "Search" button - Window 1 (See Figure 2)	3.1 The user selects to order the list by "incipit" or "Fórmula Rimática"	3.2 The user presses a letter	3.3. The user presses a "incipit" in the list
4. The system retrieves and shows the list of "incipit" of the poems that match the search criteria (sorted by "incipit" - default)	4.1 The system retrieves and shows the list of "incipit" of the poems ordered by the selected criteria: "incipit" or "Fórmula Rimática"	4.2 The system retrieves and shows the list of "incipit" of the poems which start by the selected letter	4.3. Extension to the use-case 2 - Consult a poem
5. Return to step 3			

Table 4. Description of ReMetCa Use-case 002 (Consult a poem)

Number: 002	
Use Case Name: Consult a poem	
Actor: User	
Description: Allows the user to consult metrical information of a poem	
Main flow	**Alternative flow**
1. The user clicks in one of the poem's "incipit" of the list of Use-Case 001 – Search poems	
2. The system shows all metrical information about the poem - Window 2 (see Figure 3)	
3. The user presses the print button. (optional - Extension to the use-case 3 – Print a poem).	

Table 5. Description of ReMetCa Use-case 003 (Print a poem)

Number: 003 **Use Case Name:** Print a poem **Actor:** User **Description:** Allows the user to print the metrical information of a poem	
Main flow	**Alternative flow**
1. The user clicks in the print button	
2. The system retrieves the information and opens a new window – Window 3 (see Figure 4) with the information	

Table 6 presents the data elements of Window 1 (Figure 1). In that window only one data element is identified: "Incipit." This data element is not repeatable, that is, one poem only has one "incipit"; it is and is obligatory; and it is linkable, meaning that the user can click that element to navigate to Window 2, (which is the function "Consult a poem").

Table 7 presents the data elements of Window 2 (see Figure 3). In this Window the system presents, after the user clicks in the title of a poem, metrical information of that single poem. Seven data elements can be clearly identified, none of them is

Table 6. Description of the data elements of Window 1

Window number/name: Window 1. Data elements			
Label	**Cardinality**	**Searchable**	**Link**
Incipit	1	Yes	Yes

Table 7. Description of the data elements of Window 2

Window number/name: Window 2. Data elements			
Label	**Cardinality**	**Searchable**	**Link**
Fórmula Rimática	1	No	No
Fórmula Métrica	1	No	No
Localización	1	No	No
Versos	1	No	No
Estrofas	1	No	No
Notas	0 - 1	No	No
Transcripción	1	No	No

repeated (that is, each data element only contains one single piece of information per poem). Only "Notas" is optional, all other elements are obligatory. No data element is neither searchable neither linkable in Window 2 since in this Window the user cannot search anything and cannot click in any of those elements to navigate to a new page.

Table 8 presents the data elements of Window 3 (see Figure 4). In this Window the system presents, after the user clicks the print button (in Window 2), printable metrical information of one single poem that was consulted in Window 2. Eight data elements can be clearly identified, none of them is repeated. Only "Notas" is optional, all other elements are obligatory. No data element is neither searchable neither linkable in this Window.

With the conclusion of Step 3 the Functional Requirements of ReMetCa are modeled and the data elements that support those functionalities are identified. According to Me4MAP this information will feed next activity S2 – developing the Domain Model.

In the POSTDATA case, the work-team is resorting also to other information to feed S2: a survey to final users and two case studies that are developing repertoires at the same time POSTDATA is developing the MAP. It is not in the aim of this chapter to explain how these sources of information were used to feed S2.

Developing the Domain Model

According to Me4MAP the Domain Model development is fed by the Functional Requirements, the deliverable developed in S1 activity. But Me4MAP also adds that this development may also resort to other types of information the community

Table 8. Description of the data elements of Window 3

Window number/name: Window 3. Data elements			
Label	**Cardinality**	**Searchable**	**Link**
Incipit	1	No	No
Fórmula Métrica	0 - 1	No	No
Localización	0 - 1	No	No
Item	0 - 1	No	No
Versos	0 - 1	No	No
Estrofas	0- 1	No	No
Fórmula Rimática	0 - 1	No	No
Notas	1	No	No

of practice might have, like documentation or any other type of information. In the case of the POSTDATA project the community of practice has twenty repertoires in the Web of Documents and a local repertoire in a Worksheet. This section explains how the logical models of the repertoires were analyzed and how, using a reverse engineering process, they were converted in conceptual models.

A domain model is a conceptual model that is used to explicit the concepts that exist in a certain universe of discourse. A Domain Model is used to explicit the kind of concepts the universe has and, through the use of properties, how these concepts are defined. A MAP is a semantic model that will be based in a conceptual model, assigning 1) terms of RDF vocabularies to the concepts and properties and 2) adding constraints to the terms.

This section uses real examples to show how the conceptual models were created having as starting point:

1. A MySQL dump file
2. A XML xsd file
3. A perl file with a sample of objects
4. A stylesheet with sample data

The first example presented here is the repertoire "Repertório Métrico Digital de la poesia medieval castellana" (ReMetCa), the same repertoire used to explain how the reverse engineering process was implemented (see previous sub-section). ReMetCa has a relational database implemented in MySQL. The database responsible sent to POSTDATA a MySQL dump with the database schema. It was possible to recreate the database locally and extract the logical relational model (see Figure 6) using the software MySQL Workbench[19].

The process starts by the analysis of the logical model in order to understand the concepts that each table represent.

Follows a list of the POSTDATA team reflexions and assumptions:

- A type of thing is called "table" in a relational logical model, "concept" in a conceptual model, and "class" in a semantic model
- In the process of development of a conceptual model from a logical model there is the need to eliminate details that exist because of the implementation:
  - Primary keys are not part of the "world of concepts" that conceptual models model. It is a fact that in a semantic model classes have identifiers (URIs) to implement the need to identify univocally a resource, but in a conceptual model that is not necessary
  - Foreign keys exist to explicit the relations between tables. A conceptual model explicits these relations through a line connecting concepts that

Figure 6. Logical relational model of the repertoire "Repertório Métrico Digital de la poesia medieval castellana"

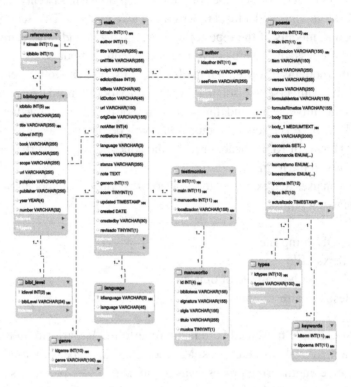

are related, and a number that defines the cardinality of the relation. A semantic model explicits the relations between classes using object properties, the line and cardinality in the concept model is sufficient to define later the object properties. Foreign keys do not exist, then, in the conceptual models

○ Tables whose properties are only keys, only exist in order to implement many-to-many relations. These tables are details of the representation and do not appear in conceptual models

○ Value tables (tables with lists of possible values for a property) are not concepts, they are instead properties of another concept with multiple or single cardinality

These last two items are introduced in a relational logical model in the process of normalization. Since this is a reverse engineer process where the goal is to arrive to a conceptual model in the context of a future semantic modeling, these items are deleted from the conceptual model.

Analyzing the logical model, the POSTDATA team identified:

- Four main tables: "main" (represents a whole poem), "poema" (represents a strophic pattern in a poem), "author" (represents the author of a poem), "bibliography" (represents a book that refers to the poem) and "manuscrito" (represents the manuscript were poems were written). These tables will be represented in the conceptual diagram as four different concepts, and the concepts will have the same properties the tables of the logical model have.
- Two tables created to express the many-to-many relationships:
  ○ "References" relates "main" to "bibliography": it expresses that one poem can be referred by many books and a book can refer many poems. This table only has one key so it does not exist in the conceptual model;
  ○ "Testimonios" relates "main" to "manuscrito": it expresses that one poem can be present in more than one manuscript and that a manuscript can have many poems. This table besides the primary key (composed by three properties) has also a property that defines the location of the poem in the manuscript. This table is represented in the conceptual model only with one property ("localizacion").
- Five tables that represent lists, these tables might be a way to control the introduction of terms by the user. In fact, all tables have two properties: a primary key and another property with the same name of the name of the table (or very similar). These tables are "genre," "bibl_level," "language," "keyword" and "types." These tables don't appear as concepts in the conceptual model since they can be replaced by a property (see Table 9). "genre," "bibl_level," "language" and "keyword" can be repeatable properties, "type" not. In the MAP definition all these fields will be terms with a vocabulary encoding scheme as range.

Table 9. Mapping of the tables that represent controlled terms to properties in the REMETCA Conceptual Model

Table & Property Logical Model	Concept & property Conceptual Model	Property Cardinality
language - language	main - language	0 - *
genre - genre	main - genre	0 - *
bibl_level - bibl_level	main – bibl-level	0 - *
type - type	StanzaPattern - type	0 - 1
keywords - idterm	StanzaPattern - keyword	0 - *

The final goal of this work is to obtain a Domain Model that will represent the community of practice universe of discourse. To achieve that, it is important to standardize the names these community gives to things since the beginning of the process. The same concept should have the same name. So, when analyzing the logical models, the POSTDATA team started immediately defining common names among all conceptual models for all concepts and properties that represent the same thing. This is the reason why when comparing the logical and the respective conceptual model names are different (neither tables, neither properties). This process is iterative, after building one model, the work-team goes back to the previous ones already developed, revise names and decide if the names are appropriate or need to change according to the new findings in the new models developed. This is done during the analysis of all models.

Table 10 presents the correspondence between Tables and Concepts in the process of building the conceptual model of ReMetCa. A similar table exists for each table that maps the properties names of the tables to the properties names of the concepts. All MAP development project should document very well all the process (as Me4MAP states). These mappings will help the owners of the repertoires to understand the correspondences between the original logical model and the final semantic model of the MAP, and will help developers in the future to migrate the data from one model to another.

The POSTDATA team used stylesheets to document the process. Figure 7 presents an excerpt of ReMetCa documentation. The stylesheet has a first row with the name of the database, a second row with the name of the first table to be documented and the correspondent name of the concept in English. If the table is not mapped the field is left empty. The stylesheet has three more columns:

Table 10. Correspondence between the tables of the Logical Model and the concepts of the Conceptual Model of ReMetCa

Logical Model Table	Conceptual Model concept
main	Work
poem	StanzaPattern
author	Author
testimonio	Manifestation
manuscrito	Manuscript
bibliography	RefBibliography

Figure 7. An excerpt of the stylesheet of ReMetCa Documentation

	A	B	C	D
1	**Name of Database**	REMETCA		
2				
3	**Entity Logical Model**	author	**Entity Conceptual Model**	Author
4	**Property Logical Model**	**Property Conceptual Model**	**Description**	
5	idauthor	PRIMARY KEY		
6	mainEntry	name	Citado según el Indice de Autoridades de la Biblioteca Nacional, aunque quitando la fecha que aparece después	
7	seeFrom	identifier		
8				
9	**Entity Logical Model**	main	**Entity Conceptual Model**	Work
10	**Property Logical Model**	**Property Conceptual Model**	**Description**	
11	idmain	PRIMARY KEY		
12	author	FOREIGN KEY REF AUTHOR		
13	title	title	Campo obligatorio. Seguimos el indice de Autoridades de la Biblioteca Nacional, en su pestaña "titulo"	
14	uniTitle	altTitle	Campo no obligatorio. Recoger otros títulos o variantes por los que pueda ser conocido el poema. Dejar en blanco si coincide con el anterior.	
15	incipit	incipit		
16	genero	genre	Referencia Hismetca. Seguimos el indice de la monografía Historia de la Métrica Medieval Castellana. Escoger el grupo al que pertenece la obra.	See Work.genre
17	edicionBase	FOREIGN KEY REF REFBIBLIOGRAPH	Edición que sirve de base al poema sobre el cual se realiza el análisis métrico. Remite a la tabla BIBLIOGRAFÍA	
18	idBeta	identifierBeta	Número de 4 digitos: Ej: 8932 del indice de Philobiblon: http://bancroft.berkeley.edu/philobiblon/son los cuatro digitos que van después de la referencia BETA	
19	idDutton	identifierDutton	Número de 4 digitos: Ej: 2897. Solamente para los poemas de cancionero recogidos en el indice de Dutton. Para el resto, dejar en blanco. Puede comprobarse la referencia en http://cancionerovirtual.liv.ac.uk pinchando en "access the editions"	
20	url	urlText	Recoger en el caso de que el texto completo (o parcial) esté disponible en web, aunque presente variantes con respecto a la edición que manejamos. Tratar de recoger siempre que sea posible la url del texto completo disponible en web, aunque no sea una edición muy fiable.	
21	origDate	origDate		
22	notAfter	notAfter	Fecha ante quem. 4 digitos numéricos. Horquilla aproximada, si no se sabe con exactitud, recoger la horquilla más amplia	
23	notBefore	notBefore	4 digitos numéricos	
24	language	language	Seleccionar castellano, a no ser que sea un texto que tenga gran parte escrita en gallego. En cualquier caso, si la lengua predominante es el castellano, las variantes o interpolaciones simplemente se citan en el campo nota.	

remetca | Work.genre | RefBibliography.documentType | Work.keyword | Work.stanzaTypologie | Work.stanzaName

Column 1: The names of the properties, as they are called originally in the database;

Column 2: The names of the properties of the concepts. New names in English are given with the concern of standardization. If a property is not mapped in the conceptual model the correspondent cell is left empty. This can happen in cases where there is a bad modulation. In case the property moves to another concept, that should be noted in the correspondent cell. Keys are noted too.

Column 3: A description of the property

There is a fourth column in case the property has a range with a set of controlled terms (e.g. the property "genre" of the concept "Work"). In the ReMetCa Case these terms are taken from the database documentation available online. In other cases the controlled terms can be found in the MySQL dump file or in the combo-boxes of the public Web interfaces of the repertoires.

To document the set of controlled terms a new sheet is created with the list of terms, the name of the sheet is given according to the following convention: "NameOfConcept.NameOfControlledVocabulary" (see Figure 8).

The conceptual model of ReMeTca is presented in Figure 9.

The data elements identified in the activity S1 – developing the Functional Requirements (see Tables 6, 7 and 8) are all present in this model. There are other concepts and properties that do not appear in Tables 6, 7 and 8. In fact, S1 did not

Figure 8. A controlled set of terms documented

	A	B	C
1	Principios poéticos		
2	Épica y juglaresca		
3	Debate		
4	Noticieros e historiográficos		
5	Poesía clerical		
6	Poesía aljamiada y clerecía rabínica		
7	Poesía lírica castellana tradicional		
8	Poesía lírica castellana cortés		
9	Poesía hagiográfica y didáctica		
10	Poesía cortesana y cancioneril		
11	Oraciones y textos litúrgicos		
12	Poemas historiográficos		
13	Prosimetra: exégesis, alegoría y ficción sentimental		
14	Romancero		
15	Poesía italianizante		
16	Dramaturgia		
17			
18			
19			
20			
21			
22			

| remetca | **Work.genre** | RefBibliography.documentType | Work.keyword | Work.s |

bring any new information to feed this model. The database has more information than the one used in the public Website. Since the Website is in construction, POST-DATA expects other functionalities to be added in the future to the ones identified (use-case 1, 2 and 3), these new functionalities might use the concepts and properties of the Conceptual Model presented in Figure 9. Some of the properties of the conceptual model might be used also to implement functionalities of the Back-end Website.

The second example presented here is the repertoire "Digital Edition of the index of Middle English Verse" (DIMEV)[20]. This repertoire uses a XML database to store data. The repertoire's responsible sent to POSTDATA a xsd file with the XML schema of the model. The software Oxygen XML editor[21] was used to create a visual image (see Figure 15 in Appendix) of the scheme. This XML scheme uses a subset of TEI[22] as data model to represent texts in a digital form, in particular the module that TEI has for poetry[23].

The process starts by analyzing the XML schema in order to understand the concepts that each element represent. We identified four concepts: "Work," "Witness,"

Figure 9. Conceptual model of the repertoire "Repertório Métrico Digital de la poesia medieval castellana"

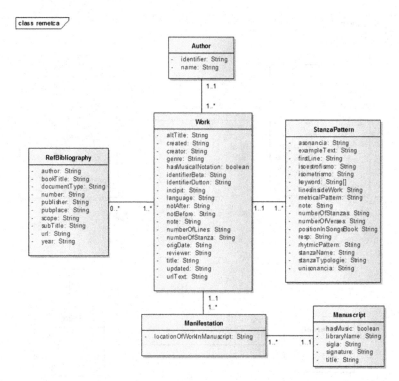

"Source" and "Interval." The main concept is the description of a "Work" (poem), a "Work" can have many "Witnesses" and a "Witness" can have many "Sources," a "Source" can have many "Intervals." "Work" has the elements "alpha," "descNote," "nimev," "imev," "name," "identifier," used only once per "Work," and "author," "ghost," "title," "subject," "verseForm," "versePattern," that are repeatable. "Witness" has the elements "allLines," "firstLines," "identifier," "ilust," "lastLines," "msAuthor," msTitle," "music" and "sourceName" that are used only once per "Witness," and "facsimile" and "edition" that are repeatable. The "Source" concept has two elements "key" and "prefix" not repeatable and the "Interval" concept has two elements "start" and "end" also not repeatable.

The UML class diagram of the conceptual model of the repertoire "DIMEV" is presented in Figure 10.

The third example presented here is the repertoire "Versologie" [24]. This repertoire stores data in perl objects. The responsible for this database sent to POSTDATA a script file in perl with a subset of data that represents the model (see Figure 11 for an excerpt of the perl file).

Figure 10. Conceptual MODEL of the repertoire "Digital Edition of the index of Middle English Verse"

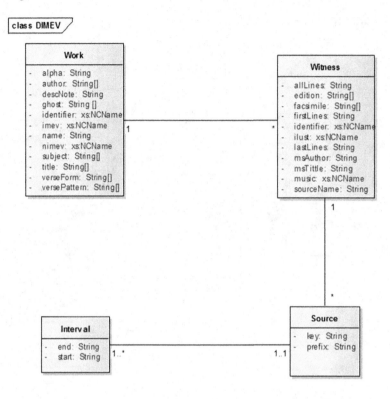

Figure 11. An excerpt of a Versologie perl script where it can be seen the data stored as objects

```perl
'head' => {

    # ============================= IDS =============================
    'id' => {
        # Id of a book from which the poem comes from
        'book' => '0001',
        # Id of a poem (unique in entire corpus - first four numbers correspond to the Id of a book
        'poem' => '0001-0000-0000-0001-0000',
    },

    # ============================= GENERAL BIBLIOGRAPHIC METADATA =============================
    'biblio' => {
        # Title of a book from which the poem comes from
        'title' => 'Na zemi a na nebi',
        # Subtitle of a book
        'subtitle' => 'Básně',
        # Year of publication of a book
        'year' => 1900,
        # Place where the book was published
        'place' => 'Praha',
        # Publisher of a book
        'publisher' => 'Unie',
        # First, second, third... edition of a book
        'edition' => 1,
        # Name of the library from which the book have been digitized & the signature of a book in library
        'signature' => 'Národní knihovna ČR, Praha: 54 H 2287',
```

The UML Class diagram of the conceptual model of "Versologie" is presented in Figure 12. The file presented in Figure 11 shows a top concept that is "Work" (poem), this top concept has several other concepts that are related to "Work": "RefBibliography," "Author," "StanzaPattern" and "Line." "Line" is related to "LinePattern" and "Word." "Person" is a class used to define a person that can be an author (sub-class of "Person" defined as the concept "Author") or an editor of books that refer "Work," these books that refer "Work" are defined in the diagram as the concept "RefBibliography". A book also can have an editor that is expressed through the relationship between "Person" and "RefBibliography." "StanzaPattern" is a pattern that exists inside a "Work." The concept "Line" represents every line of the poem ("Work"). Each "Line" has a specific pattern ("LinePattern") and is composed by words ("Word").

Both repertoires "DIMEV" and "Versologie" are on the Web of Documents so the POSTDATA team has also done the analysis of the Websites using the same reverse engineering process reported in the example of ReMetCa to model the functional requirements of those repertoires. There is no space in this chapter to present the two processes since the process is exactly the same and would not bring anything new. Both analyses did not bring any new element to the conceptual models defined in S2 – developing the Domain Model activity.

Figure 12. Conceptual model of the repertoire "Versologie"

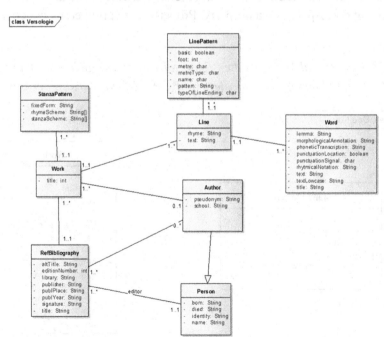

The fourth example presented here is the repertoire "Répertoire métrique de la poésie lyrique occitane des troubadours à leurs héritiers (xiiie-xve siècles)." It is a local repertoire implemented in a worksheet, in one single sheet. This file has the following columns: Domaine, Datation, Auteur, Référence, Schéma Rimique, Schéma métrique, Référence Frank, Désignation, Genre, Refrain initiale, Nbre Couplets, Réseau rimique, Tornadas, Rimes, Particularités, Mélodie, Remarques. This is apparently a flat model but some of the cells have more than one value and refer other cells. This means that there are two concepts on the sheet: "Work" (a poem) and "StanzaPattern" (the way a poem is classified). We can define more than one type of stanza pattern in the same poem.

The UML Class diagram of the conceptual model of the local repertoire "Répertoire métrique de la poésie lyrique occitane des troubadours à leurs héritiers (xiiie-xve siècles)" is shown in Figure 13.

Since this repertoire is a local Excel file there were no functional requirements to identify. The stylesheet has one only sheet with columns identifying properties, and lines, where each line is an instance of the concept and each cell has data of that instance related to the property of the column. No functionalities were identified.

All this work done with the Dimev, Versologie and Occitane databases is also documented in stylesheets. Each concept has its own list of properties, the process is the same as with the relational databases but since there are no tables, the process is slightly different. In the XML cases, elements are listed hierarchically and described, each element corresponds to a property. Properties are grouped by concept. In the

Figure 13. Conceptual Model of the "Répertoire métrique de la poésie lyrique occitane des troubadours à leurs héritiers (xiiie-xve siècles)" local repertoire

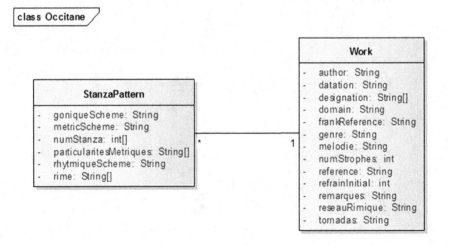

case of the perl file, each concept has also a list of properties defined in the file, and in the case of the excel file, all properties are listed since the model is very flat, but grouped by the correspondent concept (there are only two concepts).

The information that comes from all the conceptual models, together with the information that comes from S1, POSTDATA is building a common conceptual model of the European Poetry. It is important to integrate all the dimensions of all repertoires and also integrate other sources as already mentioned so POSTDATA can include as many concepts as possible in the common model.

RECOMMENDATIONS

To develop a metadata application profile is a complex task due to the uncertainty of the possible uses of the data. This specificity enhances the fact that:

- A method should be used to help to control the complexity
- The more information that can serve as input for the development of the domain model, the better

In fact, it is impossible to know all the uses the final users will give to the data. By "final users" the authors mean users that will manipulate software that uses the data, or organizations or persons that develop software that uses the available data. The more information is used as starting point for the modeling the more are the chances to define a good model. It means that many "realities" or "views" of the context will be represented in the model.

According to Me4MAP, the S1 activity (developing the Functional Requirements) and the S2 activity (Developing the Domain Model) should be done one after the other (S2 after S1) as presented in Figure 16 of Appendix. Nonetheless, in the context of POSTDATA the analysis of the Webpages of the repertoires was performed at the same time as the analysis of the databases and development of the conceptual models of those databases. In this case both S1 and S2 activities resort to existent documentation or to Web interfaces owned by the community that will use the MAP. The POSTDATA team performed the S1 activity at the same time as some activities of S2

The order in which activities S1 and S2 are performed depends on the type of resources the work-team has as starting point to do the development. Generalizing, when the development of a Domain Model (S2) is based in existent documentation or systems' analysis, this development can start at the same time as S1 since S2 is not entirely dependent on the results of S1.

Me4MAP defines the need to develop the activity "High Level Requirements." In the case of POSTDATA this activity is not yet explored, a reflexion has to be made in order to understand if there are more requirements than the ones identified due to the fact that this process is done in the context of the Semantic Web.

The POSTDATA team recommends though two changes to Me4MAP:

- Allow the S1 activity to be developed at the same time the development of the Domain Model (see Figure 14) in cases the MAP work-team resorts to existent documentation or analysis of existent systems to define the Domain Model,
- Discuss the possibility of defining the activity "Elicitation of high level requirements" as a non mandatory activity when the community of practice that will use the MAP has systems that can be the basis for functional requirements modeling.

The idea of developing a MAP using different sources such as MySQL dumps, XSD files, Perl files and stylesheets illustrates the versatility of the reverse engineering approach. A MAP development can resort to many knowledge already established in the software engineering community, since the early phases of a MAP development (domain modelling) have similarities with the early phases of software development.

Figure 14. Suggestion for new order of the activities S1 and S2 in Me4MAP

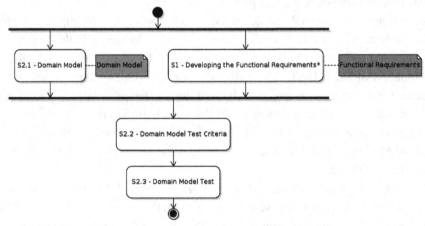

CONCLUSION AND FUTURE WORK

Poetry metrics measures and classifies poems counting syllables, accents, rhythm and rhymes to define the essential elements of the poem structure, its musicality and the type of contents that it shapes. A digital poetry metrics repertoire is a tool that gives account of metrical and rhythmical schemes of either a poetical tradition or school gathering a long corpus of poems, which are defined and classified by their main characteristics. There are many digital poetry metrics repertoires representing all European traditions, most of them in open-access in the Web of Documents. They are developed with different technologies and using different data models. Linked open Data technologies brought the possibility to open the silos of information that all these repertoires are and solve the interoperability issue that exists. For that, there is the need to define a common semantic model for all repertoires in order for them to be able to publish its data as structured Linked Open Data and become interoperable among all.

This common semantic model is a metadata application profile (MAP). The European Research Council (ERC) Starting Grant project POSTDATA is developing a MAP for the European Poetry following a method (Me4MAP) proposed recently by Curado Malta and Baptista (2013a). This chapter focus in the early stages of development of this MAP, and it shows in a very practical way what processes and techniques the POSTDATA team used to define the Functional Requirements and the Domain Model. This activities use as starting point the digital repertoires available on the Web of Documents, and a local repertoire. The modelling of the Functional Requirements resort to the analyses of the Websites by means of a reverse engineering process using the technique of use-case modelling. The definition of the Domain Model resorted to the analysis of documentation of the logical models of the databases, also by means of a reverse engineering process, to develop all the conceptual models of the repertoires. These conceptual models together with the Functional Requirements modelling and also information collected from:

1. Two Case Studies of researchers that are building a local repertoire at the same time the MAP development is in place
2. A survey that was done to final users, will be use to define the Domain Model

The POSTDATA team will continue with the activities defined by Me4MAP to develop the MAP for the European Poetry. In the near future, the testing of the Domain Model activity will be in place. This testing will be done with a Focus Group with representatives from all digital repertoires that were used as basis for the Domain Model development. After that the next main step will be the definition of the semantic model, that is, which vocabularies and terms will be used and what constraints should be applied to the elements of the model.

POSTDATA expects to have the MAP for European Poetry ready by the end of 2017.

ACKNOWLEDGMENT

The authors would like to thank all the repertoires' responsible for their availability in sharing information and discussing database issues with the POSTDATA team.

Mariana Curado Malta thanks the Polythecnic of Oporto for her 3 years' leave which opened the possibility to work in POSTDATA, a wonderful and challenging professional experience in Madrid-UNED.

This paper has been developed thanks to the research projects funded by MINECO and led by Elena González-Blanco: Acción Europa Investiga EUIN2013-50630: Repertorio Digital de Poesía Europea (DIREPO) and FFI2014-57961-R. Laboratorio de Innovación en Humanidades Digitales: Edición Digital, Datos Enlazados y Entorno Virtual de Investigación para el trabajo en humanidades, and the Starting Grant research project: Poetry Standardization and Linked Open Data:POSTDATA (ERC-2015-STG-679528), funded by European Research Council (ERC) under the European Union#s Horizon2020 research and innovation programme (http://postdata.linhd.es/).

REFERENCES

Antonelli, R. (1984). *Repertorio metrico della scuola poetica siciliana*. Palermo: Centro di Studi Filologici e Linguistici Siciliani.

Bianchi, A., Caivano, D., Marengo, V., & Visaggio, G. (2003). Iterative reengineering of legacy systems. *IEEE Transactions on Software Engineering, 29*(3), 225–241. doi:10.1109/TSE.2003.1183932

Bouillon, L., Vanderdonckt, J., & Chow, K. C. (2004). Flexible Re-engineering of Web Sites.*Proceedings of the 9th International Conference on Intelligent User Interfaces* (pp. 132–139). New York, NY, USA: ACM

Brunner, H., Wachinger, B. & Klesatschke, E. (2007). *Repertorium der Sangsprüche und Meisterlieder des 12. bis 18. Jahrhunderts*, Tübingen, Niemeyer.

Curado Malta, M., & Baptista, A. A. (2013a). A method for the development of Dublin Core Application Profiles (Me4DCAP V0.2): detailed description. In M. Foulonneau & K. Eckert (Eds.), Proc. Int'l Conf. on Dublin Core and Metadata Applications 2013 (pp. 90–103). Lisbon: Dublin Core Metadata Initiative. Retrieved from http://dcevents.dublincore.org/IntConf/dc-2013/paper/view/178/81

Curado Malta, M., & Baptista, A. A. (2013b). Me4DCAP V0. 1: A method for the development of Dublin Core Application Profiles. *Information Services & Use*, *33*(2), 161–171. doi:10.3233/ISU-130706

Curado Malta, M., & Baptista, A. A. (2013c). State of the Art on Methodologies for the Development of Dublin Core Application Profiles. *International Journal of Metadata, Semantics and Ontologies, 8*(4), 332–341.

Frank, I. (1957). *Répertoire métrique de la poésie des troubadours*, Paris, H. Champion.

Gómez Bravo, A. M. (1999). *Repertorio métrico de la poesía cancioneril del siglo XV*. Alcalá de Henares: Universidad.

Gómez Redondo, F. (2001). *Artes Poéticas Medievales*. Madrid: Laberinto.

Gorni, G. (2008). *Repertorio metrico della canzone italiana dalle origini al Cinquecento (REMCI)*. Firenze: Franco Cesati.

Hassan, S., Qamar, U., Hassan, T., & Waqas, M. (2015). Software Reverse Engineering to Requirement Engineering for Evolution of Legacy System. *Proceedings of the 2015 5th International Conference on IT Convergence and Security (ICITCS)* (pp. 1–4). IEEE. doi:10.1109/ICITCS.2015.7293021

Jacobson, I., Booch, G., Rumbaugh, J., Rumbaugh, J., & Booch, G. (1999). *The unified software development process* (Vol. 1). Addison-wesley Reading.

Linden, F., Schmid, K., & Rommes, E. (2007). The Product Line Engineering Approach. *Software Product Lines in Action*, 3–20.

Mölk, U., & and Friedrich Wolfzettel (1072). *Répertoire métrique de la poésie lyrique française des origines à 1350*, Munchen, W. Fink Verlag.

Moretti, F. (2005). *Graphs, Maps and Tress – Abstracts models for a literature theory*. London: Verso.

Müller, H. A., Jahnke, J. H., Smith, D. B., Storey, M.-A., Tilley, S. R., & Wong, K. (2000). Reverse Engineering: A Roadmap.*Proceedings of the Conference on The Future of Software Engineering* (pp. 47–60). New York, NY, USA: ACM.

Naetebus, G. (1891). *Die Nicht-Lyrischen Strophenformen Des Altfranzösischen. Ein Verzeichnis Zusammengestellt Und Erläutert.* Leipzig: S. Hirzel.

Nilsson, M., Baker, T., & Johnston, P. (2008). The Singapore Framework for Dublin Core Application Profiles. Retrieved from http://dublincore.org/documents/singapore-framework/

Nilsson, M., Baker, T., & Johnston, P. (2009). Interoperability Levels for Dublin Core Metadata. Retrieved from http://dublincore.org/documents/interoperability-levels/

Pagnotta, L. (1995). *Repertorio metrico della ballata italiana.* Milano, Napoli: Ricciardi.

Parramon i Blasco, J. (1992). *Repertori mètric de la poesia catalana medieval.* Barcelona: Curial.

Pillet, A., & Carstens, H. (1933). *Bibliographie der Troubadours.* Halle: M. Niemeyer.

Pohl, K., Böckle, G., & van Der Linden, F. J. (2005). *Software product line engineering: foundations, principles and techniques.* Springer Science & Business Media. doi:10.1007/3-540-28901-1

Pressman, R. S. (2015). *Software engineering: a practitioner's approach* (8th ed.). Palgrave Macmillan.

Raynaud, G. (1884). Bibliographie des chansonniers français des xiii. [treizième] et xiv. [quatorzième] siècles, Paris, Vieweg.

Rumbaugh, J., Jacobson, I., & Booch, G. (2004). *Unified Modeling Language Reference Manual, The.* Pearson Higher Education.

Sneed, H. M. (1995). Planning the reengineering of legacy systems. *IEEE Software,* *12*(1), 24–34. doi:10.1109/52.363168

Solimena, A. (2000). Repertorio metrico dei poeti siculo-toscani. Centro di studi filologici e linguistici siciliani in Palermo, Palermo.

Somé, S. S. (2009). A Meta-Model for Textual Use Case Description. *Journal of Object Technology,* *8*(7), 87–106. doi:10.5381/jot.2009.8.7.a2

Tavani, G. (1967). *Repertorio metrico della lingua galego-portoghese,* Roma, Edizioni dell'Ateneo.

Touber, A. H. (1975). *Deutsche Strophenformen des Mittelalters.* Stuttgart: Metzler.

W3C (2015). Semantic Web. Retrieved from https://www.w3.org/standards/semanticweb/

Zenari, M. (1999). *Repertorio metrico dei 'Rerum vulgarium fragmenta' di Francesco Petrarca*. Padova: Antenore.

KEY TERMS AND DEFINITIONS

Conceptual Model: Or conceptual data model expresses the knowledge of an organization through concepts and relations between concepts.

Functionality: A functionality is the set of functions executed by the system that transform input data in output data in a way that the user obtains a useful result.

Logical data model: A data model of a specific domain that expresses data in terms of tables with columns and relations between tables, or XML tags or object-oriented classes.

Poetry Metrics: Poetry metrics measures and classifies poems counting syllables, accents, rhythm and rhymes to define the essential elements of the poem structure, its musicality and the type of contents that it shapes.

Relational Model: A way of managing data that was defined by Cood in 1970 in the seminal document "A Relational Model of Data for Large Shared Data Banks" (see http://www.seas.upenn.edu/~zives/03f/cis550/codd.pdf).

Reverse Engineering Process: A backwards process of extracting knowledge or design from anything man-made.

ENDNOTES

[1]   See http://rpha.elte.hu/
[2]   See http://www.cirp.es/bdo/med/meddb.html
[3]   See http://www.bedt.it/BEdT_04_25/inf_home_crediti.aspx
[4]   See http://www.nouveaunaetebus.elte.hu
[5]   See http://csm.mml.ox.ac.uk
[6]   See http://webserver.erwin-rauner.de/crophius/Analecta_conspectus.htm (not available in open access)
[7]   See http://www.liederenbank.nl/
[8]   See http://www.corimu.unisi.it
[9]   See http://www.mirabileweb.it
[10] See http://dimev.net
[11] See http://icalia.es/troubadours/ca/
[12] See http://www.versologie.cz/en
[13] See http://www.remetca.uned.es

¹⁴ See Manifesto for the Digital Humanities from http://tcp.hypotheses.org/411);
      Mathew Gold's Debates in the Digital Humanities, A Companion to Digital
      Humanities from http://dhdebates.gc.cuny.edu/

¹⁵ "Web of Documents" is a term used in contrast with the term Web of Data. The
      Web of Documents is made of documents read by human beings that navigate
      between documents located in servers through hyper-links, it is the Web that
      everyone uses in a daily basis. The Web of Data or Linked Data or even the
      Semantic Web, three ways of expressing similar concepts, have technologies
      that "enable people to create data stores on the Web, build vocabularies, and
      write rules for handling data" (W3C, 2015)

¹⁶ Only draft versions are published so far. The first version of Me4MAP was
      submitted to an international research journal and is waiting for approval. The
      POSTDATA team is using this first version of Me4MAP not yet published

¹⁷ See http://www.oxfordlearnersdictionaries.com/definition/english/
      functionality?q=functionality

¹⁸ See http://www.remetca.uned.es

¹⁹ See http://www.mysql.com/products/workbench/

²⁰ See http://dimev.net

²¹ See https://www.oxygenxml.com/

²² Text Encoding Initiative, see http://www.tei-c.org

²³ See http://www.tei-c.org/release/doc/tei-p5-doc/en/html/VE.html

²⁴ See http://metro.ucl.cas.cz/kveta/

APPENDIX

Figure 15. Digital Edition of the index of Middle English Verse XML schema

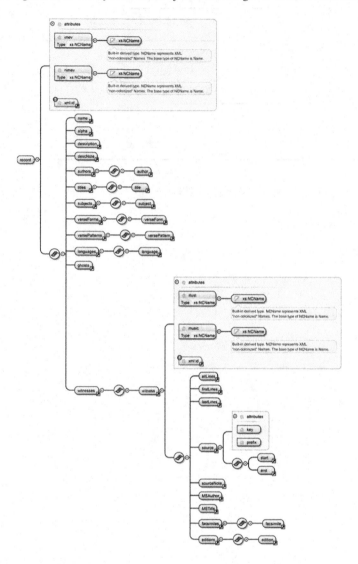

Figure 16. Me4MAP order of activities S1 and S2

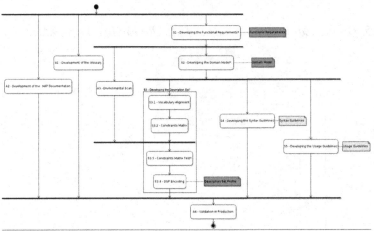

Chapter 8
Involving Data Creators in an Ontology–Based Design Process for Metadata Models

João Aguiar Castro
University of Porto, Portugal

Yulia Karimova
University of Porto, Portugal

Ricardo Carvalho Amorim
University of Porto, Portugal

João Rocha da Silva
University of Porto, Portugal

Rúbia Gattelli
University of Porto, Portugal

Cristina Ribeiro
INESC TEC/ DEI - University of Porto, Portugal

ABSTRACT

Research data are the cornerstone of science and their current fast rate of production is disquieting researchers. Adequate research data management strongly depends on accurate metadata records that capture the production context of the datasets, thus enabling data interpretation and reuse. This chapter reports on the authors' experience in the development of the metadata models, formalized as ontologies, for several research domains, involving members from small research teams in the overall process. This process is instantiated with four case studies: vehicle simulation; hydrogen production; biological oceanography and social sciences. The authors also present a data description workflow that includes a research data management platform, named Dendro, where researchers can prepare their datasets for further deposit in external data repositories.

DOI: 10.4018/978-1-5225-2221-8.ch008

INTRODUCTION

As the research environment is increasingly driven by data, research data management is gradually becoming a very important requirement for research projects. In the absence of proper management, expensive and irreplaceable research data may never realize their reuse potential; at the same time, their availability usually declines steadily as the publications age (Vines et al., 2014). While this is a problem for large-scale projects, it is even more prevalent in the context of research groups, or single researchers, in the long-tail of science (Heidorn, 2008), that often operate with very limited resources to ensure sustainability of their data.

To deal with this pressing issue, an increasing number of research funders are demanding research grant applicants to include data management plans in their project proposals - especially if public funds are required. These data management plans state, among other things, where and how the data will be deposited, preserved and kept accessible after the formal conclusion of the project. Major research funding providers are demanding such data management plans with recent calls for projects – examples include the European Commission under Horizon2020 (European Commission, 2013), and the National Science Foundation, in the US (National Science Foundation, 2011). Some publishers have also started to request data as supplementary materials to the submitted articles, under the assumption that their readers should be able to validate or replicate the presented results. Nature, for instance, requests authors to disclose research materials as a condition for the publishing of research papers. Another example is an Open Access publisher, PLOS ONE, that demands a full, unrestricted access to the original data for each of the submitted manuscripts. Following these trends data management is already an important concern for the scientific community.

The investment in research data management is important for many reasons: not only does it improve the chances of reproducibility and verifiability of the research results but can also prevent fraud. Another advantage of promoting data reuse relies on decreasing data duplication and the inherent research efforts to produce them. This allows researchers to directly focus their work in the project's specific goals, leaving more time to pursue an extensive validation or other research activities.

Research data management workflows involve both practical issues faced by the process stakeholders as well as technical ones. Sound technological solutions to support institutional repositories have been presented to reduce the technical issues, and we have seen great progress in that regard; solving the practical issues is, however, a challenge that is far from being settled, as it depends on fostering the interest of researchers to be active stakeholders in the data management workflow, more precisely in the description of their data. Data description assumes a critical nature in this workflow as it enables researchers with interest in a dataset to find and reuse it. Thus, the dissemination and preservation of research data strictly relies on metadata (Treloar and Wilkinson, 2008). Practical and technical issues are therefore related, and the need for high-quality metadata drives the technical developments often seen in research data management infrastructures.

However, data description is very demanding and time consuming, let alone the research process itself, so researchers are progressively investing in metadata creation, dealing with it during their daily activities.

This involves producing data from diverse sources and extracting their production context that is often kept in laboratory notebooks. By nature, such records follow an unstructured approach, strongly dependent on the researchers' perspective. When this is the case, researchers generate metadata that may lose their value upon the project's closure, as their interpretation can be problematic for external parties. In fact, an international survey demonstrate that researchers agree on the satisfaction of data saving in the short-term and the capacity to analyse the data they are creating (more than 70 per cent); however, the same does not apply for storing the data beyond the lifetime of a project, as only 44 per cent of them were satisfied with the access to long-term research data (Tenopir et al., 2011).

It is becoming clear that researchers must be perceived as central players in data description tasks, as long as they are motivated to assume such a role. Nevertheless, the short-term benefits of this activity, together with data management, are not always tangible for them as publications drive most of the academic reward system (Martone, 2013).

In this chapter the authors focus on data description as their approach targets the motivation of researchers to describe their data as soon as possible in the research workflow. Their past experience, along with emergent cases showed that postponing data description to the end of a project's cycle - when researchers naturally become focused on other projects - is very likely to yield poor metadata. This chapter is organised as follows: The next section provides the context of this work as it addresses data description and available data repository solutions. This section ends with a presentation of Dendro, a platform for data organization and description, in development by our research team at the University of Porto. The Modelling Process section discusses the role of researchers and data curators in data description activities and details the steps in the development of the domain-specific metadata models. In the section Case Studies the process is instantiated with four case-studies from the vehicle simulation, hydrogen production, biological oceanography and social sciences domains.

Background

The intensive rate at which research data is being produced has a strong impact in both the quantity and the multiple shapes of data that researchers are handling, making research data indexing one of the most complex tasks in the management of these assets. In contrast with publications, datasets are not very expressive by nature (often purely numerical) and require contextual information so that third parties, and other members of the research team, can understand them. Otherwise, their significance will be lost over time and research data won´t be reused. A scenario where research data becomes obsolete is to be avoided since many resources are spent in their production and maintenance. Therefore, metadata appears as a good solution to prevent research data from being wasted (Wilson, 2007).

Defined by "data about data" (NISO, 2004), metadata is an essential resource for data discovery, contextualization, detailed processing, and reuse in the long run. Metadata has become an indispensable component for the management of research data and for scientific communication in general (Willis, Greenberg & White, 2012). However, to produce adequate metadata for research data is a cumbersome task, and it is recognized that the documentation of data calls for the participation of re-searchers, who have to consider the trade-off between performing a time-consuming task with the no obvious short-term rewards for their effort. Hence, it is normal that researchers might feel discouraged to address data description consistently (Qin & Li, 2013), even though it has been demonstrated that datasets that are linked to detailed metadata records have improved citation rates (Piwowar, 2007). Although data citation is not yet generalized, data journals are gaining popularity among research groups (Candela, Castelli, Manghi & Tani, 2015). Data journals mirror the publication model, while also being pointers to datasets, and their papers are more easily citable than datasets. Data papers are also a source of information for the development of metadata models and a result of timely capture of metadata by researchers, thus demonstrating their willingness to perform such tasks, if the motivation is right (in this case, the citation of their data papers).

Data description needs can be radically different between domains, or even in the same domain, depending on the research group culture, data management pro-ficiency, funding agency requirements or others. By taking so many formats, from statistics to interviews, research data demands contextual expertise so that descrip-tion requirements for each domain can be fully satisfied (Cox & Pinfield, 2013).

A practical classification is to group research data under three categories from which data description strategies can be derived (National Science Foundation, 2005) (Willis, Greenberg & White, 2012). Observational data are the result of the measurements that are associated with specific locations and time, and once captured are unique and are usually archived indefinitely. Experimental data are embedded in laboratorial experiments and are produced under controlled environments, such as testing the reaction of combined chemical elements. This type of data is typically reproducible depending on the availability of information providing their context. Computational data are produced in computer model or simulation experiments and its replication require that all configuration settings are provided, such as the software involved in the capture of data along with the values for the corresponding input variables. Other types of data are those created in governmental, business, public and private life contexts that may also be useful for scientific applications (Borgman, 2012).

Metadata Standards

The limited number of research datasets that are shared by researchers can be attributed to the difficulties to deliver the metadata records containing information regarding the conditions on which the datasets are created (Faniel & Yakel, 2012). A possible approach to achieve higher quality metadata is to balance generic and domain-specific metadata. By using generic elements, from available metadata standards, in their descriptions, researchers are contributing to a more uniform and interoperable representation of their datasets, albeit only partially addressing data reuse issues. A more exhaustive approach requires the use of domain-specific descriptors for an in-depth and accurate description.

In this sense, scientific metadata standards are proliferating among several communities. This is the case of the Content Standard for Digital Geospatial Metadata (Federal Geographic Data Committee, 1998), that provide a common set of terminology and definitions for the documentation of geospatial data. Other examples are the Ecological Metadata Language (Fegraus & Andelman, 2005), documented in a modular manner to describe ecological data, and the Darwin Core (Wieczorek, 2012), which is composed by a set of standards to facilitate the sharing of datasets across the biological diversity community. The social, behavioral and economics community have developed the Data Documentation Initiative, an international standard for data description in these domains (Vardigan, Heus & Wendy, 2008). Other available scientific metadata standards are listed in the UK Digital Curation Centre´s Disciplinary Metadata Catalogue, which is part of an initiative by the Research Data Alliance Metadata Standards Directory Working Group (Ball et al., 2014).

To another extent it is pivotal to highlight the role of the European Commission, under the INSPIRE directive 2007/2/EC, in proposing an infrastructure for spatial information data sharing across public sector organizations (Bartha & Kocsis, 2011). The INSPIRE metadata recommendations include elements for the identification of resources, their geographic and temporal references and for the conformity with implementing rules on the interoperability of spatial datasets and services. Nevertheless, the INSPIRE directive considers the possibility for users and systems to combine elements from other metadata standards, if these are prescribed by international standards, to achieve more detailed descriptions.

However, even these metadata standards, tailored for scientific applications, are not without limitations, and their complexity and specificity makes their compatibility with the fast-paced growth of research data vulnerable. Furthermore, no single metadata standard is able to encompass the needs of every domain without compromising description accuracy, and many initiatives are seeking to modify or extend existing ones, in conformance with their local needs (Qin & Li, 2013; Wessels et al., 2014).

Realizing these limitations, some authors argue that application profiles are suitable solutions to deal with the diversity of domains and their metadata requirements (Heery and Patel, 2000). In this context the Dublin Core community, with the Singapore framework, is proposing a set of guidelines that application profiles designers must follow to ensure maximum interoperability and reusability of digital resources (Nilsson, Baker & Johnston, 2008). Included in these guidelines are the definition of the functional requirements of an application profile, the encoding syntax, and most importantly the domain model. This model includes the identification of the conceptual entities for the domain, which must be described to match metadata functional requirements (Qin, Ball & Greenberg, 2012).

Ontologies for Research Data

Ontologies have been recognized as essential tools for the description of resources on the Semantic Web (Berners-Lee, Hendler & Lassila, 2001), as they are knowledge representation structures that have the ability to capture the meaning of each descriptor used in a metadata record in a machine-processable way. A dimension of the convenience of adopting ontologies for research data management is that they can promote the necessary vocabulary agreement (Noy & McGuinness, 2000), thus establishing the common semantics of concepts shared by distinct entities.

Ontology representation serves as a means to obtain the expressive, accurate and unambiguous syntaxes, desirable in today's research data production contexts (Li et al., 2013). Essentially, formal ontologies are capable of setting the semantic baseline from which research data description issues can be tackled, and eventually escalate data reuse (Mena-Gárces, García-Barriocanal, Sicilia & Sánchez-Alonso, 2011), since they can be shared and evolved with great flexibility to establish relationships between datasets and concepts from different domains.

Being aware of the advantages of adopting ontologies for the description of research assets, many scientific communities are working to deliver research-oriented ontologies. A good example is the Common European Research Information Format

(CERIF) (Jörg, 2010), which is being adopted by numerous organizations and was first intended as a data exchange format for records describing projects. Despite its initial rigid format, CERIF has evolved to provide richer semantics, while its core set ensures interoperability between records. Another example is EXPO, an ontology that formalizes generic knowledge about scientific experimental design, methodology and results representation. According to the developers of EXPO, its main advantage is the fact that generic knowledge about experiments can be organized consistently in only one place, to ensure clear updating and non-redundancy (Soldatova & King, 2006). For a more specific application the Earth System Grid (ESG) and the Extensible Observation Ontology (OBOE) have been developed for the earth sciences and ecology disciplines, respectively. The ESG ontology has search and retrieval of datasets as its primary function (Pouchard et al., 2003), while OBOE is a formal ontology for generic scientific observation and measurement semantic representation (Madin et al., 2007).

Despite the fitness of these ontologies to model the knowledge structure of their domains, one may argue that they are too fine-grained, particularly ESG and OBOE, to be of practical use in an operational data management workflow targeting data description (Castro, Rocha da Silva and Ribeiro, 2014).

Data Repositories

Following the recent requirements in research data management, several platforms are being developed and integrated in diverse research workflows. Dealing with research data from several domains can be an ambitious task when different requirements are in place (Willis et al., 2012). These requirements are often related, at a lower level, with data description and preservation capabilities; these are, however, very likely to affect their longevity and reuse chances. On the other hand, at a higher level, user experience and integration capabilities are also crucial to ensure, among other achievements, that the platforms are adopted by their end users. An important factor that is currently influencing the way these tools are being developed is the fact that researchers are being increasingly asked to collaborate in the management of their own data. This makes sense, as they are the ones who can ideally provide better insight about its production context and meaning.

Data management services such as Figshare or Zenodo reflect these tendencies by presenting their users simple, yet capable interfaces for data deposit and description. They often take into account both the advances in the specification of preservation guidelines and the emergence of metadata standards to describe the deposited resources (Amorim et al., 2015a). Nevertheless, it is often common to find limitations regarding the specificity of the metadata standards that they adopt, as they have to provide data description to a large number of domains. On the other hand, depending on the requirements of institutions when considering the implementation of a platform for data management, hiring such services may be costly in the long run, and often poses serious limitations to the implementation of local requirements or platform customization. In this regard, several open source communities are actively developing solutions that can be locally installed and deeply customized to meet such requirements, while keeping a set of features that enable data dissemination through the established protocols. An example of these platforms is CKAN, which, although being used mainly by governments to disclose government-related data and contribute to administration transparency, also shows value when applied to the needs of research institutions. Also worth mentioning, other repositories initially developed to target research publications, such as DSpace and ePrints, are concerned with accompanying the tendencies which are materialized through the development of additional customizations or plug-ins to improve the capabilities of the platforms for the publication of research outputs (Amorim et al., 2015a).

When considering larger-scale projects that are also tackling research data management, the European-wide project EUDAT provides a collaborative environment that integrates both file management and sharing into a single, remotely accessed platform (EUDAT, n/a). Each of the active modules is developed following a specific project and its integration with the entire system is frequently updated, also allowing processing raw data directly from the platform and the connection with existing data dissemination protocols. This integrated research data management environment also incorporates the notion of domain-specific metadata. When depositing a dataset in the repositories that are integrated in EUDAT (such as GBIF, CLARIN, etc.), users must fill in a set of generic metadata descriptors and can also fill in additional descriptors, depending on the target repository. In this sense, a dataset from the biodiversity domain can have a different set of descriptors than one from the linguistics domain, for example.

Either implemented at an institutional level or as an online service, the number of available data management platforms is growing. Disciplinary data repositories, or similar platforms, usually provide scientific metadata standards that enable researchers to deliver more accurate versions of their metadata. The Inter-university Consortium for Political and Social Research (ISCPSR) uses the Data Documentation Initiative metadata, which can be exported as eXtensible Markup Language (XML), while also providing Dublin Core, Machine Readable Cataloguing (MARC) and DataCite versions of the exported metadata. Initiatives, such as the Global Biodiversity Information Facility, and INSPIRE, aim to standardized the way resources are described via the Ecological Metadata Language and the ISO 11915 for geographic information, respectively.

However, when data repositories are implemented with no specific community in mind the metadata is often generic and do not promote the reuse potential of the datasets (Assante, Candela, Castelli & Tani, 2016). Moreover, data repositories promote description at the deposit stage when it is already late to capture all the desirable information to reuse the dataset, while many datasets never reach this stage. Therefore, it is convenient to adopt flexible solutions that address the needs of researchers from different domains, and encourage data description early in the research data life-cycle.

Dendro, A Collaborative Platform for Data Organization and Description

It is acknowledged that data description should start as soon as possible in the research workflow, ideally as a complement task to be performed during the production of the datasets. This is the moment where researchers are still fully involved in the research process and are more aware of the conditions that originate their data. For instance, recording an event temperature long after its occurrence will surely impact metadata reliability. Dendro, a platform being developed by the authors' research group at the University of Porto, aims to tackle such issues as it offers researchers the opportunity to promptly register the underlying values of metadata for datasets, which is a desirable condition to obtain good quality metadata (Rocha da Silva, Ribeiro & Lopes, 2014).

In order to make researchers active stakeholders in the overall description process, data management solutions need to be easily adopted, and Dendro follows a file management structure logic in a similar manner to Dropbox – a tool that most researchers are acquainted to work with – along with collaborative capabilities, thus allowing individuals from the same research team to incrementally annotate metadata records. This collaborative facet, common in semantic wikis, is handy to ease the data description effort, while also allowing a research team to keep track of the resource's change log. Furthermore, Dendro is a fully open-source solution for multiple domain dataset description through an extensible, triple-store based data model.

Data curators are also key stakeholders in the Dendro platform workflow. This platform is founded in a flexible data model that data curators can manipulate and expand. The process to evolve the data model is fairly simple, the authors believe, as data curators with limited programming skills can create ontologies using tools like Protégé, and load them into Dendro. These ontologies are then materialized as descriptors in the Dendro user interface, to be combined with other ontologies previously loaded. As shown in Figure 1, descriptors from generic ontologies were already ingested in Dendro, namely the Friend of a Friend ontology and an ontology version of Dublin Core metadata standard, together with domain specific ones that the authors have created in previous experiences (Castro, Rocha da Silva & Ribeiro, 2014).

Although the creation of ontologies does not require programming skills, it does require conceptual modelling expertise and a thorough analysis of the concepts of the domain being modelled. Furthermore, the ability to add new descriptors into Dendro is fully controlled by the data curator, thus avoiding concept redundancy. This is one of the benefits of working with ontologies, since they enable the incremental approach of adding new descriptors as a data curator, or a researcher, sees fit. All the generic and domain-specific ontologies, and correspondent descriptors, are available and searchable to all researchers while using Dendro. Yet, it is easy for a researcher to be overwhelmed as more and more descriptors are introduced. To prevent this, Dendro has a description recommendation module, driven by the usage patterns, to assist researchers in building their own application profile, since the information of past interactions of a particular user is used to tailor the metadata sheets to the description needs of the same user (Rocha da Silva, 2016).

Dendro is expected to act as a platform for data organization and description, based on the principle that researchers are creating documented versions of their datasets early in the research workflow. By the time data reach a final stage in the research life cycle, and a final publication is written, core data can be packaged and sent to an external data repository and follow the regular deposit procedures. Moreover, if the process is executed quickly enough and is successful, the researcher can still cite the datasets in the publication itself, satisfying the requests of funding agencies and publishers.

Figure 1. A view over an open project in the Dendro platform

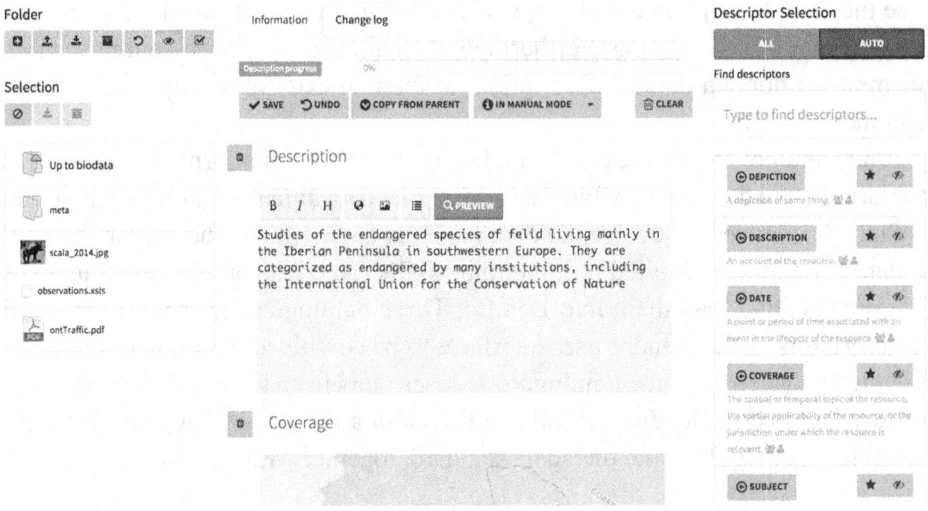

In short, Dendro aims to make the deposit process as simple as possible for users, while integrating with external platforms for the sake of interoperability. LabTablet, an electronic laboratory notebook solution, also being developed by the authors' research group is one example of the Dendro integration capabilities (Amorim et al., 2015b). Dendro also integrates with EUDAT, allowing researchers to export their described data to EUDAT's B2Share. The metadata gathered in Dendro is pre-processed to filter descriptors recognized by the EUDAT platform, through the existing API, while the complete metadata record is exported as an RDF file.

Modelling Process

Taking into account that every research domain or experiment configuration is likely to induce new data description requirements, a close collaboration between a panel of researchers working in different research domains at the University of Porto and the authors is currently assembled.

This panel of researchers is broad enough to gather a collection of datasets that correspond to the different types of research data: experimental, observational and computational data. The research domains represented in this research panel are diverse, including members from the analytical chemistry, fracture mechanics and hydrogen production research groups, which generate experimental data. Other groups are working mostly with observational data and are related with an astronomy laboratory, biodiversity campaigns and social and behavioral studies. Other members of this panel work in computational research environments, namely an operational research team that studies optimization problems, a research group that is currently evaluating the performance of electrical buses, and a team from the computational fluid dynamics area. Altogether, this research panel - and their datasets - provide a rich testing scenario for the definition of the metadata models that are convenient to apply in very particular data production environments, while taking into consideration a broader application and shared needs with other research contexts.

The main objective of this collaboration is to develop the metadata models that best suit the description needs of researchers, by selecting a set of descriptors that meet the daily terminology they are applying when working or communicating with their colleagues. Capturing familiar concepts that researchers can actually understand, and use in more casual descriptions, will likely mitigate existing barriers to data description processes, as it can reduce the complexity of using scientific metadata standards tailored for describing data at the end of the research cycle by trained professionals (Qin & Li, 2013). Hence, it is of utmost importance to promote the engagement between data curators and researchers in the definition of the metadata tools that will fit the latter expectations (Martinez-Uribe & Macdonald, 2009).

The Role of Researchers and Data Curators in Data Description

Academic institutions are ideal backgrounds for providing research data management services, and if some are already engaged in research data activities, others are considering doing so. In fact, data management services were pointed out has one of the top trends for academic libraries (Tenopir, Birch & Allard, 2012). Ideally, institutions should provide the infrastructures and services to support research data management, sharing and reuse (Heidorn, 2011).

Yet, institutions often lack the resources and struggle to support researchers' data management requirements (Rice & Haywood, 2011). A possible solution relies on having data curators, or other information specialists, as stakeholders on these services, as they can be part of grant proposal teams as data curation consultants for example. In big data projects, it is not unusual to have data scientists with domain expertise to perform data-related activities. Nevertheless, the same does not apply in the long-tail of science that may fall short in resources to deal with research data issues.

Data curators are aware of metadata best-practices and are becoming very participative in this environment, as they can assist researchers to foster data dissemination by improving metadata quality (Gore, 2011). Data curators and information scientists in general, can make good use of their skills, but in the long run their contribution can be less effective if researchers are not motivated to collaborate in the overall research data management process. Data curators have limited knowledge concerning domain-specific disciplines or research endeavours in general, being counter-productive for them to address data documentation activities in a wide variety of fields. Thus, the heterogeneity of scientific disciplines can prove to be overwhelming for data curators. Exclusively depending on them for data management can delay the whole process, considering that most institutions cannot delegate a data curator for each department or research group and, if this were done, it could yield unsustainable costs for small or medium-scale institutions. Therefore, despite their general metadata skills, by themselves, data curators will not be capable to provide timely metadata to face the fast pace at which research data is created, and eventually, this situation will result in a bottleneck in the research data workflow (Wilson, 2007).

Given these circumstances, researchers should be considered key stakeholders in data description and in the development of data management tools, such as ontologies. Taking into account their expertise in domain terminology and regular involvement in research environments, researchers, as data creators, are valuable candidates to produce accurate metadata records (Crystal & Greenberg, 2005). In this sense, collaboration between researchers and data curators is crucial, and both parties should co-exist in the development of the vocabularies to support metadata activities—researchers by providing insight on the domain terminology, and data curators, as information management experts, by working together to make datasets reach a larger audience.

Steps in the Development of the Domain-Specific Metadata Models

A first moment in the definition of the domain-specific metadata models is a meeting with both stakeholders in the description process, the data curator and the researchers. This initial meeting consists in an in-depth interview (Legard, Keegan & Ward, 2003) conducted by the data curator. The interview is a good methodological approach in this case since it provides the curator rich insight on domain knowledge. This knowledge includes information about the procedures and instruments that are used in research activities, data collection methodologies, in addition to how the research teams are handling, storing and sharing their data with their collaborators.

The interview is also the moment where researchers, in most of the cases, become aware of research data management problems and start to formulate them for the first time (struggling to find an illustrative in their archives; not being able to interpret a dataset originated by a colleague). During the interview, participant researchers also identify, by themselves, some research data management opportunities, such as the ability to partially disclose their data or consenting the access to the associated metadata record only, thus allowing other researchers, provided they are interested, to request access to the corresponding dataset.

The authors are applying an adapted version of the Data Curation Profile Toolkit script, translated into Portuguese, in order to "capture requirements for specific data generated by researchers as articulated by the researchers themselves", helping in the data processes decision making, while being flexible to be applied to any scientific sub-domain.

The questions in the interview can either be generic or specific as the following examples illustrate:

If you (the researcher) have to describe the research process as a series of data stages, what happens to the data in each of these stages?
How are the datasets organized and described? Do you use any standards?
Do you share the datasets you are working with anyone? Under which condition?

A better practice before running this interview is to allow researchers to read and consider the answer to each question. For instance, by sending the interview form by e-mail beforehand may result in more detailed responses. The authors argue that via this interaction data curators will obtain domain knowledge starting from the domain expert's point of view, and the domain expert can also gain a perspective on research data management from someone with prior experience on this matter. The performed interviews were recorded, with informed consent by the researchers, and also transcribed in portuguese. Since we work with four case studies, with results to be treated separately, there was no need to apply any software to analyse the contents of the interviews.

Furthermore, and to prevent researchers unavailability to participate full-time in the definition of the metadata models for their domain, the authors apply content analysis to the documents produced by the researchers, depending on the availability. Defined as a systematic, replicable technique for compressing many words of text into fewer content categories, traditionally applied to communication studies (Lewis, Zamith & Hermida, 2013), content analysis is a suitable technique that may be applied to other scenarios (Stemlerk, 2001). In this work content analysis was performed manually in order to extract the main domain concepts to include in the metadata models as descriptors.

The criteria for selecting these relevant concepts takes into consideration many variables or environmental features that are at the core of a given research configuration outlined in the document under scope, such as spatial and temporal variables, instrumentation, collected materials, type of samples and other parameters. For instance, a methodology section of a published paper is a natural source of information regarding the production context of the data to describe, as illustrated by the following experimental setup section in one of the papers scrutinized:

One of the most critical components of the simulation of a vehicle dynamics is the driving cycle on which all the vehicle calculations are based. (Perrotta et al., 2012)

This sentence provides the clue that the compound concept "drivingCycle" must be included in a vocabulary that is oriented to describe an experiment regarding vehicle dynamics, and the authors follow the same logic to derive some others concepts in their metadata models. Furthermore, for a better understanding of technical language one can resort to scientific dictionaries, thesauri, wikis, taxonomies and other controlled vocabularies.

Both the interview and the content analysis are useful tools to elaborate conceptual maps for the domain that are, in turn, at the core of the developed metadata models. To design a conceptual map is therefore the third step in the process to structure and formalize the knowledge of the data workflow for a selected domain. After the definition of the conceptual map, and having established the relation between classes and their properties, the key concepts are sought in metadata standards, particularly scientific ones, giving preference to those already formalized as lightweight ontologies.

After a selection of domain descriptors, another session is scheduled to propose those concepts to the researchers, and they are then also asked about the contextual information necessary to provide enough scientific evidence for others to verify, replicate, and reproduce the experiments from which the datasets were gathered. Finally the researchers are invited to validate the metadata model by evaluating the recommended concepts, and they can suggest new ones, remove or even rephrase the concepts. From the experience of the authors, the interaction with the researchers takes a total of three sessions, with a duration that can range between one and two hours.

When this cycle is complete, the chosen concepts are ready to be formalized as data properties in a lightweight ontology. All the concepts were given annotations specifying their *rdf:labels* and *rdf:comments*, since a natural language description of the concepts is adequate to facilitate their interpretation by humans and, mainly, because Dendro use the annotation properties in the ontologies to build its resource description interface. Moreover, lightweight ontology has weak constraints (Corcho, 2006), and their design is convenient due to their simplicity, when compared to highly specialized ontologies with granularities that are far too fine. Therefore, lightweight ontologies are easily processable by machines and easily managed by data curators, which makes them adequate for a research data management system, particularly for the use in resource descriptions tasks. Controlled vocabularies and thesauri can be represented via lightweight ontologies, and these vocabularies are usually used to assign metadata to web resources (Lassila & Mcguiness, 2001). The available Friend of Friend ontology is a good example of a widely used lightweight ontology. Finally, the developed lightweight ontologies, detailed in the next section, use concepts from existing metadata standards, if available, and purpose-built ones otherwise.

The domain-specific metadata models derived from the described process are built for particular domain requirements in collaboration with domain experts - thus they do not intend to comprehensively portray a scientific domain, but are focused in the data description needs of small research groups that are creating datasets in such domains. Also, these metadata models do not convey the notion of application profile, but rather a set of concepts that were identified together with domain researchers, that are to be combined with other descriptors to obtain richer metadata records. In return the application profiles are built as a consequence of the researchers' interactions with Dendro.

CASE STUDIES

Recognizing that every research domain, or experiment configuration, has different data description requirements, a collaboration with a panel of researchers from several domains at the University of Porto was established. The authors' goal is to provide researchers with the descriptors that enable them to obtain comprehensive and accurate metadata records. These domain-specific descriptors are expected to be simple and within the terminology used by the researchers, so they can be easily adopted in the production of well-documented versions of their datasets.

It is worth mentioning that the descriptors are only defined once in the domain-specific ontologies. This means that if two different domains require the same descriptor in their metadata models, this descriptor is only included in one of the ontologies, due to Dendro´s ability to draw descriptors from many ontologies at the same time and combine them in a single metadata record. This saves time, but the best benefit is fostering interoperability through concept reuse.

Research: A Generic Lightweight Ontology

In order to accommodate the domain-specific ontologies that are being developed, a lightweight Research ontology, that models generic multi-domain concept has been defined. The Research lightweight ontology consist in few classes that represent the structure of research types, using concepts like Experiment and Simulation, and comprehensive domain-agnostic properties such as the instrumentation, software, or method applied to capture the data.

By the time a new lightweight domain-specific ontology is developed one can subclass *Experiment* with a specific type of experiment (*HydrogenProduction*), from which the data properties identified to describe datasets in this domain can be instantiated. The developed lightweight ontologies are then loaded into Dendro; this process was already fully explored in two research domains (Castro, Rocha da Silva & Ribeiro, 2014). Figure 2 shows a partial view of the incremental integration of domain-specific descriptors (in this case hydrogen production and vehicle simulation descriptors) in the Research ontology.

A Vehicle Simulation Case Study

At the time of the interview the Vehicle Simulation research group was conducting experiments to assess specific parameters related to the performance of electrical buses in an urban environment. This performance evaluation is highly dependent on datasets containing the bus routes, such as the geographic coordinates, latitude and longitude where the bus will go through. These data are provided by a bus company

Figure 2. Domain-specific elements integrated with the generic Research ontology

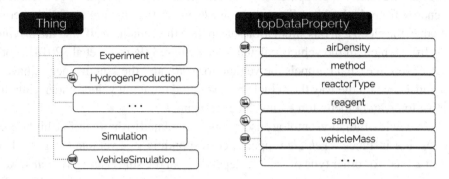

and each route has an associated file with the line schedules, allocated driver and distances covered. Other files contain technical vehicle properties provided by the manufacturer. To complement these data, researchers also need specific environmental information, such as the air coefficient or the surface roughness, which can easily be retrieved from the web, according to the interviewed researcher.

When this information is gathered researchers are in condition of running a simulation as close as possible to reality in a laboratorial context. After each simulation new datasets are created, and those are liable to different interpretations and can be analysed, or reused, according to any specific research criteria, thus justifying the potential value that these datasets hold to launch new projects. For instance, traffic engineers can use the data to study congestion points; others can use them to optimize the bus routes. Access to these data, in the words of the researcher, can also reduce field work endeavours, since the alternative is to go to the street and manually count the traffic data.

So far the research group working on electrical bus performance does not follow any particular research data management guidelines. The datasets are mainly organized as Excel spreadsheets, and when new external data arrives it is stored via Dropbox, and regular backups are made. For the purpose of searching for data, researchers basically trust their personal e-mail to keep track of all the entries. The research group does not describe their data, although the simulation variables can be part of a "ReadMe" file. This makes exploring the data harder than if they were registered as metadata entries in a proper information system.

To calculate specific electric bus performance parameters the vehicle simulation researchers have developed a mathematical model (Perrotta et al., 2012), that is prone to be changed over time. This model includes several subsystems; one that computes the required energy for a vehicle to complete a driving cycle and another that uses the kinetic energy of the vehicle to calculate the possible amount of energy that can be recovered from the regenerative braking. Other subsystems are related to the batteries and supercapacitors and evaluate if these are capable of absorbing the energy from the braking. There are high-level entities that are essential to contextualize the electrical bus simulation set-up, like the vehicle itself, and the driving cycle from which all the vehicle calculations are based (Perrotta et al., 2014). Both the tractive force, that compels the vehicle forward, and the kinetic energy, have a great influence on the way the vehicle behaves, and the input values underlying the tractive force and kinetic force must be documented.

The vehicle simulation ontology uses properties related to the identified high-level entities. For instance a *vehicle* property, corresponding to a vehicle category, like "electric bus" (or other type of vehicle depending on the study) and a *vehicleModel* property that records a very specific property used in the simulation (eBus-12), where defined in this ontology. Likewise, since there are many available driving cycle standards to be used in vehicle simulations, the *drivingCycle* property was also defined. These are properties with the potential to create access points to the datasets, as they can yield information that distinguishes a dataset from others. All the other properties deal with a set of variables that constrain the entire simulation and are tied to the calculation of the tractive force and of the kinetic energy. Values concerning the *aerodynamicDragCoefficient*, and the *roadSurfaceCoefficient*, are contextual environmental variables that influence the performance of the vehicle under scope, and therefore must be annotated to help others interpret, or reproduce, the outputs from a vehicle simulation (Table 1).

However, since the mathematical model is expected to evolve, so does the vehicle simulation ontology if needed. At a given time researchers can be focused on evaluating the battery's performance and battery attributes can easily be added to the ontology.

A Biological Oceanography Case Study

The Biological Oceanography domain in this case study includes researchers from three different groups at the Universidade Federal do Rio Grande, in south Brazil, namely: the Decapods Crustaceans Laboratory, a Laboratory of Ichthyology, and the Ecological Benthic Invertebrate Laboratory. A researcher from each group have collaborated with this work, thus the metadata model, and corresponding ontology for this domain, uses concepts that relates to each one of them.

The data production occurs in the context of three subareas in the Biological Oceanography domain that aim to assess the ecological interaction between marine and estuarine organisms along with their environmental parameters. These subareas are fishes, decapod crustaceans and benthic invertebrate organism´s ecology. The activities of these research groups are split in two moments designated as field and laboratory activities. Field activities concern biological material collection events

Table 1. The properties of the Vehicle Simulation ontology

aerodynamicDragCoefficient: A number used in calculating the aerodynamic drag of a vehicle
airDensity: The mass per unit of air in terms of weight per unit of volume
controllerEfficiency: The efficiency of the motor controller
drivingCycle: A series of data points representing the speed of the vehicle versus time
gearRatio: The relationship between the number of turns made by a driving gear to complete a full turn of the driven gear
gravitationalAcceleration: The acceleration of an object cause by the force of gravitation
roadSurfaceCoefficient: Used in determining the influence of the road surface properties in rolling resistance
tireRadius: The forward speed divided by the spin rate, for a free rolling wheel
vehicle: The vehicle used in the simulation
vehicleFrontalArea: The vehicle front end dimension
vehicleMass: The mass of the vehicle
vehicleModel: A parameter used to designate the vehicle

(ordinarily called collection) and environmental parameters registration, which produce mainly observational data. The laboratorial activities regard all the necessary interaction with the biological material collected in the field, which may involve some sort of experiments, producing both observational and experimental data. The data resulting from these laboratory activities are called "biotic data".

The biological material collected consists of the organisms studied by the researchers (fishes, crustaceans and benthos) and sediments (substrate deposited on the bottom of water bodies). Environmental parameters may be recorded during the collection events or be independent, collected according to previously stipulated intervals. They are called by the researchers as "abiotic data" and the main ones are: water temperature, salinity, transparency and depth of the water. The two field activities apply methods and use specific instruments and tools to gather all sorts of biological material and environmental variables.

So far researchers in this case study use mainly spreadsheets to manage their data, first in paper for field data, and then Excel for safeguarding. The electronic files are simple and contain, at the headings, the performed measurements, abbreviated temporal and spatial references, sometimes accompanied by captions that are easily interpreted by the laboratory staff. The data is often organized in the available computers, and eventually saved in the cloud, depending on each researcher. The interviewed researchers give priority to raw data for storage and preservation, since raw data can originate new studies, and processed data are already documented in publications.

Regarding data sharing, it is usually up to each researcher to decide whether data from their projects can be disclosed or not, because there are no established guidelines or commitments for this purpose. As a result, these initiatives are not based on standardized procedures and no data repositories are involved at this stage. Ultimately, sharing research data is only done if two or more institutions are involved in a single project. Nevertheless, the research team acknowledges that this collaborative scenario is gaining relevance and becoming more frequent as new projects begin. This collaborative environment flourishes mostly within the University, where data sharing occurs through the exchange of digital files containing biotic and abiotic data between laboratories.

For both field activities sampling events, spatial and temporal data are recorded. These were key elements during the process of building a Biological Oceanography ontology. Spatial data elements refer to the name of the place of a given event, specific sampling points, coordinates, among other. The temporal information is represented via the date of the events, their periodicity and the season when they occur.

After the field events the collected material is processed in the laboratory. The biological material captured consists in organisms and sediment, which are separated in a triage process. At this stage, researchers calculate the sediment elements, the individuals are separated by species and an inventory is made along with several measurements. In order to describe some of these processes the following properties were defined in the biological oceanography ontology: *individualCount*; *individualPerSpecies*; *speciesCount; observedWeight*. Other parameters also include what species were captured, the individual's sex and its life stage to address this description the properties *scientificName*, *sex* and *lifeStage* are also properties in this ontology.

To address methodology issues it is important for researchers to annotate a description of the sampling procedures used in the research project, and the final destination of a sample after the analyses are made also needs to be recorded.

The Biological Oceanography combines elements from different metadata standards or ontologies, namely descriptors taken from the Ecological Metadata Language (eml. prefix), from the Darwin Core standard (dwc. prefix), and others from the Ocean Biogeographic Information System (n/a) database repository metadata profile, which is an extension of Darwin Core (obis. prefix). All the remaining descriptors were included as suggested by the researchers from this case study, as illustrated in Table 2.

A Hydrogen Production Case Study

The research group at the CEFT (Transport Phenomena Research Center, Energy branch) is focused on studying phenomena related to large-scale hydrogen production via chemical hydrides. The main purpose of this research workgroup is to instanta-

Table 2. The properties of the Biological Oceanography ontology

eml.beginDate: A single time stamp signifying the beginning of some time period, like a sampling event period
eml.commonName: Specification of applicable common names, may be general descriptions of a group of organisms if appropriate
eml.endDate: A single time stamp signifying the end of some time period, like a sampling event period
eml.geographicDescription: A short text description of a dataset's geographic areal domain
dwc.lifeStage: The age class or life stage of the biological individual(s) at the time the sampling event
dwc.individualCount: The number of individuals represented present at the time of the sampling event
individualPerSpecies: The quantity of individuals caught per species in a sampling event
obis.observedWeight: The total biomass found in a collection/record event
speciesCount: The total number of species caught in a sampling event
sampleDestination: Describes the final destination of a sample after used in the research analysis
sampleIdentification: An identifier created at collection time to identify the specimen collected
eml.samplingDescription: Allows for a text-based/human readable description of the sampling procedures used in the research project.
dwc.samplingEffort: The amount of effort expended during an event.
samplingPeriodicity: This field expresses the time interval between sampling events.
dwc.scientificName: The full scientific name, with authorship and date information if known.
dwc.sex: The sex of the biological individual(s) collected.
eml.singleDataTime: Is intended to describe a single date and time for an event.

neously produce hydrogen to feed diverse Proton Exchange Membrane (PEM) fuel cells that can be used in a variety of portable devices such as cell phones or MP3 players. The experiments in this area focus on five main objectives, as follows:

1. Reactor optimization (smaller and lighter, with an ideal geometry);
2. Performance improvements through systematic feeding of reagent solution;
3. Storage of hydrogen in a liquid-based state through diverse additions (polymers, ionic fluids and other solutions);
4. Reaction output recycling;
5. Development of a kinetic model for the whole reaction.

Experimental data from this group is mainly stored in spreadsheets along with information associated with the environment where data was produced - temperature, involved compounds, pressure and other relevant measurements. Several connected sensors are used to extract this information, which is gathered with a specific software - LabView - that then exports them to the spreadsheet. Their workflow is divided in three main stages: first they produce raw data, which is then subject to error and consistency checking. At the last stage, raw data is then processed and refined to extract results and obtain conclusions about the performance of the procedure and the quality of the outputs. From the preservation point of view though, researchers identified the outputs of the first stage as the most important data to be deposited and preserved.

Concerning the collaborative scenario, the research team often resorts to traditional communication tools such as e-mail to share documents and data among them. In other cases data is copied from the researcher's personal computer to external hard drives, individually managing each access request.

When presented with the advantages of having research data published and accessible to either the workgroup or the scientific community, the interviewed researcher stated that it would be convenient to be able to test the reproducibility of their data and to retrieve the data associated with a specific publication, together with the associated metadata. To make their data findable and in conditions to be reproduced, hydrogen production researchers need to ensure that their descriptions include the predefined settings of the experiments. These settings involve the *additive*, *catalyst*, *reagent*, *reactorType*, and the type of *hydrolysis* used to perform the analysis. This kind of information serves as a pointer to facilitate the retrieval of datasets in this context, as a researcher may be interested only in a dataset containing the results of a powder reused *Nickel-Ruthenium* based *catalyst* experiment (Ferreira et al., 2010). Additionally, since the amount of water used in the experiment (*hydractionFactor*) and the number of times a catalyst was reused (*numberOfReutilization*) influence the hydrogen generation results, the corresponding values also need to be recorded. In the final stage of the experiment the researchers evaluate the results in conformance with the "*gravimetricCapacity*" and the "*hydrogenGenerationRate*", which determine if the experiment performance was positive or negative. All the datasets have valid results but only a few have satisfactory battery performance, and these are candidates to be used in the development of the fuel cell type PEM. If these values are registered the researchers can later easily identify the datasets that contain positive or negative values, and all results can be important for further analysis. Table 3 shows the descriptors that were selected to describe hydrogen production datasets.

A Social Sciences Case Study

Researchers from the social sciences domain deal with data from diverse sources related to interventions at different levels. The cases considered here concern the direct interaction with different social groups and the analysis of either their behaviours or their beliefs towards a specific subject. The produced data is extracted

Table 3. The properties of the Hydrogen Production ontology

additive: Type of additive used in the experiment.
catalyst: Type of catalyst used in the experiment.
gravimetricCapacity: Gravimetric hydrogen storage capacity.
hydrationFactor: Amount of water used in the experiment = 2+x.
hydrogenGenerationRate: Amount of hydrogen per minute.
hydrolysis: Type of hydrolysis reaction.
numberOfReutilization: Number of catalyst reutilizations.
reactorType: Type of reactor used in the experiment.
reagent: Type of reagent used in the experiment

from interviews - structured or unstructured transcriptions from such interviews, personal observations or reports, photos, videos or other multimedia-based support.

Data from these projects are considered to be very sensitive, as it concerns personal private information that needs to be hidden before the disclosure of data. Although some researchers already have procedures to anonymize data such as encouraging interviewees to use fictitious names, maintaining the overall validity of their data, this was often skipped in favour of a quicker access to raw data. When first approached, researchers from this domain showed awareness of recent, emergent data management practices. Projects from this domain were occasionally referred for data preservation, and there were already some guidelines for this purpose.

However, the guidelines were not available at the beginning of their projects, so some of the involved teams didn't actually put them into practice. The result was that their daily outputs were mainly deposited and managed individually by each author in their own storage solutions, lacking the other contextual description that would otherwise accompany such resources. Due to their diversity in terms of data sources, these researchers resorted to different tools to allow them to individually and occasionally share specific items. This often incurred extra time consuming tasks as some of these artefacts were hard to find. Among these tools, Dropbox and personal email were the main platforms in place to achieve such a collaborative environment.

From the interview with one of the lead researchers, having access to the data associated to a publication would be of a great interest if this data could be fully interpreted. This requires recording parameters such as the date of production, the characteristics of the interviewed population (if applicable), and the point of collection. Nevertheless, from a reuse point of view, this researcher did not see a substantial benefit in having data available to the scientific community and would rather have it managed within a smaller community. This is due to the fact that each newly created project already involves gathering new data, as old data tends to lose meaning and importance in this area.

After the domain analysis and the interview with a lead researcher, we were able to identify some of the data description requirements, specifically tailored to help researchers from this domain to better understand data produced by other collaborators in the same area. Some initiatives already have impact in this field, such as the Data Documentation Initiative that proposes a set of metadata guidelines to describe data from the social sciences domain, and is also useful to other domains that may directly or indirectly involve interviews. From this stage, we selected a set of Data Documentation Initiative (ddi. prefix) elements that were mostly needed for the purpose of data description in this specific case study. As data from this domain greatly benefits from clear identification of the interviewed population, spatial coverage, involved methodologies and time span for the interviews, the selected descriptors are listed in Table 4.

Lessons Learned

Our metadata model design process is based on the premise that researchers are accountable for the description of the data they produce, as long as expressive descriptors are provided to them. Thus, researchers are not only stakeholders in data description, but also in the definition of the concepts to include in the domain-specific ontologies. The design of the lightweight ontologies itself was a rather straightforward process, since these are not as exhaustive and complex from a modelling perspective, while their implementation as a part of the data model of Dendro is expedited.

Table 4. The properties of the Social Sciences ontology

ddi.dataCollectionDate: Provides a data range of dates for the described data collection event
ddi.dataCollectionMethodology: Describes the methodology used for collecting data
ddi.dataCollectionSoftware: Describes the software used for collecting data
ddi.dataSource: Describes the source of provenance of the data
ddi.externalAid: Any support given to the interviewee such as text cards, images or audiovisual aid
ddi.kindOfData: Briefly describes the kind of data documented in the logical product(s) of a group unit such as Qualitative, Quantitative or Mixed
ddi.methodology: Metadata regarding the methodologies used concerning data collection, determining the timing and repetition patterns for data collection, and sampling procedures
ddi.sampleSize: Size of the sample from which data was requested
ddi.samplingProcedure: Describes the type of sample, sampling design and provide details on drawing the sample
ddi.universe: Describe a universe which may also be known as a population

Yet, the main challenges of this work were related to the interaction between the data curator and the researchers, mostly due to the lack of published material or related work in this context, which certainly would add value to the dynamics of the first interactions with the researchers.

We also dealt with the researchers' neglect regarding research data management, specifically when data description is not, yet, a common practice for the majority of the research groups. In our conversations with the researchers, we observed a general belief that their current attitude towards data management is already good enough, despite the difficulties in sharing research data between group members, or finding a dataset of interest. Furthermore, this collaboration started upon request from our side, which may have limited researchers' willingness to actively partici-pate. Therefore, it is important to clearly show researchers the benefits of having their data described in order to motivate them; otherwise the many deterrents will prevent them from performing data description. However, the research groups in our case studies were motivated to be engaged in this work, and others are showing the interest to collaborate in the future.

Another aspect to consider is the researchers' availability to participate in the meetings. Although we adopt the same approach in all of our case studies, the amount of time to complete the process was very disparate between them. For instance, the meetings with the researchers from the Hydrogen Production group were conducted over a period of time of no more than two weeks and the meetings occurred in their work place. On the other hand, the meetings with the Vehicle Simulation researcher were scattered over a period of three months and, mostly, in our work place. So, this kind of engagement is time consuming and needs to be carefully planned.

There are two additional aspects to consider. One is the quality of the metadata that we are able to capture with the metadata models proposed, the other is the Dendro platform workflow. Thus, we have conducted data description experiments with the researchers to assess the use of the ontologies and of the Dendro recommendation system (Rocha da Silva, 2016). The results were promising, since researches were able to reuse the concepts that they identify for their domains, but also the concepts that have other ontologies as a source. We also verified, in an informal fashion, that some researchers left out some concepts from their domain ontology. This may be related to the fact that the resources they create may use a different set of concepts, making it hard to define an application profile comprehensively enough to describe all research data from a specific domain. Moreover, we intervene as little as possible in the experiment and the descriptions could have been more detailed if researchers were assisted to deliver metadata records ready for publication. A junior researcher, who participated in this study, stated that the Dendro platform was not useful for him since it had no descriptors of interest. This feedback alone strengthens our belief that researchers will not adhere to data description unless familiar descriptors are provided to them.

Further work is necessary to estimate which of the defined concepts are really relevant to the researcher and which are not, and to work on extended versions of the ontologies. From these experiments we have gathered evidence on description accuracy, since Dendro, at the time, did not validate the introduced metadata values. This prompted us to the development of controlled vocabularies. A first attempt to model the controlled vocabularies as a part of the ontologies has already been tested in the Hydrogen Production domain. Preliminary results indicate that researchers are able to create metadata records with more detail, in less time, when compared to the experiments without the controlled vocabularies (Karimova, 2016).

This line of work will continue to be guided by the feedback provided by the researchers, as we gather more and more research groups from the University of Porto. We expect that the knowledge obtained working together with the researchers, in the context of the data description experiments, will consistently improve our approach to develop ontology-based metadata models, and consequently pave the way to involve researchers in data description activities.

CONCLUSION

Digital technologies, and the way they quickly evolve, raise as many challenges for research data management as they bring opportunities for the research community, that are still to be fully grasped. The landscape of contemporary science is highly impacted by the availability of research data. This imposes many challenges, as researchers now have to deal with the correct management of these assets.

Metadata has been described as an important instrument for research data management, particularly by allowing data description in the first place, and its later retrieval and interpretation. Metadata production comes at a cost, and technologies have created the conditions for the upsurge of instruments that can be of great value to create metadata records. The scientific community is increasingly conscious of the potential of these instruments, such as ontologies, hence efforts have been made to deliver the vocabularies that improve the chances of data reuse.

In this scenario there is a space for researchers and data curators to partner and take advantage of their combined skills to develop domain vocabularies. To make data reuse more likely to succeed, it is important that researchers pay particular attention to the description of their data from the moment they begin to produce it, surpassing the problems caused by the mere adoption of ad-hoc practices to keep data safe. On the other hand, as research data management is a matter of concern for data curators, these should guarantee the deposit of research data into appropriate repositories, ensuring its correct indexing and classification.

The ontologies, derived from our metadata model design process, are not intended to fully represent the domains from which they derived; instead they capture the particular data description needs of the panel of researchers, detailed in the case studies. If the researchers need to provide extra contextual information, the corresponding properties can easily be added to the ontology and incorporated by the Dendro platform.

The developed ontologies, together with others from the panel of researchers, were loaded to Dendro as a part of an ongoing data description experiment. Preliminary results are showing that researchers can make good use of the descriptors that have been selected for their domains, while also using descriptors from other domain-specific ontologies, along with generic ones to improve the richness of their metadata records. Moreover, by exploring the vocabularies that they helped to build in the first place, in a concrete data platform use case scenario, researchers have developed a sharper awareness towards data management, and introduce their own recommendations to improve the proposed data description workflow.

Ultimately, the authors want to document successful stories of either individuals or research groups, with no prior data management knowledge, that have completed a research data lifecycle, from the moment of data creation up to the point where research data are submitted to a data repository and are ready to be reused and cited by third parties.

ACKNOWLEDGMENT

This work is financed by the ERDF – European Regional Development Fund through the Operational Programme for Competitiveness and Internationalisation - COMPETE 2020 Programme and by National Funds through the Portuguese funding agency, FCT - Fundação para a Ciência e a Tecnologia within project POCI-01-0145-FEDER-016736. João Aguiar Castro is supported by the FCT – Fundação para a Ciência e a Tecnologia (Portuguese Foundation for Science and Technology) under the PhD Grant PD/BD/114143/2015. João Rocha da Silva was supported by PhD grant SFRH / BD / 77092 / 2011 provided by the Portuguese funding agency, Fundação para a Ciência e a Tecnologia (FCT), during this work.

We would like to thank the reviewers for the pertinent feedback that has allowed us to improve this work.

REFERENCES

Amorim, R. C., Castro, J. A., Rocha da Silva, J., & Ribeiro, C. (2015a). A Comparative Study of Platforms for Research Data Management: Interoperability, Metadata Capabilities and Integration Potential. In New Contributions in Information Systems and Technologies. doi:10.1007/978-3-319-16486-1_10

Amorim, R. C., Castro, J. A., Rocha da Silva, J., & Ribeiro, C. (2015b). Engaging researchers in data management with LabTablet, an electronic laboratory notebook. *Proceedings of the Symposium on Languages, Applications and Technologies (SLATE '15)*. doi:10.1007/978-3-319-27653-3_21

Assante, M., Candela, L., Castelli, D., & Tani, A. (2016). Are Scientific Data Repositories Coping with Research Data Publishing? *Data Science Journal, 15*(6), 1–24. doi:10.5334/dsj–2016–006

Ball, A., Chen, S., Greenberg, J., Perez, C., Jeffery, K., & Koskela, R. (2014). Building a disciplinary metadata standards directory. *Proceedings of IDCC '14*.

Bartha, G., & Kocsis, S. (2011). Standardization of Geographic Data: The European INSPIRE Directive. *European Journal of Geography, 22*, 79–89.

Berners-Lee, T., Hendler, J., & Lassila, O. (2001). The Semantic Web. *Scientific American, 284*(5), 34–43. doi:10.1038/scientificamerican0501-34 PMID:11396337

Borgman, C. L. (2012). The conundrum of sharing research data. *Journal of the American Society for Information Science and Technology, 63*(6), 1059–1078. doi:10.1002/asi.22634

Candela, L., Castelli, D., Manghi, P., & Tani, A. (2015). *Data Journals: A survey*. Journal of the Association for Information Science and Technology, n/a, 90–103. doi:10.1002/asi.23358

Castro, J. A., Rocha da Silva, J., & Ribeiro, C. (2014). Creating lightweight ontologies for dataset description. Practical applications in a cross-domain research data management workflow. *Proceedings of the IEEE/ACM Joint Conference on Digital Libraries (JCDL)*. doi:10.1109/JCDL.2014.6970185

Corcho, O. (2006). Ontology based document annotation: trends and open research problems. *International Journal of Metadata, Semantics and Ontologies, 1*(1), 47–57. Retrieved from http://inderscience.metapress.com/index/8XNM4JJYF5JU6MXP.pdf

Cox, A. M., & Pinfield, S. (2013). Research data management and libraries: Current activities and future priorities. *Journal of Librarianship and Information Science, 46*(4), 299–316. doi:10.1177/0961000613492542

Crystal, A., & Greenberg, J. (2005). Usability of a metadata creation application for resource authors. *Library & Information Science Research*, *27*(2), 177–189. doi:10.1016/j.lisr.2005.01.012

EUDAT. (n/a). Retrieved from: http://eudat.eu/

European Commission. (2013). *Multi-beneficiary General Model Grant Agreement.* Retrieved from http://ec.europa.eu/research/participants/data/ref/h2020/mga/sme/h2020-mga-sme-1-multi_en.pdf

Faniel, I. M., & Yakel, E. (2011). Significant Properties as Contextual Metadata. *Journal of Library Metadata*, *11*(3-4), 155–165. doi:10.1080/19386389.2011.629959

Federal Geographic Data Committee. (1998). *Content standard for digital geospatial metadata, Version 2.0.*

Fegraus, E., Andelman, S., Jones, M. B., & Schildhauer, M. (2005). Maximizing the value of ecological data with structured metadata: An introduction to Ecological Metadata Language (EML) and principles for metadata creation. *Bulletin of the Ecological Society of America*, *86*(3), 158–168. doi:10.1890/0012-9623(2005)86[158:MTVOED]2.0.CO;2

Ferreira, M. J. F., Gales, L., Fernandes, V. R., Rangel, C. M., & Pinto, M. F. R. (2010). Alkali free hydrolysis of sodium borohydride for hydrogen generation under pressure. *International Journal of Hydrogen Energy*, *35*(18), 9869–9878. doi:10.1016/j.ijhydene.2010.02.121

Gore, S. A. (2011). e-Science and data management resources on the Web. *Medical Reference Services Quarterly*, *30*(2), 167–177. doi:10.1080/02763869.2011.562778 PMID:21534116

Heery, R., & Patel, M. (2000). Application profiles: mixing and matching metadata schemas. *Ariadne*, 25. Retrieved from http://www.ariadne.ac.uk/issue25/app-profiles/

Heidorn, P. B. (2011). The Emerging Role of Libraries in Data Curation and E-science. *Journal of Library Administration*, *51*(7-8), 662–672. doi:10.1080/01930826.2011.601269

Heidorn, P. B.P. Bryan Heidorn. (2008). Shedding Light on the Dark Data in the Long Tail of Science. *Library Trends*, *57*(2), 280–299. doi:10.1353/lib.0.0036

Jörg, B. (2010). CERIF: The Common European Research Information Format Model. *Data Science Journal*, *9*(July), 24–31.

Karimova, Y. (2016). *Vocabulários controlados na descrição de dados de investigação no Dendro* [Master Dissertation]. Retrieved from http://handle.net/10216/85221

Lassila, O., & Mcguinness, D. (2001). *The Role of Frame-Based Representation on the Semantic Web*. Retrieved from ftp://ftp.ksl.stanford.edu/pub/KSL_Reports/KSL-01-02.html

Leegard, R., Keegan, J., & Ward, K. (2003). In-depth Interviews. In J. Ritchie and J. Lewis (Ed.), Qualitative research practice: A guide for social science students and researchers (pp. 138–169). London: Sage

Lewis, S. C., Zamith, R., & Hermida, A. (2013). Content Analysis in an Era of Big Data: A Hybrid Approach to Computational and Manual Methods. *Journal of Broadcasting & Electronic Media, 57*(1), 34–52. doi:10.1080/08838151.2012.761702

Li, Y., Kennedy, G., Ngoran, F., Wu, P., & Hunter, J. (2013). An ontology-centric architecture for extensible scientific data management systems. *Future Generation Computer Systems, 29*(2), 641–653. doi:10.1016/j.future.2011.06.007

Madin, J., Bowers, S., Schildhauer, M., Krivov, S., Pennington, D., & Villa, F. (2007). An ontology for describing and synthesizing ecological observation data. *Ecological Informatics, 2*(3), 279–296. doi:10.1016/j.ecoinf.2007.05.004

Martinez-Uribe, L., & Macdonald, S. (2009). User engagement in research data curation. In *Research and Advanced Technology for Digital Libraries,* LNCS (Vol. *5714,* pp. 309–314). Retrieved from http://www.springerlink.com/content/7mnq1 3x34717p48310.1007/978-3-642-04346-8_30

Martone, M. E. (2013). Brain and Behavior: We want you to share your data. *Brain and Behavior, 4*(1). doi:10.1002/brb3.192 PMID:24653948

Mena-Garcés, E., García-Barriocanal, E., Sicilia, M.-A., & Sánchez-Alonso, S. (2011). Moving from dataset metadata to semantics in ecological research: A case in translating EML to OWL. *Procedia Computer Science, 4,* 1622–1630. doi:10.1016/j.procs.2011.04.175

National Information Standards Organization. (2004). Understanding Metadata. MD: NISO Press. doi:10.1017/S0003055403000534

National Science Foundation. (2005). *Long-Lived Digital Data Collections: Enabling Research and Education in the 21st Century*. Retrieved from: http://www.nsf.gov/pubs/2005/nsb0540/nsb0540.pdf

National Science Foundation. (2011). Grants.Gov Application Guide A Guide for Preparation and Submission of NSF Applications via Grants.gov. Retrieved from http://www.nsf.gov/pubs/policydocs/grantsgovguide0113.pdf

Nilsson, M., Baker, T., & Johnston, Pete. (January, 2008). *The Singapore Framework for Dublin Core Application Profiles*. Retrieved from http://dublincore.org/documents/singapore-framework/

Noy, N. F., & Mcguinness, D. L. (2000). *Ontology Development 101*: A *Guide to Creating Your First Ontology*. Retrieved from http://protege.stanford.edu/publications/ontology_development/ontology101.pdf

Ocean Biogeographic Information System. (n. d.). Retrieved from http://www.iobis.org/

Perrotta, D., Macedo, J. L., Rossetti, R. J. F., De Sousa, J. F., Kokkinogenis, Z., Ribeiro, B., & Afonso, J. L. (2014). Route Planning for Electric Buses: A Case Study in Oporto. *Procedia: Social and Behavioral Sciences*, *111*, 1004–1014. doi:10.1016/j.sbspro.2014.01.135

Perrotta, D., Teixeira, A., Silva, H., Ribeiro, B., & Afonso, J. (2012). Electrical Bus Performance Modeling for Urban Environments. *SAE Int. J. Alt. Power*, *1*(1), 34–45. doi:10.4271/2012-01-0200

Piwowar, H. A., Day, R. B., & Fridsma, D. S. (2007). *Sharing detailed research data is associated with increased citation rate. PLoS ONE*, *2*(3), e308. doi:10.1371/journal.pone.0000308 PMID:17375194

Pouchard, L., Cinquini, L., & Strand, G. (2003). The Earth System Grid Discovery and Semantic Web Technologies. In *Workshop for Semantic Web Technologies for Searching and Retrieving Scientific Data - 2nd International Semantic Web Conference* (pp. 1–6).

Qin, J., & LI, K. (2013). How Portable Are the Metadata Standards for Scientific Data? A Proposal for a Metadata Infrastructure.*Proceedings of the International Conference on Dublin Core and Metadata Applications* (pp. 25–34).

Qin, J., Ball, A., & Greenberg, J. (2012). Functional and Architectural Requirements for Metadata: Supporting Discovery and Management of Scientific Data.*Proceedings of the International Conference on Dublin Core and Metadata Applications* (pp. 62–71).

Rice, R., & Haywood, J. (2011). Research data management initiatives at University of Edinburgh. *International Journal of Digital Curation*, 6(2), 232–244. Retrieved from http://www.ijdc.net/index.php/ijdc/article/view/194 doi:10.2218/ijdc.v6i2.199

Rocha da Silva, J. (2016). *Usage-driven Application Profile Generation Using Ontologies* [Doctoral Dissertation]. Retrieved from (http://hdl.handle.net/10216.83993)

Rocha da Silva, J., Castro, J. A., Ribeiro, C., Honrado, J., Lomba, Â., & Gonçalves, J. (2014). Beyond INSPIRE: An Ontology for Biodiversity Metadata Records. In *On the Move to Meaningful Internet Systems: OTM 2014 Workshops* (Vol. 8842, pp. 597–607). doi:10.1007/978-3-662-45550-0_61

Rocha da Silva, J., Castro, J. A., Ribeiro, C., & Lopes, J. C. (2014). Dendro: collaborative research data management built on linked open data. *Proceedings of the 11th European Semantic Web Conference.* Retrieved from http://2014.eswc-conferences. org/sites/default/files/eswc2014pd_submission_54.pdf

Rocha da Silva, J., Ribeiro, C., Barbosa, J., Gouveia, M., & Lopes, J. C. (2013). UPBox and Data Notes: a collaborative data management environment for the long tail of research data. *Proceedings of the iPres 2013 Conference.*

Rocha da Silva, J. R., Cristina, R., & Lopes, J. C. (2012). Semi-automated application profile generation for research data assets. *Proceedings of the Metadata and Semantics Research Conference (MTSR '12).* Retrieved from http://www.springer. com/series/7899

Soldatova, L. N., & King, R. R. D. (2006). An ontology of Scientific Experiments. *Journal of the Royal Society, Interface*, 3(11), 795–803. doi:10.1098/rsif.2006.0134 PMID:17015305

Stemler, S. (2001). An overview of Content Analysis. *Practical Assessment, Research & Evaluation*, 7(17), 137–146.

Tenopir, C., Allard, S., Douglass, K., Aydinoglu, A. U., Wu, L., Read, E., & Frame, M. et al. (2011). Data Sharing by Scientists: Practices and Perceptions. *PLoS ONE*, 6(6), e21101. doi:10.1371/journal.pone.0021101 PMID:21738610

Tenopir, C., Birch, B., & Allard, S. (2012). *Academic libraries and research data services.* Current practices and plans for the future - An ACRL White Paper.

Treloar, A., & Wilkinson, R. (2008). Rethinking Metadata Creation and Management in a Data-Driven Research World. *Proceedings of the IEEE Fourth International Conference on eScience* (pp. 782–789). doi:10.1109/eScience.2008.41

Vardigan, M., Heus, P., & Thomas, W. (2008). Data Documentation Initiative: Toward a Standard tor the Social Sciences. *The International Journal of Digital Curation, 3*(1), 107–113. Retrieved from http://onlinelibrary.wiley.com/doi/10.1002/cbdv.200490137/abstract doi:10.2218/ijdc.v3i1.45

Vines, T. H., Albert, A. Y. K., Andrew, R. L., Débarre, F., Bock, D. G., Franklin, M. T., & Rennison, D. et al. (2014). The availability of research data declines rapidly with article age. *Current Biology, 24*(1), 94–97. doi:10.1016/j.cub.2013.11.014 PMID:24361065

Wessels, B., Finn, R. L., Linde, P., Mazzetti, P., Nativi, S., Riley, S., & Wyatt, S. et al. (2014). *Issues in the development of open access to research data.* Prometheus. *Critical Studies in Innovation, 32*(1), 49–66. doi:10.1080/08109028.2014.956505

Wieczorek, J., Bloom, D., Guralnick, R., Blum, S., Döring, M., Giovanni, R., & Vieglais, D. et al. (2012). Darwin core: An evolving community-developed biodiversity data standard. *PLoS ONE, 7*(1), e29715. doi:10.1371/journal.pone.0029715 PMID:22238640

Willis, C., Greenberg, J., & White, H. (2012). Analysis and Synthesis of Metadata Goals for Scientific Data. *Journal of the American Society for Information Science and Technology, 63*(8), 1505–1520. doi:10.1002/asi.22683

Wilson, A. J. (2007). Toward Releasing the Metadata Bottleneck A Baseline Evaluation of Contributor-supllied Metadata. *Library Resources & Technical Services, 51*(1), 16–28. doi:10.5860/lrts.51n1.16

KEY TERMS AND DEFINITIONS

Biological Oceanography: Studies of marine species and their influence and evolution in different marine ecosystems.

Data Repository: A platform designed to provide a layer of data storage with additional management capabilities that can range from data description to dataset preservation.

Hydrogen Production: Set of procedures and studies to evaluate and improve the performance of large-scale hydrogen generation.

Ontology: A formal representation of classes, properties and relations, which can help representing knowledge in a machine-readable format while allowing reasoning.

Research Data Management: Set of tasks for a proper data handling ensuring their transition from the researcher's daily outputs up to their later deposit and long-term preservation.

Social Sciences: Studies that target social groups as a mean to extract valuable information about their social interactions and evaluate their involvement in society and citizenship.

Vehicle Simulation: Studies related to simulation of traffic interaction and behaviour to achieve a faithful representation of real-world scenarios.

Compilation of References

Abode Systems. (n.d.). Adobe XMP developer center. Retrieved May 15, 2016, from http://www.adobe.com/devnet/xmp.html

Ahlers, D. (2013). Assessment of the accuracy of GeoNames gazetteer data. In C. Jones & R. Purves (Eds.), *Proceedings of the 7th Workshop on Geographic Information Retrieval, GIR '13,* New York, NY, USA (pp. 74-81). doi:10.1145/2533888.2533938

Amorim, R. C., Castro, J. A., Rocha da Silva, J., & Ribeiro, C. (2015a). A Comparative Study of Platforms for Research Data Management: Interoperability, Metadata Capabilities and Integration Potential. In New Contributions in Information Systems and Technologies. doi:10.1007/978-3-319-16486-1_10

Amorim, R. C., Castro, J. A., Rocha da Silva, J., & Ribeiro, C. (2015b). Engaging researchers in data management with LabTablet, an electronic laboratory notebook. *Proceedings of the Symposium on Languages, Applications and Technologies (SLATE '15).* doi:10.1007/978-3-319-27653-3_21

Antonelli, R. (1984). *Repertorio metrico della scuola poetica siciliana.* Palermo: Centro di Studi Filologici e Linguistici Siciliani.

Assante, M., Candela, L., Castelli, D., & Tani, A. (2016). Are Scientific Data Repositories Coping with Research Data Publishing? *Data Science Journal, 15*(6), 1–24. doi:10.5334/dsj–2016–006

Athanasiadis, N., Sotiriou, S., Zervas, P., & Sampson, D. G. (2014). The Open Discovery Space Portal: A Socially-Powered and Open Federated Infrastructure. In D. G. Sampson, D. Ifenthaler, J. M. Spector, & P. Isaias (Eds.), *Digital Systems for Open Access to Formal and Informal Learning* (pp. 11–23). USA: Springer International Publishing.

Baghdadi, N., Leroy, M., Maurel, P., Cherchali, S., Stoll, M., Faure, J. F.,... Pacholc-zyk, P. (2015, September). The Theia land Data Centre. *Proceedings of International Society of Photogrammetry and Remote Sensing Conference – RSDI Workshop*, Montpellier, France.

Baker, T., & Coyle, K. (2009). Guidelines for Dublin Core Application Profiles. Retrieved April 12, 2016, from http://dublincore.org/documents/profile-guidelines/

Ball, A., & Thangarajah, U. (2012). *RAIDmap application developer guide*. Retrieved from http://opus.bath.ac.uk/30098

Ball, A., Chen, S., Greenberg, J., Perez, C., Jeffery, K., & Koskela, R. (2014). Building a disciplinary metadata standards directory. *Proceedings of IDCC '14*.

Ball, A., Darlington, M., Howard, T., McMahon, C., & Culley, S. (2012). Visualizing research data records for their better management. *Journal of Digital Information*, *13*(1). Retrieved from https://journals.tdl.org/jodi/article/view/5917/5892

Ball, A., Patel, M., McMahon, C., Green, S., Clarkson, J., & Culley, S. (2006). A grand challenge: Immortal information and through-life knowledge management (KIM). *International Journal of Digital Curation*, *1*(1), 53–59. doi:10.2218/ijdc.v1i1.5

Barker, P., & Campbell, L. (2014, April 23-25). Learning Resource Metadata Initiative: Using Schema.org to Describe Open Educational Resources. Proc. of the Open-CourseWare Consortium Global 2014 (OCWC Global 2014), Ljubljana, Slovenia.

Bartha, G., & Kocsis, S. (2011). Standardization of Geographic Data: The European INSPIRE Directive. *European Journal of Geography*, *22*, 79–89.

Berners-Lee, T., Hendler, J., & Lassila, O. (2001). The Semantic Web. *Scientific American*, *284*(5), 34–43. doi:10.1038/scientificamerican0501-34 PMID:11396337

Bianchi, A., Caivano, D., Marengo, V., & Visaggio, G. (2003). Iterative reengineering of legacy systems. *IEEE Transactions on Software Engineering*, *29*(3), 225–241. doi:10.1109/TSE.2003.1183932

Boneva, I., & Prud'hommeaux, E. (2016) *Shape Expressions Language*. Retrieved from https://shexspec.github.io/spec

Booch, G., Jacobson, I., & Rumbaugh, J. (1999). *The unified software development process* (1st ed.). Addison-Wesley Professional.

Borgman, C. L. (2012). The conundrum of sharing research data. *Journal of the American Society for Information Science and Technology, 63*(6), 1059–1078. doi:10.1002/asi.22634

Bouillon, L., Vanderdonckt, J., & Chow, K. C. (2004). Flexible Re-engineering of Web Sites.*Proceedings of the 9th International Conference on Intelligent User Interfaces* (pp. 132–139). New York, NY, USA: ACM

Bradner, S. (1997). *Key words for use in RFCs to Indicate Requirement Levels.* Harvard University. Retrieved from http://www.ietf.org/rfc/rfc2119.txt

Brockmans, S., Colomb, R. M., Haase, P., Kendall, E. F., Wallace, E. K., Welty, C., & Xie, G. T. (2006, November). A model driven approach for building OWL DL and OWL full ontologies. *Proceedings of theInternational Semantic Web Conference* (pp. 187-200). Berlin: Springer. doi:10.1007/11926078_14

Brunner, H., Wachinger, B. & Klesatschke, E. (2007). *Repertorium der Sangsprüche und Meisterlieder des 12. bis 18. Jahrhunderts*, Tübingen, Niemeyer.

C.U.R.L. Exemplars in Digital Archives. (2000). Metadata for digital preservation: The Cedars Project outline specification. Retrieved from http://www.webarchive. org.uk/wayback/archive/20050111120000/http://www.leeds.ac.uk/cedars/colman/ metadata/metadataspec.html

Candela, L., Castelli, D., Manghi, P., & Tani, A. (2015). *Data Journals: A survey.* Journal of the Association for Information Science and Technology, n/a, 90–103. doi:10.1002/asi.23358

Caplan, P. (2006). Preservation metadata. In S. Ross & M. Day (Eds.), DCC Digital Curation Manual. Edinburgh, UK: Digital Curation Centre. Retrieved from http:// www.dcc.ac.uk/resource/curation-manual/chapters/preservation-metadata/

Castro, J. A., Rocha da Silva, J., & Ribeiro, C. (2014). Creating lightweight ontologies for dataset description. Practical applications in a cross-domain research data management workflow. *Proceedings of theIEEE/ACM Joint Conference on Digital Libraries (JCDL).* doi:10.1109/JCDL.2014.6970185

Cattani, A. D., Laville, J.-L., Gaiger, L. I., & Hespanha, P. (2009). *Dicionário Internacional da Outra Economia.* CES.

CEN. (2005). CWA 15248:2005. Guidelines for machine-processable representation of Dublin Core Application Profiles. European Committee of Standardization. Retrieved from http://dublincore.org/moinmoin-wiki-archive/architecturewiki/attachments/cen-cwa15248.pdf

Clark, J., & Makoto, M. (2001) *RELAX NG Specification*. Retrieved from http://relaxing.org/spec-20011203.html

Conole, G. (2013). *Open Educational Resources. In Designing for Learning in an Open World* (pp. 225–243). NY, USA: Springer International Publishing. doi:10.1007/978-1-4419-8517-0

Consultative Committee for Space Data Systems. (2002). *Reference model for an Open Archival Information System (OAIS)* (Blue Book No. CCSDS 650.0-B-1). Retrieved from http://www.ccsds.org/documents/650x0b1.pdf

Consultative Committee for Space Data Systems. (2012). *Reference model for an Open Archival Information System (OAIS)* (Magenta Book No. CCSDS 650.0-M-2). Retrieved from http://www.ccsds.org/documents/650x0m2.pdf

Corcho, O. (2006). Ontology based document annotation: trends and open research problems. *International Journal of Metadata, Semantics and Ontologies*, 1(1), 47–57. Retrieved from http://inderscience.metapress.com/index/8XNM4JJYF5JU6MXP.pdf

Cossu, R., Pacini, F., Brito, F., Fusco, L., Santi, E. L., & Parrini, A. (2010, October). GENESI-DEC: a federative e-infrastructure for Earth Science data discovery, access, and on-demand processing. *Proceedings of the 24th International Conference on Informatics for Environmental Protection*.

Cox, A. M., & Pinfield, S. (2013). Research data management and libraries: Current activities and future priorities. *Journal of Librarianship and Information Science*, 46(4), 299–316. doi:10.1177/0961000613492542

Coyle, K., & Baker, T. (2008). *Guidelines for Dublin Core Application Profiles*. Retrieved from http://dublincore.org/documents/profile-guidelines/index.shtml

Coyle, K., & Baker, T. *Guidelines for Dublin Core Application Profiles*. (2009) Retrieved 16 from http://dublincore.org/documents/profile-guidelines

Crystal, A., & Greenberg, J. (2005). Usability of a metadata creation application for resource authors. *Library & Information Science Research*, 27(2), 177–189. doi:10.1016/j.lisr.2005.01.012

Curado Malta, M. (2014). *Contributo metodológico para o desenvolvimento de perfis de aplicação no contexto da Web Semântica*. University of Minho. Retrieved from http://hdl.handle.net/1822/30262

Curado Malta, M., & Baptista, A. A. (2013a). A method for the development of Dublin Core Application Profiles (Me4DCAP V0.2): detailed description. In M. Foulonneau & K. Eckert (Eds.), Proc. Int'l Conf. on Dublin Core and Metadata Applications 2013 (pp. 90–103). Lisbon: Dublin Core Metadata Initiative. Retrieved from http://dcevents.dublincore.org/IntConf/dc-2013/paper/view/178/81

Curado Malta, M., & Baptista, A. A. (2013a). A method for the development of Dublin Core Application Profiles (Me4DCAP V0.2): detailed description. In M. Foulonneau & K. Eckert (Eds.), Proc. Int'l Conf. on Dublin Core and Metadata Applications 2013 (pp. 90–103). Lisbon: Dublin Core Metadata Initiative; Retrieved from http://dcevents.dublincore.org/IntConf/dc-2013/paper/view/178/81

Curado Malta, M., & Baptista, A. A. (2013c). State of the Art on Methodologies for the Development of Dublin Core Application Profiles. *International Journal of Metadata, Semantics and Ontologies, 8*(4), 332–341.

Curado Malta, M., & Baptista, A. A. (2015). A DCAP for the Social and Solidarity Economy. In M. Curado Malta & S. A. B. G. Vidotti (Eds.), *2015 Proceedings of the International Conference on Dublin Core and Metadata Applications* (pp. 20–29). S. Paulo, Brazil: DCMI.

Curado Malta, M., Centenera, P., & Gonzalez-Blanco, E. (2016). POSTDATA – Towards publishing European Poetry as Linked Open Data. In V. Charles & L. G. Svensson (Eds.), *International Conference on Dublin Core and Metadata Applications*. North America: Dublin Core Metadata Initiative. Retrieved from http://dcevents.dublincore.org/IntConf/dc-2016/paper/view/440

Curado Malta, M., & Baptista, A. A. (2012). State of the Art on Methodologies for the Development of a Metadata Application Profile. *Metadata and Semantics Research, 343*(July), 61–73. doi:10.1007/978-3-642-35233-1_6

Curado Malta, M., & Baptista, A. A. (2013b). Me4DCAP V0. 1: A method for the development of Dublin Core Application Profiles. *Information Services & Use, 33*(2), 161–171. doi:10.3233/ISU-130706

Curado Malta, M., & Baptista, A. A. (2014). A panoramic view on metadata application profiles of the last decade. *International Journal of Metadata. Semantics and Ontologies*, *9*(1), 58. doi:10.1504/IJMSO.2014.059124

Curado Malta, M., Baptista, A. A., & Parente, C. (2014). Social and Solidarity Economy Web Information Systems: State of the Art and an Interoperability Framework. *Journal of Electronic Commerce in Organizations*, *12*(1), 35–52. doi:10.4018/jeco.2014010103

Currier, S. (2008). Metadata for Learning Resources: An Update on Standards Activity for 2008. *Ariadne*, *55*(2).

D'Souza, D., Aamod, S., & Birchenough, S. (1999). First-class extensibility for UML – packaging of profiles, stereotypes, patterns. In R. France & B. Rumpe (Eds.), *UML'99 – The Unified Modeling Language,* LNCS (Vol. 1723, pp. 265–277). Springer Berlin Heidelberg. doi:10.1007/3-540-46852-8_19

Darlington, M. (2012). *REDm-MED project final report to JISC*. University of Bath. Retrieved from http://www.ukoln.ac.uk/projects/redm-med/reports/redm-med_final_report_v1.pdf

Darlington, M., Thangarajah, U., & Ball, A. (2012). *RAIDmap application user guide*. University of Bath. Retrieved from http://opus.bath.ac.uk/30097

Day, M. (2004). Preservation metadata. In G. E. Gorman & D. G. Dorner (Eds.), *Metadata applications and management* (pp. 253–273). London: Facet Publishing.

De la Prieta, F., Gil, A., Rodríguez, S., & Martín, B. (2011). BRENHET2, A MAS to Facilitate the Reutilization of LOs through Federated Search. In J. M. Corchado, J. B. Pérez, K. Hallenborg, P. Golinska, & R. Corchuelo (Eds.), *Trends in Practical Applications of Agents and Multiagent Systems. AISC* (Vol. 90, pp. 177–184). Heidelberg: Springer. doi:10.1007/978-3-642-19931-8_22

Desconnets, J. C., Chahdi, H., & Mougenot, I. (2014, November). Application profile for Earth Observation images. *Proceedings of theResearch Conference on Metadata and Semantics Research* (pp. 68-82). Springer International Publishing.

Desconnets, J. C., Libourel, T., Maurel, P., Miralles, A., & Passouant, M. (2001, September). Proposition de structuration des métadonnées en géosciences: Spécificité de la communauté scientifique. Proceedings of Journées Cassin 2001: Géomatique et espace rural (pp. 69-82).

Dublin Core Metadata Element Set (DCMES). Version 1.1 (2004). Reference description. Retrieved from http://dublincore.org/documents/2004/12/20/dces/

Dublin Core Metadata Initiative Usage Board. (2012) *DCMI Metadata Terms*. Retrieved from http://dublincore.org/documents/dcmi-terms/

Dublin Core Metadata Initiative. *History of the Dublin Core Metadata Initiative*. Retrieved from http://dublincore.org/about/history/

Dublin Core. (2012). Dublin Core Metadata Element Set, Version 1.1. (2012). Retrieved from http://www.dublincore.org/documents/dces/

Duranti, L., Eastwood, T., & MacNeil, H. (1997). The preservation of the integrity of electronic records. Vancouver, BC: University of British Columbia; Retrieved from http://www.interpares.org/UBCProject/index.htm

Durrieu, S., & Deshayes, M. (1994). Méthode de comparaison dimages satellitaires pour la détection des changements en milieu forestier. Application aux monts de Lacaune. *Annales des Sciences Forestieres*, *51*(2), 147–161. doi:10.1051/forest:19940205

Duval, E., Smith, N., & Van Coillie, M. (2006, July 5-7). Application profiles for learning. *Proc. of theIEEE International Conference on Advanced Learning Technologies (ICALT)*, Kerkrade, The Netherlands (pp. 242–246). doi:10.1109/ICALT.2006.1652415

Duval, E., Hodgins, W., Sutton, S., & Weibel, S. L. (2002). Metadata Principles and Practicalities. *D-Lib Magazine*, 8.

Education Network Australia. (2006). EdNA resources metadata application profile 1.0. Retrieved from http://edna.wikispaces.com/EdNA+Metadata+Standard+1.1

Ehlers, U. D. (2011). Extending the Territory: From Open Educational Resources to Open Educational Practices. *Journal of Open, Flexible, and Distance Learning*, *15*(2), 1–10.

Eiter, T., Ianni, G., Krennwallner, T., & Polleres, A. (2008). Rules and ontologies for the semantic web. In *Reasoning Web* (pp. 1–53). Springer Berlin Heidelberg. doi:10.1007/978-3-540-85658-0_1

EUDAT. (n/a). Retrieved from: http://eudat.eu/

European Commission. (2013). *Multi-beneficiary General Model Grant Agreement.* Retrieved from http://ec.europa.eu/research/participants/data/ref/h2020/mga/sme/h2020-mga-sme-1-multi_en.pdf

Faniel, I. M., & Yakel, E. (2011). Significant Properties as Contextual Metadata. *Journal of Library Metadata, 11*(3-4), 155–165. doi:10.1080/19386389.2011.629959

Federal Geographic Data Committee. (1998). *Content standard for digital geospatial metadata, Version 2.0.*

Fegraus, E., Andelman, S., Jones, M. B., & Schildhauer, M. (2005). Maximizing the value of ecological data with structured metadata: An introduction to Ecological Metadata Language (EML) and principles for metadata creation. *Bulletin of the Ecological Society of America, 86*(3), 158–168. doi:10.1890/0012-9623(2005)86[158:MTVOED]2.0.CO;2

Ferreira, M. J. F., Gales, L., Fernandes, V. R., Rangel, C. M., & Pinto, M. F. R. (2010). Alkali free hydrolysis of sodium borohydride for hydrogen generation under pressure. *International Journal of Hydrogen Energy, 35*(18), 9869–9878. doi:10.1016/j.ijhydene.2010.02.121

Frank, I. (1957). *Répertoire métrique de la poésie des troubadours*, Paris, H. Champion.

Friesen, N. (2009). Open educational resources: New possibilities for change and sustainability. *International Review of Research in Open and Distance Learning, 10*(5). doi:10.19173/irrodl.v10i5.664

Friss-Christensen, A., Ostländer, N., Lutz, M., & Bernard, L. (2007). Designing Service Architectures for Distributed Geoprocessing: Challenges and Future Directions. *Transactions in GIS, 11*(6), 799–818. doi:10.1111/j.1467-9671.2007.01075.x

Gaspéri, J., Houbie, F., Woolf, A., & Smolders, S. (2012). Earth observation metadata profile of Observations & Measurements. Retrieved from https://portal.opengeospatial.org/files/?artifact_id=47040

Gayte, O., Libourel, T., Cheylan, J. P., & Lardon, S. (1997). *Conception des systèmes d'information sur l'environnement. Géomatique.* Paris, France: Edition Hermès.

GLOBE. (2011). *GLOBE metadata application profile specification document. Version 1.* Retrieved from http://www.globe-info.org/images/ap/globe_lom_ap_v1.0.pdf

Compilation of References

Gómez Bravo, A. M. (1999). *Repertorio métrico de la poesía cancioneril del siglo XV*. Alcalá de Henares: Universidad.

Gómez Redondo, F. (2001). *Artes Poéticas Medievales*. Madrid: Laberinto.

Gore, S. A. (2011). e-Science and data management resources on the Web. *Medical Reference Services Quarterly*, *30*(2), 167–177. doi:10.1080/02763869.2011.5627 78 PMID:21534116

Gorni, G. (2008). *Repertorio metrico della canzone italiana dalle origini al Cinquecento (REMCI)*. Firenze: Franco Cesati.

Ha, K. H., Niemann, K., Schwertel, U., Holtkamp, P., Pirkkalainen, H., & Boerner, D. et al.. (2011). A novel approach towards skill-based search and services of open educational resources. *Proc. of Metadata and Semantic Research* (pp. 312–323). Berlin: Springer. doi:10.1007/978-3-642-24731-6_32

Halpin, T., & Morgan, T. (2008). *Information Modeling and Relational Databases* (2nd ed.). Burlington: Morgan Kaufman.

Hassan, S., Qamar, U., Hassan, T., & Waqas, M. (2015). Software Reverse Engineering to Requirement Engineering for Evolution of Legacy System. *Proceedings of the 2015 5th International Conference on IT Convergence and Security (ICITCS)* (pp. 1–4). IEEE. doi:10.1109/ICITCS.2015.7293021

Hayes, P., & McBride, B. (2004). RDF semantics. Retrieved from http://www.w3.org/TR/2004/REC-rdf-mt-20040210/

Heery, R., & Patel, M. (2000). Application profiles: mixing and matching metadata schemas. *Ariadne*, 25. Retrieved from http://www.ariadne.ac.uk/issue25/app-profiles/

Heery, R., & Patel, M. (2000). Application profiles: Mixing and matching metadata schemas. *Ariadne*, 25. Retrieved from http://www.ariadne.ac.uk/issue25/app-profiles/

Heery, R., & Patel, M. (2000). Application Profiles: Mixing and Matching Metadata Schemas. *Ariadne*, I25.

Heidorn, P. B. (2011). The Emerging Role of Libraries in Data Curation and E-science. *Journal of Library Administration*, *51*(7-8), 662–672. doi:10.1080/01930 826.2011.601269

Heidorn, P. B.P. Bryan Heidorn. (2008). Shedding Light on the Dark Data in the Long Tail of Science. *Library Trends*, *57*(2), 280–299. doi:10.1353/lib.0.0036

Hevner, A., & Chatterjee, S. (2010). Design Research in Information Systems - Theory and Practice. (R. Sharda & S. Voß, Eds.) (Integrated). Springer.

Hevner, A. R. (2007). A three cycle view of design science research. *Scandinavian Journal of Information Systems*, *19*(2), 4.

Hitzler, P., & Parsia, B. (2009). Ontologies and rules. In *Handbook on Ontologies* (pp. 111–132). Springer Berlin Heidelberg. doi:10.1007/978-3-540-92673-3_5

Hunt, A., & Thomas, D. (2000). *The pragmatic programmer: From journeyman to master*. Reading, MA: Addison-Wesley.

IEEE Learning Technology Standards Committee (LTSC). (2005). Final Standard for Learning Object Metadata. Retrieved from http://ltsc.ieee.org/wg12/files/IEEE_1484_12_03_d8_submitted.pdf

Iiyoshi, T., & Kumar, M. V. (Eds.). (2008). *Opening up education: The collective advancement of education through open technology, open content, and open knowledge*. London, UK: MIT Press.

IMS Global Learning Consortium (GLC). (2005). IMS Application Profile Guidelines Technical Manual. Retrieved from http://www.imsglobal.org/ap/apv1p0/imsap_techv1p0.html

InterPARES project. Project overview. (n. d.). Retrieved from http://www.interpares.org/

ISA. (2015). DCAT Application Profile for data portals in Europe. Version 1.1. Interoperability Solutions for European Public Administration. European Union. Retrieved from https://joinup.ec.europa.eu/node/137964/

ISA. (2015b). GeoDCAT-AP: A geospatial extension for the DCAT application profile for data portals in Europe. Working Group Draft 7. Interoperability Solutions for European Public Administration. European Union. Retrieved from https://joinup.ec.europa.eu/asset/dcat_application_profile/asset_release/geodcat-ap-v10

Islam, A. S., Bermudez, L., Fellah, S., Beran, B. & Piasecki, M. (2004). Implementation of the Geographic Information-Metadata (ISO 19115: 2003) Norm using the Web Ontology Language (OWL). *Transactions in GIS*.

ISO. (2003). *Geographic Information Metadata, ISO 19115*. Geneva, Switzerland: International Organization for Standardization.

ISO. (2004). *ISO 19106:2004. Geographic information — Profiles*. Geneva, Switzerland: International Organization for Standardization.

ISO. (2007). *ISO/TS 19139:2007. Geographic information — Metadata — XML schema implementation*. Geneva, Switzerland: International Organization for Standardization.

ISO. (2009). *ISO19115-2:2009. Geographic information — Metadata — Part 2: Extensions for imagery and gridded data*. Geneva, Switzerland: International Organization for Standardization.

ISO. (2011). *ISO 19156:2011, 2014. Geographic information – Observations and Measurements*. Geneva, Switzerland: International Organization for Standardization.

ISO/IEC. (2011). *ISO/IEC 19788-1:2011 Information technology – Learning, education and training – Metadata for learning resources - Part 1: Framework*. International Organization for Standardization.

Jacobson, I., & Ng, P. W. (2004). *Aspect-oriented software development with use cases (addison-wesley object technology series)*. Addison-Wesley Professional.

Jörg, B. (2010). CERIF: The Common European Research Information Format Model. *Data Science Journal*, 9(July), 24–31.

Kalz, M., Specht, M., Nadolski, R., Bastiaens, Y., Leirs, N., & Pawlowski, J. (2010). OpenScout: Competence based management education with community-improved open educational resources. In S. Halley, C. Birch, D.T. Tempelaar, M. McCuddy, N. Hernández Nanclares, S. Reeb-Gruber, W.H. Gijselaers, B. Rienties, and E. Nelissen, (Eds.), *Proc. of the17th Conference on Education Innovation in Economics and Business (EDiNEB '11)* (pp. 137-146). Maastricht, The Netherlands: FEBA ERD Press.

Karimova, Y. (2016). *Vocabulários controlados na descrição de dados de investigação no Dendro* [Master Dissertation]. Retrieved from http://handle.net/10216/85221

Kazmierski, M., Desconnets, J. C., Guerrero, B., & Briand, D. (2014, June). Accessing Earth Observation data collections with semantic-based services.*Proceedings of the 17th AGILE Conference on Geographic Information Science, Connecting a Digital Europe through Location and Place*, Castellon, Spain.

Klerkx, J., Vandeputte, B., Parra Chico, G., Santos Odriozola, J. L., Van Assche, F., & Duval, E. (2010). How to share and reuse learning resources: the Ariadne experience.*Proc. of the 5th European Conference on Technology Enhanced Learning (EC-TEL '10)* (pp. 183–196). Heidelberg: Springer. doi:10.1007/978-3-642-16020-2_13

Lamb, J. (2001). Sharing best methods and know-how for improving generation and use of metadata. In *New Techniques and Technologies for Statistics and Exchange of Technology and Know-how* (pp. 175-194).

Lane, A. & McAndrew, P. (2010). Are open educational resources systematic or systemic change agents for teaching practice? *British Journal of Educational Technology, 41*(6), 952-962.

Lassila, O., & Mcguinness, D. (2001). *The Role of Frame-Based Representation on the Semantic Web*. Retrieved from ftp://ftp.ksl.stanford.edu/pub/KSL_Reports/KSL-01-02.html

Lechat, M. P. (2007). Economia social, economia solidária, terceiro setor: do que se trata? *Civitas- Revista de Ciências Sociais, 2*(1), 123–140.

Leegard, R., Keegan, J., & Ward, K. (2003). In-depth Interviews. In J. Ritchie and J. Lewis (Ed.), Qualitative research practice: A guide for social science students and researchers (pp. 138–169). London: Sage

Lewis, S. C., Zamith, R., & Hermida, A. (2013). Content Analysis in an Era of Big Data: A Hybrid Approach to Computational and Manual Methods. *Journal of Broadcasting & Electronic Media, 57*(1), 34–52. doi:10.1080/08838151.2012.761702

Library of Congress. (2014) *BIBFRAME Profiles: Introduction and Specification*. Retrieved from http://www.loc.gov/bibframe/docs/bibframe-profiles.html

Library of Congress. (2016). PREMIS: Preservation metadata maintenance activity. Retrieved from http://www.loc.gov/standards/premis/

Linden, F., Schmid, K., & Rommes, E. (2007). The Product Line Engineering Approach. *Software Product Lines in Action*, 3–20.

Livre Blanc. (1998). *L'information géographique française dans la société de l'information*. Rapport CNIG/AFIGEO.

Li, Y., Kennedy, G., Ngoran, F., Wu, P., & Hunter, J. (2013). An ontology-centric architecture for extensible scientific data management systems. *Future Generation Computer Systems*, *29*(2), 641–653. doi:10.1016/j.future.2011.06.007

Lupovici, C., & Masanès, J. (2000). *Metadata for the long-term preservation of electronic publications*. The Hague, The Netherlands: Koninklijke Bibliotheek. Retrieved from https://www.kb.nl/sites/default/files/docs/NEDLIBmetadata.pdf

Madin, J., Bowers, S., Schildhauer, M., Krivov, S., Pennington, D., & Villa, F. (2007). An ontology for describing and synthesizing ecological observation data. *Ecological Informatics*, *2*(3), 279–296. doi:10.1016/j.ecoinf.2007.05.004

Maguire, D. J., & Longley, P. A. (2005). The emergence of geoportals and their role in spatial data infrastructures. *Computers, Environment and Urban Systems*, *29*(1), 3–14. doi:10.1016/S0198-9715(04)00045-6

Mallory, M. (2015). RIOxx (Research Interoperability Opportunities Extensions) http://www.rioxx.net. Technology Services Quarterly, 32(4).

Malta, M. C., & Baptista, A. A. (2012). State of the art on methodologies for the development of a metadata application profile. *International Journal of Metadata. Semantics and Ontologies*, *8*(4), 332–341. doi:10.1504/IJMSO.2013.058416

Manouselis, N., Kastrantas, K., Sanchez-Alonso, S., Cáceres, J., Ebner, H., Palmer, M., & Naeve, A. (2009). Architecture of the Organic.Edunet Web Portal. *International Journal of Web Portals*, *1*(1), 71–91. doi:10.4018/jwp.2009092105

Martinez-Uribe, L., & Macdonald, S. (2009). User engagement in research data curation. In *Research and Advanced Technology for Digital Libraries,* LNCS (Vol. *5714*, pp. 309–314). Retrieved from http://www.springerlink.com/content/7mnq1 3x34717p48310.1007/978-3-642-04346-8_30

Martone, M. E. (2013). Brain and Behavior: We want you to share your data. *Brain and Behavior*, *4*(1). doi:10.1002/brb3.192 PMID:24653948

Mason R.T., & Ellis T. J. (2009). Extending SCORM LOM. *Issues in Informing Science and Information Technology*, 6.

Mason, J., & Galatis, H. (2007). Theory and practice of application profile development in Australian education and training. *Proc. of the 2007 International Conference on Dublin Core and Metadata Applications: application profiles: theory and practice (DCMI '07)*, Singapore (pp. 43-52).

Maurel, P., & Faure, J. F. · Cantou, J.P., Desconnets, J.C., Teisseire, M., Mougenot, I., Martignac, C. & Bappel E. (2015, September). The GEOSUD remote sensing data and services infrastructure. *Proceedings of the International Society of Photogrammetry and Remote Sensing Conference – RSDI Workshop*. Montpellier, France.

McGreal, R. (2008). A typology of learning object repositories. In: H. H. Adelsberger, Kinshuk, J. M. Pawlovski & D. Sampson, (Eds.), International Handbook on Information Technologies for Education and Training (2nd ed., pp. 5-18). New York: Springer. doi:10.1007/978-3-540-74155-8_1

McGreal, R. (2004). *Online Education Using Learning Objects*. Washington, D.C.: Falmer Press.

McMahon, C. (2015). Design informatics: Supporting engineering design processes with information technology. *Journal of the Indian Institute of Science*, *95*(4), 365–378. Retrieved from http://journal.library.iisc.ernet.in/index.php/iisc/article/view/4585

Megalou, E., & Kaklamanis, C. (2014). Photodentro LOR, The Greek National Learning Object Repository. *Proc. of the 8th International Technology, Education and Development Conference (INTED '14)* (pp. 309-319).

Mena-Garcés, E., García-Barriocanal, E., Sicilia, M.-A., & Sánchez-Alonso, S. (2011). Moving from dataset metadata to semantics in ecological research: A case in translating EML to OWL. *Procedia Computer Science*, *4*, 1622–1630. doi:10.1016/j.procs.2011.04.175

Mölk, U., & and Friedrich Wolfzettel (1072). *Répertoire métrique de la poésie lyrique française des origines à 1350*, Munchen, W. Fink Verlag.

Moretti, F. (2005). *Graphs, Maps and Tress – Abstracts models for a literature theory*. London: Verso.

Mougenot, I., Desconnets, J. C., & Chahdi, H. (2015). A DCAP to promote easy-to-use data for multiresolution and multitemporal satellite imagery analysis. *Proceedings of the International Conference on Dublin Core and Metadata Applications*, Sao Paulo, Brazil.

Müller, H. A., Jahnke, J. H., Smith, D. B., Storey, M.-A., Tilley, S. R., & Wong, K. (2000). Reverse Engineering: A Roadmap. *Proceedings of the Conference on The Future of Software Engineering* (pp. 47–60). New York, NY, USA: ACM.

Naetebus, G. (1891). *Die Nicht-Lyrischen Strophenformen Des Altfranzösischen. Ein Verzeichnis Zusammengestellt Und Erläutert.* Leipzig: S. Hirzel.

National Archives of Australia. (1999). Recordkeeping metadata standard for commonwealth agencies. Retrieved from http://pandora.nla.gov.au/nph-wb/20000510130000/http://www.naa.gov.au/www.naa.gov.au/recordkeeping/control/rkms/contents.html

National Archives of Australia. (2015). Australian government recordkeeping metadata standard, version 2.2. Retrieved from http://www.naa.gov.au/records-management/publications/agrkms/

National Information Standards Organization. (2004). Understanding Metadata. MD: NISO Press. doi:10.1017/S0003055403000534

National Library of Australia. (1999). Preservation metadata for digital collections. Retrieved from http://pandora.nla.gov.au/pan/25498/20020625-0000/www.nla.gov.au/preserve/pmeta.html

National Library of New Zealand. (2003). *Metadata standards framework – preservation metadata (revised).* Retrieved from http://digitalpreservation.natlib.govt.nz/assets/Uploads/nlnz-data-model-final.pdf

National Science Foundation. (2005). *Long-Lived Digital Data Collections: Enabling Research and Education in the 21st Century.* Retrieved from: http://www.nsf.gov/pubs/2005/nsb0540/nsb0540.pdf

National Science Foundation. (2011). Grants.Gov Application Guide A Guide for Preparation and Submission of NSF Applications via Grants.gov. Retrieved from http://www.nsf.gov/pubs/policydocs/grantsgovguide0113.pdf

Nilsson, B.J. (2008). *The Singapore Framework for Dublin Core Application Profiles.* Retrieved from http://dublincore.org/documents/singapore-framework/

Nilsson, M. (2008) *Description Set Profiles: A constraint language for Dublin Core Application Profiles.* Retrieved from http://dublincore.org/documents/dc-dsp/

Nilsson, M. (2008). Description Set Profiles: A constraint language for Dublin Core Application Profiles [misc]. Retrieved April 6, 2016, from http://dublincore.org/documents/2008/03/31/dc-dsp/

Nilsson, M., Baker, T., & Johnston, P. (2008) *The Singapore Framework for Dublin Core Application Profiles*. Retrieved from http://dublincore.org/documents/Singapore-framework

Nilsson, M., Baker, T., & Johnston, P. (2008). The Singapore Framework for Dublin Core Application Profiles. Retrieved February 10, 2015, from http://dublincore.org/documents/singapore-framework/

Nilsson, M., Baker, T., & Johnston, P. (2008). The Singapore Framework for Dublin Core Application Profiles. Retrieved from http://dublincore.org/documents/singapore-framework/

Nilsson, M., Baker, T., & Johnston, P. (2009). Interoperability Levels for Dublin Core Metadata. Retrieved from http://dublincore.org/documents/interoperability-levels/

Nilsson, M., Baker, T., & Johnston, P. (2009). Interoperability Levels for Dublin Core Metadata. Retrieved October 10, 2016, from http://dublincore.org/documents/interoperability-levels/

Nilsson, M., Baker, T., & Johnston, Pete. (January, 2008). *The Singapore Framework for Dublin Core Application Profiles*. Retrieved from http://dublincore.org/documents/singapore-framework/

Nilsson, M., Miles, A. J., Johnston, P., & Enoksson, F. (2009). Formalizing Dublin Core Application Profiles–Description Set Profiles and Graph Constraints. In Metadata and Semantics (pp. 101-111). Springer US. doi:10.1007/978-0-387-77745-0_10

NISO. (2004). *Understanding Metadata. National Information Standards Organisation*. Baltimore, USA: NISO Press.

Noy, N. F., & Mcguinness, D. L. (2000). *Ontology Development 101*: A *Guide to Creating Your First Ontology*. Retrieved from http://protege.stanford.edu/publications/ontology_development/ontology101.pdf

Ocean Biogeographic Information System. (n. d.). Retrieved from http://www.iobis.org/

Ochiai, K., Nagamori, M., & Sugimoto, S. (2014). A Metadata Schema Design Model and Support System Based on an Agile Development Model. In M. Kindling & E. Greifeneder (Eds.), iConference 2014 Proceedings (pp. 921–927). article, Illinois: iSchools. http://doi.org/ doi:0.9776/14314

OCLC/RLG Preservation Metadata, & the Implementation Strategies Working Group. (2005). *Data dictionary for preservation metadata*. Retrieved from http://www.loc.gov/standards/premis/v1/premis-dd_1.0_2005_May.pdf

OCLC/RLG Working Group on Preservation Metadata. (2001). *Preservation metadata for digital objects: A review of the state of the art*. Retrieved from http://www.oclc.org/content/dam/research/activities/pmwg/presmeta_wp.pdf

OCLC/RLG Working Group on Preservation Metadata. (2002). *Preservation metadata and the oais information model: A metadata framework to support the preservation of digital objects*. Retrieved from http://www.oclc.org/content/dam/research/activities/pmwg/pm_framework.pdf

OECD. (2007). Giving knowledge for free: The emergence of open educational resources. Retrieved from http://www.oecd.org/dataoecd/35/7/38654317.pdf

OGC. (2007). OGC Catalogue Services Specification 2.0.2 – ISO Metadata Application Profile (1.0.0). Retrieved from http://portal.opengeospatial.org/files/?artifact_id=21460

OMG. (2006). Meta Object Facility (MOF) Core Specification OMG Available Specification Version 2.0. Retrieved from http://doc.omg.org/formal/2006-01-01.pdf

OMG. (2015). OMG Unified Modeling Language TM (OMG UML). Version 2.5. Retrieved from http://www.omg.org/spec/UML/2.5/PDF

OSGEO. (2007). Geodata metadata model. Retrieved from https://wiki.osgeo.org/wiki/Geodata_Metadata_Model

OSGEO. (2008). DC4GLite, Dublin Core Lightweight Profile for Geospatial. Retrieved from https://wiki.osgeo.org/wiki/DCLite4G

Otón, S., Ortiz, A., de-Marcos, L., de Dios, S. M., García, A., García, E., & Barchino, R. et al. (2012). *Developing Distributed Repositories of Learning Objects*. INTECH Open Access Publisher. doi:10.5772/29447

Pagnotta, L. (1995). *Repertorio metrico della ballata italiana*. Milano, Napoli: Ricciardi.

Parramon i Blasco, J. (1992). *Repertori mètric de la poesia catalana medieval*. Barcelona: Curial.

Perrotta, D., Macedo, J. L., Rossetti, R. J. F., De Sousa, J. F., Kokkinogenis, Z., Ribeiro, B., & Afonso, J. L. (2014). Route Planning for Electric Buses: A Case Study in Oporto. *Procedia: Social and Behavioral Sciences*, *111*, 1004–1014. doi:10.1016/j.sbspro.2014.01.135

Perrotta, D., Teixeira, A., Silva, H., Ribeiro, B., & Afonso, J. (2012). Electrical Bus Performance Modeling for Urban Environments. *SAE Int. J. Alt. Power*, *1*(1), 34–45. doi:10.4271/2012-01-0200

Pillet, A., & Carstens, H. (1933). *Bibliographie der Troubadours*. Halle: M. Niemeyer.

Piwowar, H. A., Day, R. B., & Fridsma, D. S. (2007). *Sharing detailed research data is associated with increased citation rate. PLoS ONE*, *2*(3), e308. doi:10.1371/journal.pone.0000308 PMID:17375194

Pohl, K., Böckle, G., & van Der Linden, F. J. (2005). *Software product line engineering: foundations, principles and techniques*. Springer Science & Business Media. doi:10.1007/3-540-28901-1

Pouchard, L., Cinquini, L., & Strand, G. (2003). The Earth System Grid Discovery and Semantic Web Technologies. In *Workshop for Semantic Web Technologies for Searching and Retrieving Scientific Data - 2nd International Semantic Web Conference* (pp. 1–6).

Powell, A., Nilsson, M., Naeve, A., Johnston, P., & Baker, T. (2007). DCMI Abstract Model. DCMI Recommendation. Retrieved from http://dublincore.org/documents/abstract-model/

Prause, C., Ternier, S., de Jong, T., Apelt, S., Scholten, M., Wolpers, M., & Duval, E. et al. (2007, September 18). Unifying learning object repositories in mace. *Proc. of the 1st International Workshop on Learning Object Discovery & Exchange (LODE '07)*, Lassithi, Greece.

PREMIS Editorial Committee. (2011). *PREMIS data dictionary for preservation metadata, version 2.1*. Washington, DC: Library of Congress. Retrieved from http://www.loc.gov/standards/premis/v2/premis-2-1.pdf

Pressman, R. S. (2015). *Software engineering: a practitioner's approach* (8th ed.). Palgrave Macmillan.

Public Record Office Victoria. (2000). PROS 99/007 Standard for the management of electronic records, version 1.2. Retrieved from http://pandora.nla.gov.au/pan/22965/20021222-0000/www.prov.vic.gov.au/vers/standards/pros9907.htm

Qin, J., & LI, K. (2013). How Portable Are the Metadata Standards for Scientific Data? A Proposal for a Metadata Infrastructure.*Proceedings of the International Conference on Dublin Core and Metadata Applications* (pp. 25–34).

Qin, J., Ball, A., & Greenberg, J. (2012). Functional and Architectural Requirements for Metadata: Supporting Discovery and Management of Scientific Data.*Proceedings of the International Conference on Dublin Core and Metadata Applications* (pp. 62–71).

Raynaud, G. (1884). Bibliographie des chansonniers français des xiii. [treizième] et xiv. [quatorzième] siècles, Paris, Vieweg.

Research Libraries Group, Working Group on Preservation Issues of Metadata. (1998). *Final report*. Retrieved from https://web.archive.org/web/20040216202156/http://www.rlg.org/preserv/presmeta.html

Rice, R., & Haywood, J. (2011). Research data management initiatives at University of Edinburgh. *International Journal of Digital Curation*, 6(2), 232–244. Retrieved from http://www.ijdc.net/index.php/ijdc/article/view/194 doi:10.2218/ijdc.v6i2.199

Rocha da Silva, J. (2016). *Usage-driven Application Profile Generation Using Ontologies* [Doctoral Dissertation]. Retrieved from (http://hdl.handle.net/10216.83993)

Rocha da Silva, J. R., Cristina, R., & Lopes, J. C. (2012). Semi-automated application profile generation for research data assets. *Proceedings of the Metadata and Semantics Research Conference (MTSR '12)*. Retrieved from http://www.springer.com/series/7899

Rocha da Silva, J., Castro, J. A., Ribeiro, C., & Lopes, J. C. (2014). Dendro: collaborative research data management built on linked open data. *Proceedings of the 11th European Semantic Web Conference*. Retrieved from http://2014.eswc-conferences.org/sites/default/files/eswc2014pd_submission_54.pdf

Rocha da Silva, J., Castro, J. A., Ribeiro, C., Honrado, J., Lomba, Â., & Gonçalves, J. (2014). Beyond INSPIRE: An Ontology for Biodiversity Metadata Records. In *On the Move to Meaningful Internet Systems: OTM 2014 Workshops* (Vol. 8842, pp. 597–607). doi:10.1007/978-3-662-45550-0_61

Rocha da Silva, J., Ribeiro, C., Barbosa, J., Gouveia, M., & Lopes, J. C. (2013). UPBox and Data Notes: a collaborative data management environment for the long tail of research data. *Proceedings of the iPres 2013 Conference.*

Rogers, C., & Tennis, J. T. (2016). *General Study 15 – Application profile for authenticity metadata.* InterPARES 3 Project. Retrieved from http://www.interpares.org/ip3/display_file.cfm?doc=ip3_canada_gs15_final_report.pdf

Rumbaugh, J., Blaha, M., Premerlani, W., Eddy, F., & Lorensen, W. E. (1991). Object-oriented modeling and design, 199 *(1)*. Englewood Cliffs, NJ: Prentice-hall.

Rumbaugh, J., Jacobson, I., & Booch, G. (2004). *Unified Modeling Language Reference Manual, The.* Pearson Higher Education.

Sampson, D. G., & Zervas, P. (2013). Learning object repositories as knowledge management systems. *Knowledge Management & E-Learning: An International Journal, 5*(2), 117-136.

Sampson, D. G., Zervas, P., & Chloros, G. (2012). Supporting the process of developing and managing LOM application profiles: The ASK-LOM-AP tool. *IEEE Transactions on Learning Technologies, 5*(3), 238–250. doi:10.1109/TLT.2011.39

Schema.org. (n. d.). XML Schema 1.1.

Schneider, G., & Winters, J. P. (2001). *Applying use cases: a practical guide (Second Edi). book.* Boston: Addison-Wesley.

Scholarly Works Application Profile. (2009). Retrieved from http://www.ukoln.ac.uk/repositories/digirep/index/Scholarly_Works_Application_Profile#Introduction

Sen, A. (2004). Metadata Management: Past, present and future. *Decision Support Systems, 37*(1), 151–173. doi:10.1016/S0167-9236(02)00208-7

Shu, Y., Liu, Q., & Taylor, K. (2016). Semantic validation of environmental observations data. *Environmental Modelling & Software, 79*, 10–21. doi:10.1016/j.envsoft.2016.01.004

Smith, N., Van Coillie, M., & Duval, E. (2006). Guidelines and support for building Application profiles in e-learning. *Proc. of the CEN/ISSS WS/LT Learning Technologies Workshop on Availability of alternative language versions of a learning resource in IEEE LOM* (pp. 1-26). Brussels: CEN Workshop Agreements.

Sneed, H. M. (1995). Planning the reengineering of legacy systems. *IEEE Software*, *12*(1), 24–34. doi:10.1109/52.363168

Soldatova, L. N., & King, R. R. D. (2006). An ontology of Scientific Experiments. *Journal of the Royal Society, Interface*, *3*(11), 795–803. doi:10.1098/rsif.2006.0134 PMID:17015305

Soley, R. (2000). Model driven architecture. OMG white paper.

Solimena, A. (2000). Repertorio metrico dei poeti siculo-toscani. Centro di studi filologici e linguistici siciliani in Palermo, Palermo.

Somé, S. S. (2009). A Meta-Model for Textual Use Case Description. *Journal of Object Technology*, *8*(7), 87–106. doi:10.5381/jot.2009.8.7.a2

Starr, J., Ashton, J., Brase, J., Bracke, P., Gastl, A., Gillet, J., & Ziedorn, F. (2011). *DataCite metadata schema for the publication and citation of research data, version 2.2*. DataCite Consortium; doi:10.5438/0005

Steinacker, A., Ghavam, A., & Steinmetz, R. (2001). Metadata standards for web-based resources. *IEEE MultiMedia*, *8*(1), 70–76. doi:10.1109/93.923956

Stemler, S. (2001). An overview of Content Analysis. *Practical Assessment, Research & Evaluation*, *7*(17), 137–146.

Tavani, G. (1967). *Repertorio metrico della lingua galego-portoghese*, Roma, Edizioni dell'Ateneo.

Tenopir, C., Birch, B., & Allard, S. (2012). *Academic libraries and research data services*. Current practices and plans for the future - An ACRL White Paper.

Tenopir, C., Allard, S., Douglass, K., Aydinoglu, A. U., Wu, L., Read, E., & Frame, M. et al. (2011). Data Sharing by Scientists: Practices and Perceptions. *PLoS ONE*, *6*(6), e21101. doi:10.1371/journal.pone.0021101 PMID:21738610

Ternier, S., Verbert, K., Parra, G., Vandeputte, B., Klerkx, J., Duval, E., & Ochoa, X. et al. (2009). The Ariadne Infrastructure for Managing and Storing Metadata. *IEEE Internet Computing*, *13*(4), 18–25. doi:10.1109/MIC.2009.90

The William and Flora Hewlett Foundation. (2013). White Paper: Open Educational Resources. Breaking the Lockbox on Education. Retrieved from http://tinyurl.com/oerhewlett

Totschnig, M. (2007). Open ICOPER Content Space Implementation of 2nd Generation of Open ICOPER Content Space including Integration Mini Case Studies.

Touber, A. H. (1975). *Deutsche Strophenformen des Mittelalters*. Stuttgart: Metzler.

Treloar, A., & Wilkinson, R. (2008). Rethinking Metadata Creation and Management in a Data-Driven Research World. *Proceedings of the IEEE Fourth International Conference on eScience* (pp. 782–789). doi:10.1109/eScience.2008.41

Tucker, C. J. (1979). Red and photographic infrared linear combinations for monitoring vegetation. *Remote Sensing of Environment, 8*(2), 127–150. doi:10.1016/0034-4257(79)90013-0

UNESCO. (2002). *Forum on the Impact of Open Courseware for Higher Education in Developing Countries-Final Report*. Retrieved from http://goo.gl/eOkgdD

UNESCO. (2012, June 20-22). 2012 World Open Educational Resources (OER) Congress. UNESCO, Paris. Retrieved from http://tinyurl.com/unescoparis2012

University of Pittsburgh, School of Information Sciences. (1996). Metadata specifications derived from the fundamental requirements: A reference model for business acceptable communications. Retrieved from http://web.archive.org/web/20000302194819/www.sis.pitt.edu/~nhprc/meta96.html

Vardigan, M., Heus, P., & Thomas, W. (2008). Data Documentation Initiative: Toward a Standard tor the Social Sciences. *The International Journal of Digital Curation, 3*(1), 107–113. Retrieved from http://onlinelibrary.wiley.com/doi/10.1002/cbdv.200490137/abstract doi:10.2218/ijdc.v3i1.45

Vines, T. H., Albert, A. Y. K., Andrew, R. L., Débarre, F., Bock, D. G., Franklin, M. T., & Rennison, D. et al. (2014). The availability of research data declines rapidly with article age. *Current Biology, 24*(1), 94–97. doi:10.1016/j.cub.2013.11.014 PMID:24361065

W3C (2015). Semantic Web. Retrieved from https://www.w3.org/standards/semanticweb/

W3C. (2014). Data Catalog Vocabulary (DCAT). W3C Recommendation. Retrieved from https://www.w3.org/TR/vocab-dcat/

W3C. (2015). W3C - Linked Data. Retrieved November 19, 2016, from https://www.w3.org/standards/semanticweb/data

Walsh, T. (2010). *Unlocking the gates: How and why leading universities are opening up access to their courses*. Princeton, NJ: Princeton University.

Warren, R., & Champion, E. (2014). Linked Open Data Driven Game Generation. *In Proceedings of the 13th International Semantic Web Conference – Part II (ISWC '14)* (pp. 358-373). New York: Springer.

Weibel, S., Kunze, J., Lagoze, C. & Wolf, M. (1998). *Dublin core metadata for resource discovery* (No. RFC 2413).

Wessels, B., Finn, R. L., Linde, P., Mazzetti, P., Nativi, S., Riley, S., & Wyatt, S. et al. (2014). *Issues in the development of open access to research data*. Prometheus. *Critical Studies in Innovation, 32*(1), 49–66. doi:10.1080/08109028.2014.956505

Wieczorek, J., Bloom, D., Guralnick, R., Blum, S., Döring, M., Giovanni, R., & Vieglais, D. et al. (2012). Darwin core: An evolving community-developed biodiversity data standard. *PLoS ONE, 7*(1), e29715. doi:10.1371/journal.pone.0029715 PMID:22238640

Wiley, D. A. (2002). The instructional use of learning objects. Bloomington, USA: Association for Educational Communications and Technology (AECT) Press.

Willis, C., Greenberg, J., & White, H. (2012). Analysis and Synthesis of Metadata Goals for Scientific Data. *Journal of the American Society for Information Science and Technology, 63*(8), 1505–1520. doi:10.1002/asi.22683

Wilson, A. J. (2007). Toward Releasing the Metadata Bottleneck A Baseline Evaluation of Contributor-supllied Metadata. *Library Resources & Technical Services, 51*(1), 16–28. doi:10.5860/lrts.51n1.16

Wolf, M., & Wicksteed, C. (1998). *Date and time formats*. World Wide Web Consortium. Retrieved from http://www.w3.org/TR/1998/NOTE-datetime-19980827

Woodley, M. S. (2008). Crosswalks, metadata harvesting, federated searching, metasearching: Using metadata to connect users and information. In M. Baca (Ed.), *Introduction to metadata* (3rd ed., pp. 38–62). Los Angeles, CA: Getty Research Institute.

World Wide Web Consortium. (2013, September 10-11) *RDF Validation Workshop; Practical Assurances for Quality RDF Data*. Washington, DC. Retrieved from https://www.w3.org/2012/12/rdf-val/

World Wide Web Consortium. (2014) *RDF Shapes Working Group Charter*. Retrieved from https://www.w3.org/2014/data-shapes/charterWorldWideWebConsortium

Yamada, T. (2013). Open educational resources in Japan. In G. Dhanarajan & D. Porter (Eds.), Open educational resources: An Asian perspective (pp. 85-105). Vancouver: Commonwealth of Learning and OER Asia

Zenari, M. (1999). *Repertorio metrico dei 'Rerum vulgarium fragmenta' di Francesco Petrarca*. Padova: Antenore.

Zepheira. (n. d.). *Bibframe Lite*. Retrieved from http://bibfra.me/view/lite/

Zervas, P., Alifragkis, C., & Sampson, D. G. (2014a). A quantitative analysis of learning object repositories as knowledge management systems. *Knowledge Management & E-Learning: An International Journal*, 6(2), pp. 156-170.

Zervas, P., Kalamatianos, A., & Sampson, D. G. (2014b). A Systematic Analysis of Metadata Application Profiles of Learning Object Repositories in Europe. In R. Huang & N. S. Chen (Eds.), *The New Development of Technology Enhanced Learning* (pp. 75–91). Berlin: Springer. doi:10.1007/978-3-642-38291-8_5

About the Contributors

Mariana Malta holds a PhD in Information Systems & Technologies from the University of Minho, Portugal. She is an electrical and software engineer from the Faculty of Engineering, University of Oporto, Portugal. She is an associate professor in the Polytechnic of Oporto since 1998. She is currently on leave to work as a researcher in the European Research Council (ERC) Starting Grant Project "POST-DATA", where she is the leading information modeler. POSTDATA is located in the Universidad Nacional de Educación a Distancia at the Laboratory of Digital Humanities. Mariana is interested in semantic modeling and development of application profiles, more particularly in the study and development of methods for the development of application profiles. She is one of the authors of Me4MAP a method for the development of metadata application profiles.

Ana Alice Baptista is a professor at the Information Systems Department and a researcher at ALGORITMI Center, both at University of Minho, Portugal. She graduated in computer engineering and has a PhD on Information Systems and Technologies. As an independent member of the Dublin Core Metadata Initiative (DCMI) Governing Board she was elected chair-elect of DCMI. She also co-chairs the DCMI Education & Outreach Committee (DC-EOC). She is also a member of the Elpub conference series Executive Committee. She participated in several R&D projects and she was an evaluator of project proposals under FP7. She has authored or co-authored more than 60 articles. Her main areas of interest include Metadata, Linked Data and the Open Movement both under their technological and social perspectives.

***

Paul Walk has had a long-term involvement in developing, supporting and advocating the use of institutional repositories. With a focus on technical infrastructure and information standards, he is an active participant in COAR's Next-generation Repositories working group and is the technical author of the successful RIOXX metadata application profile. Paul also works closely with the Dublin Core Metadata Initiative and is current Chair of the DCMI Governing Board Paul is currently Head of Technology Strategy and Planning at EDINA, University of Edinburgh.

Ricardo Carvalho Amorim is a researcher at the University of Porto and currently holds a Master's degree in Informatics and Computing Engineering, focusing on the fields of mobile computing and research data management.

Alex Ball joined the University of Bath in 2005 as a Research Officer in UKOLN, a centre of expertise in digital information management, where he specialized in digital curation and scientific metadata. He joined the Digital Curation Centre in 2009, where he provided guidance and support on research data management, maintained catalogues of domain metadata standards and research data tools, edited the International Journal of Digital Curation, and coordinated the metadata aspects of the UK Research Data Discovery Service project. He began his current role as Research Data Librarian at the University of Bath in 2015. He is a co-moderator of the Dublin Core Science and Metadata Community, and co-chair of the Research Data Alliance Metadata Standards Catalog Working Group.

João Aguiar Castro has a master degree in Information Science, and is currently a Digital Media PhD student at the Faculty of Engineering of the University of Porto. He is a research data management researcher, with a particular interest in the definition of the metadata models for the description of research data from different research domains.

Paloma Centenera holds a Computer Engineer PhD (Universidad Politécnica de Madrid / Universidad Pontificia de Comillas), a Master in Economics and Innovation Management (Universidad Complutense de Madrid) and a Master in Libraries and Digital Information Services (Universidad Carlos III de Madrid). She has been a professor of Engineering in the Universidad Pontifical de Salamanca and she is currently working as a researcher in the European Research Council (ERC) Starting Grant Project "POSTDATA". This project is located in the Universidad Nacional de Educación a Distancia at the Laboratory of Digital Humanities.

Hatim Chahdi received his Master's degree in computer science from the University of Montpellier in 2013. He is currently pursuing a PhD in knowledge engineering and Machine learning. His current research focuses on efficient knowledge modeling and processing, knowledge integration in semi-supervised clustering and image analysis using incomplete background knowledge.

Karen Coyle is a librarian with over thirty years of experience with library technology. She now consults in a variety of areas relating to digital libraries. Karen has published dozens of articles and reports, most available on her web site, kcoyle. net. She has served on standards committees including the MARC standards group (MARBI), NISO committee AX for the OpenURL standard, and was an ALA representative to the e-book standards development that led to the ePub standard. She follows, writes, and speaks on a wide range policy areas, including intellectual property, privacy, and public access to information. As a consultant she works primarily on metadata development and technology planning. She is currently investigating the possibilities offered by the semantic web and linked data technology.

João Rocha da Silva is an Informatics Engineering PhD working at the Faculty of Engineering of the University of Porto. He specializes on research data management, applying the latest Semantic Web Technologies to the adequate preservation and discovery of research data assets.

Mansur Darlington is a cognitive scientist with a particular interest in the development of information and knowledge methods for supporting engineering designers in their professional activities.

Jean-Christophe Desconnets is a geomatic scientist at IRD (Research Institute for Developping countries), involved at MICADO research team of UMR ESPACE-DEV (joint research unit). He has two complementary competences. The first one is an environmental competence in water science and the other one in computer science. Jean-Christophe Desconnets is specialized in Spatial Data Infrastructure design with emphasis on semantic discovery and data processing capabilities. He is involved in various European and international projects. He has participated to the design and the implementation of various environmental spatial data infrastructure or data sharing platform in the framework of INSPIRE, GEOSS. Currently, he is involved with the ANR Equipex-GEOSUD project, implemented a Remote Sensing Data Infrastructure.

Rubia Gattelli is a Librarian with a Master degree in Information Science at Faculty of Engineering of University of Porto, Portugal. Works in a library specialized in Oceanography at University of Rio Grande, south of Brazil.

Elena González-Blanco is a Faculty member of the Spanish Literature and Literary Theory Department at Universidad Nacional de Educación a Distancia UNED (Open University) of Spain in Madrid. Her main research and teaching areas are Comparative Medieval Literature, Metrics and Poetry, and Digital Humanities. She holds a Ph.D. in Spanish Literature, a M.A. in Digital Libraries and Information Systems, a M.A. in Spanish Philology and an M.A. in Classics. She is the Director of the Digital Humanities Lab at UNED: LINHD (Laboratorio de Innovación en Humanidades Digitales) http://linhd.uned.es, constituent member of the first Clarin-K Center. She leads two Post-graduate diplomas: one on Digital Humanities, and the other on Digital Scholarly Editing, and the yearly summer school www.linhd.uned.es/formacion, and she is also the coordinator of the institutional linked data project UNEDATA http://unedata.uned.es. She was recently awarded with a European Research Council (ERC) Starting Grant. She is though the principal investigator of the ERC POSTDATA project.

Yulia Karimova holds a Master's Degree in Information Science.

Chris McMahon is Professor of Engineering Design in the Department of Mechanical Engineering at the University of Bristol, a post he has held since September 2012. He previously worked at the University of Bristol from 1984 to 2002. From 2002 to 2012, he worked at the University of Bath as Reader then Professor and Director of its Innovative Design and Manufacturing Research Centre. Prior to 1984 he was a Production and Design Engineer in the railway and automotive industries. His research interests are in engineering design, especially concerning the application of computers to the management of information and uncertainty in design, design automation, product life cycle management, design education, and design for sustainability, areas in which he has published over 250 refereed papers, a textbook, and a number of edited books. Professor McMahon is a Chartered Engineer, Fellow of the Institution of Mechanical Engineers (UK), and a founder member of the Design Society, for which he was President from 2010 to 2013. He is an active member of the scientific committees of various international journals and conferences.

Isabelle Mougenot Ph. D. is an associate professor in computer science at the University of Montpellier. She is currently involved in the MICADO research team (belonging to ESPACE-DEV research unit) that is conducting a number of interdisciplinary projects on joint aspects of computer science, geomatics and applied mathematics for environmental studies.

Cristina Ribeiro holds a PhD in Informatics from Universidad Nova de Lisboa. She is an Assistant Professor at the Department of Informatics Engineering, University o Porto, a Researcher at INESC-Porto, and teaches undergraduate and graduate courses in Information Retrieval, Markup Languages, and Knowledge Representation. Her research interests include information retrieval, multimedia databases, and digital repositories.

Demetrios G. Sampson has received a Diploma in Electrical Engineering from the Democritus University of Thrace, Greece in 1989 and a Ph.D. in Electronic Systems Engineering from the University of Essex, UK in 1995. Since October 2015, he has been a Professor of Learning Technologies at the School of Education, Curtin University, Western Australia. He was a Professor of Digital Systems for Learning and Education at the Department of Digital Systems, University of Piraeus, Greece (2003-2015) and a Research Fellow at the Information Technologies Institute (ITI), Centre of Research and Technology Hellas (CERTH), since 2000. He is the Founder and Director of the Advanced Digital Systems and Services for Education and Learning (ASK) since 1999. He has been a Visiting Professor and/or Research Scholar at the School of Computing and Information Systems, Athabasca University, Canada (2010), the Information Management Department, National Sun Yat-sen University, Taiwan (2011), the University of Tunis (2012, 2013), the Faculty of Education, Beijing Normal University, China (2013), Department of Educational Technology, Peking University Beijing, China (2013), Department of Learning Technologies, University of North Texas, USA (2013), School of Education, Curtin University, Australia (2015). His main scientific interests are in the area of Learning Technologies. He is the co-author of more than 385 publications in scientific books, journals and conferences with at least 3810 known citations (h-index: 28). He has received 9 times Best Paper Award in International Conferences on Advanced Learning Technologies. He is a Senior and Golden Core Member of IEEE and he was the elected Chair of the IEEE Computer Society Technical Committee on Learning Technologies (2008-2011). He is a member of the ICT Advisory Board of the Arab League Educational, Cultural and Scientific Organisation (ALESCO) since March 2014. He is the Editor-in-Chief of the Educational Technology and Society Journal (5-year impact factor 1.376). He has served or serves as Member of the Steering Committee of the IEEE Transactions on Learning Technologies (5-year impact factor 1.697), Member of the Advisory Board of the Journal of King Saud University - Computer and Information Sciences and the International Journal of Digital Literacy and Digital Competence, Member of the Editorial Board of 23 International/National Journals and a Guest Editor in 30 Special Issues of International Journals. His participation in the organization of scientific conferences involves: General and/or Program Committee and/or Honorary Chair in 40 International Conferences, Program Committees Member in 405 International/National Scientific Conferences.

He has been a Keynote/Invited Speaker in 67 International/National Conferences. He has been project director, principle investigator and/or consultant in 65 R&D projects with external funding at the range of 14 Million € (1991-2016). He is the recipient of the IEEE Computer Society Distinguished Service Award (July 2012).

Panagiotis Zervas has received a Diploma in Electronics and Computer Engineering from the Technical University of Crete, Greece in 2002, a Master's Degree in Computational Science from the Department of Informatics and Telecommunications of the National and Kapodistrian University of Athens, Greece in 2004 and a PhD from the Department of Digital Systems, University of Piraeus, Greece in 2014. His PhD research dealt with Methods and Systems for supporting Open Access and Reuse to Educational Resources and Practices. He is the co-author of more than 95 scientific publications with at least 520 known citations (h-index 12). He has received 5 times Best Research Paper Awards in International Conferences on Learning Technologies (July 2014, July 2011, April 2010, November 2010, July 2007). He has been a Member of the Advanced Digital Systems and Services for Education and Learning (ASK) since 2003 and he is currently, a Post-Doc Researcher in ASK. He is a member of the Executive Board of the IEEE Technical Committee on Learning Technology and the Technical Manager of the Educational Technology and Society Journal.

Index

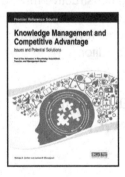

Support Your Colleagues and Stay Current on the Latest Research Developments

Become a Reviewer

In this competitive age of scholarly publishing, constructive and timely feedback significantly decreases the turn-around time of manuscripts from submission to acceptance, allowing the publication and discovery of progressive research at a much more expeditious rate.

The overall success of a refereed journal is dependent on quality and timely reviews.

Several IGI Global journals are currently seeking highly qualified experts in the field to fill vacancies on their respective editorial review boards. Reviewing manuscripts allows you to stay current on the latest developments in your field of research, while at the same time providing constructive feedback to your peers.

Reviewers are expected to write reviews in a timely, collegial, and constructive manner. All reviewers will begin their role on an ad-hoc basis for a period of one year, and upon successful completion of this term can be considered for full editorial review board status, with the potential for a subsequent promotion to Associate Editor.

Join this elite group by visiting the IGI Global journal webpage, and clicking on "**Become a Reviewer**".

Applications may also be submitted online at:
www.igi-global.com/journals/become-a-reviewer/.

Applicants must have a doctorate (or an equivalent degree) as well as publishing and reviewing experience.

If you have a colleague that may be interested in this opportunity, we encourage you to share this information with them.

Any questions regarding this opportunity can be sent to:
journaleditor@igi-global.com.

Printed in the United States
By Bookmasters